# An African Voice

## DATE DUE

| | | | |
|---|---|---|---|
| | | | |
| | | | |
| | | | |
| | | | |
| | | | |
| | | | |
| | | | |
| | | | |
| | | | |
| | | | |
| | | | |
| | | | |
| | | | |
| | | | |
| | | | |
| | | | |
| | | | |
| | | | |
| | | | |

The Library Store     #47-0102

D1275793

# An African Voice

The Role of the Humanities in African Independence

# Robert W. July

Duke University Press    Durham 1987

© 1987 Duke University Press
All rights reserved
Printed in the United States of America on
acid-free paper ∞
Library of Congress Cataloging-in-Publication Data
appear on the last printed page of this book.

JAN

*Remember the laughter . . .*

# Contents

Preface ix
Prologue: A Candle at Kilimanjaro 1

## Part 1 The Crisis of Independence

**1** Colonial Legacies 7
The Ambiguities of Colonialism 7 Antecedents 8 The Shock of
Colonialism 11 Neocolonial Influences 14 The Urge for Cultural
Independence 18
**2** *Présence Africaine* and the Expression of Cultural Freedom 20
The Meaning of Independence: Julius Nyerere and Sékou Touré 20
The First International Congress of Black Writers and Artists 24
Negritude 29 *Présence Américaine* 33 Pan-Africanism or
Communism? 39 A Congress Cultural or a Congress Political? 41

## Part 2 The Arts and Cultural Independence

**3** The Visual Arts and African Independence 47
The Humanist and the Intangibles of Independence 47 The Decline
of Excellence 48 Oku Ampofo and the Akwapim Six 52
**4** The Independent African Theater 59
African Theatrics 59 Ibadan University and the Eclectic Theater of
Nigeria 62 The Pedagogical Theater of Efua Sutherland 73

**5** Africans Dance 82
Africa Still Dances 82  The Musician 84  The Catalyst 91  The
Dancer 96  *Les Ballets Africains* 103
**6** Literary Perspectives of Cultural Independence  107
Three Novels 107  Independence 108  Uncertainty 116
Affirmation 120


**Part 3  Educational Independence**

**7** The Search for a Usable Past  129
The Uses of History 129  Negro Nations and Their Culture 134
History at Ibadan 140  The Question of Oral Tradition 147  A
Usable Past 153
**8** The Idea of an African University  157
Early Educational Theories 157  African Education at University
College of the Gold Coast 161  Nkrumah at Legon 165  Nkrumah
Chooses a Vice-Chancellor 172
**9** Organizing Africana  177
The Pros and Cons of African Studies 177  African Studies in
Ghana 183  The African Studies Institute—University of Ibadan 192


**Part 4  A Modern African Civilization**

**10** The African Personality and Europe  201
Identity Quandaries 201  The Assault of Scientific Racism 202
Black Orpheus 208  The Flight from Europe—Frantz Fanon 212
The Flight from Europe—Medicine in Africa 217  The African
Identity and the New African Philosophy 220
**11** An African Voice  227
Bellagio 227  In Defense of African Culture 229  Technology and
African Culture 232  The Evolution of an African Designer 237
An African Voice 243


Notes  245
Bibliography  257
Index  263

# *Preface*

During the mid-1960s, shortly after most African nations achieved independence, I wrote *The Origins of Modern African Thought*, a book that concerned itself with the flux of ideas supporting the nationalist and independence movements in Africa following the conclusion of the Second World War. The book's thesis argued the importance of Western thought and institutions in the ideology that fueled independence in Africa, an influence dating back at least to the beginning of the nineteenth century. To be sure, there were other forces at work, Islam, for instance, as well as traditional customs and beliefs. Nevertheless, it seemed to be the westernizing element, small but pervasive, that had provided the main engine of modernization and eventually of independence.

This present volume, *An African Voice*, is also a study of ideas surrounding African independence, a sequel account that treats a different but related aspect of the independence process. While Western ideas and institutions played a decisive role in creating a modern Africa, there were Africans who hesitated, doubtful, who viewed the uncritical importation of Western concepts and paraphernalia as inimical, even dangerous, to the achievement of a genuine independence. Their concern was expressed in two forms. First, they felt that the mere granting of national sovereignty by a former colonial overlord did not, in itself, comprise or insure true independence, not political, not economic, and certainly not cultural. Indeed, they feared that just the opposite might result, that by embracing Western culture Africa might lose its freedom, degenerating into a collection of client states and economic satellites guided by an adulterant version of Western civilization ill adapted to the African environment.

Their second argument flowed from the first. Despite the existence and obvious advantages to Africa of Western endowments, they insisted, there was much life and validity in the ways of traditional Africa, that Africans would discard their inheritance at Africa's peril, that indigenous cultures and institutions might well provide the firmest foundation for building economically healthy, politically autonomous, and psychically secure African societies. This did not mean a turning away from the West, its establishments and tenets already deeply embedded in African life, nor did it mean an unreflective romantic appeal to an African past. Rather it meant a search for modernized versions of traditional culture that might be married to those imports from the West that were seen to be relevant and beneficial to African life. Then might true independence be achieved, drawing strength from the best of both Western and African civilization.

Those Africans who argued the importance of an indigenous African civilization represented diverse walks of life. Nevertheless many of the more eloquent or effective exponents were humanists—artists, writers, musicians, educators, as well as political figures of a philosophic or reflective bent of mind—those whose work caused them to dwell more fully on matters of culture while affording the opportunity to give public utterance to their views. For the most part, they were men of two worlds, educated usually in the West and fully aware of the Western contribution to modern Africa. At the same time their taproots were securely fixed in Africa, their critical or artistic faculties sensitive to indigenous custom, their concern to identify and reshape the best of the old ways to be used again in the world of modern Africa.

This volume, *An African Voice*, describes the activities of a number of African humanists concerned with cultural independence through a renascent indigenous civilization. The list is not complete and not meant to be. It is exemplary rather than inclusive, using particular cases to illustrate developments in a broad range of the arts and humanities that argued the importance of traditional civilization as the means to cultural independence. The study concentrates primarily on the two decades following the end of the Second World War, and it is apparent, moreover, that many of the examples are drawn from West Africa, more particularly from Ghana and Nigeria. This is not by design but by circumstance. During the years covered in this work, West Africa was in better position than most other regions of the continent to produce persons who were both conscious of the impact of the West and self-conscious about the importance of Africa's own traditions and institutions. This does not reflect parochialism, however. Whatever their geographic origins, in their ideas and aspirations these individuals can be said truly to represent all of black Africa.

Finally, I should say that those whose work I have set out to describe were not operating in an artistic vacuum; their motivation was highly social and political. My analysis, therefore, makes no effort at aesthetic assessments; rather it views the exertions of these humanists as contributions to their social or political milieu.

The argument does not quite end there, however. The years directly after the Second World War were particularly receptive to the revival of indigenous culture, a reaffirmation of an African identity to accompany political freedom, and above all to throw off at long last the self-hate of dependence and inferiority, of slavery and colonialism, in favor of a positive self-assurance and confidence in Africa and its values. At the same time the urge toward modernization intensified among peoples seeking the fruits of independence, arguing that Africa discard its old ways and follow Europe toward those Western achievements of prosperity and material plenty. Thus the old ambivalence remained between the traditionalists and the Westernizers, intensified, if anything, more than ever in need of a reconciliation that would guide Africa in its new freedom, drawing on the best of both the African and Western worlds. Then, at last, secure in the validity of an evolving culture, Africans might speak with their own voice, to make a unique African contribution to the civilization of a wider world.

I have organized my book into four sections. After a brief prologue, the first part comprises two chapters and deals with the granting of political sovereignty and the problems and possibilities that emerged with the arrival of independence. The second section, chapters 3 through 6, reviews the activities of individuals and movements in the arts and humanities, specifically such fields as the visual arts, theater, music, dance, and literature. Part 3, involving chapters 7, 8, and 9,

examines particular developments within some of the new African universities relating to the reexamination and revival of traditional history
and culture, as well as the university's role in the new independent Africa. The final section, chapters 10 and 11, inquires into the quality of
modern African civilization, a culture that seems to be taking form as
an integral, combining elements drawn both from the West and from
Africa's own traditional institutions and values.

This book quite simply could not have been written without the help
of a large number of individuals who contributed most generously of
their time and wisdom, many assisting with correspondence, others sub-
mitting to lengthy personal interviews. It is with a sense of deepest
gratitude that I mention them hereinunder—Dapo Adelugba, J. F. A.
Ajayi, Oku Ampofo, Ephraim Amu, Lord Ashby, Geoffrey Axworthy,
Peter Benson, Joel Colton, Michael Crowder, Pathé Diagne, Amady Ali
Dieng, K. O. Dike, Mme Alioune Diop, Cheikh Anta Diop, Dorothy
Hodgkin, Thomas Hodgkin, Abiola Irele, Graham Irwin, Camera
Ladji, Bill Marshall, Davidson Nicol, J. H. Nketia, Demas Nwoko, Conor
Cruise O'Brien, B. A. Ogot, Albert Opoku, J. Rabemananjara, Wole
Soyinka, Efua Sutherland, and Bakary Traoré.

I must also thank the Rockefeller Foundation for the generous Humanities Fellowship that made possible the fieldwork on which much
of my text is based.

# An African Voice

# Prologue
## A Candle at Kilimanjaro

It tasted good. To the surging crowds at the Lagos racecourse, to the thousands who packed the polo grounds in Accra, to the multitudes that lined the streets of Nairobi, Kampala, Abidjan, Freetown, or Dar es Salaam, it tasted very good indeed.

"It is the hour of truth," proclaimed President Senghor in Dakar.

"At long last the battle has ended!" Kwame Nkrumah exulted, watching the red, green, and gold colors of Ghana fluttering in the night breeze. "Ghana . . . is free forever."

By great and small alike the pronouncements of statesmen were echoed in the streets. Moving with Accra's crowds, Martin Luther King repeated Nkrumah's words, "free forever," and pondered their implications for blacks in America. "Today is the most important day for Nigeria," said another in Lagos, his anonymity making him spokesman for all. "Today, this is the last day of the colonial regime."[1]

They came at different times, these independence rites of passage, but there was a basic sameness about the festivities. Perhaps it was the repetition of essential formalities, perhaps a predictable reaction of people with heightened aspirations and exuberance to match, perhaps the pattern set by Ghana's ceremonies that memorable March day in 1957. By October 1964, when Zambia's turn had come, some twenty-five independence celebrations later, seasoned connoisseurs of these events were assessing the mood as they watched the familiar revelers singing and dancing their way through streets bedecked with flags and bunting against a backdrop of late-blooming jacaranda, flame trees, and bougainvillea. It was a more emotional affair than most, they concluded, probably because of Zambia's ebullient leader, Kenneth Kaunda, whose personality shone so warmly over all things.

Outside Lusaka, a large stadium had been constructed with stands on two sides abutting a rocky rise on the third. Here, during the evening of the last day before independence, the crowds gathered to witness the final climactic spectacles leading to that magic midnight moment when one more new nation would be born. On the floodlit field, hordes of dancers surged forward, group succeeding group, as they shouted, sang, and pranced to the insistent rhythms of the drums. All this was authentically African; so were the acrobatic stilt dancers with their prodigious gyrations as well as the masked figures, bizarre yet powerful and mysterious. In time the program shifted to exhibitions of regimental marching, executed by Zambian guardsmen in bright tunics moving with massed precision to the accompaniment of brass flourishes and bagpipes. The ecstatic spectators roared in delight.

Brilliantly staged, the evening's activities now moved to their climax. As midnight approached, the sense of excitement quickened, warming the packed stands and the thousands more crowded on the dark hillside against the shivering winds that whipped about the stadium. All at once the moment was at hand. Amidst a sudden and profound silence, Prime Minister Kaunda and the retiring British governor-general walked slowly to the middle of the field. Caught in a circle of light, they stood alone, surrounded by the stillness and the black night; then the lights left them and shifted to the flagstaff as the Union Jack descended for the last time, quickly to be replaced by the green of the Zambian flag.

"A fresh strong green, designed to challenge the sky as the trees and grass do." Such was the observation of Doris Lessing, who brought an artist's eye to the occasion. As the flags changed, she went on, the silence was transformed into an uproar, waves of ululation from the dark hillside, shouting all around, drumming in the night air, and the booming of guns, while overhead the sky flashed and crackled with fireworks. Nearby, she noticed a young girl, who had been reduced to helpless laughter by the din. Down on the field, as the Zambian flag rose, a woman rolled over and over across the dusty expanse until she came to rest at the foot of the flagpole. Mrs. Lessing thought the incident prearranged, though appropriate theater, all the same.[2]

This was familiar enough—the midnight ceremony of the flags, the gay crowds, the colorful entertainment. What impressed visitors as well was the lavishness of the arrangements wherever they were mounted. Small or large, and all impecunious by world standards, most countries seemed incapable of economies at this consummate moment of history. In Nairobi, for example, Kenyan independence was marked by a mammoth civic ball attended by 1,700 guests who consumed 500 cases of soft drinks, 120 cases of champagne, and 200 cases of spirits, along with mountains of food. The party was estimated to cost £12,000, but this was far from a memorable figure. Ghana allocated £600,000 for her celebrations, including allowances of £20,000 for fireworks, £10,000 for a regatta, and £25,000 to provide the Accra air terminal with a decorative pool and garden. Even tiny Gambia scheduled a full week of festivities that included durbahs, concerts, inland safaris, and exhibitions by the famed griot praise singers of the country.

Not to be outdone, Julius Nyerere and his careful ministers allowed a good half-million pounds for their formalities; nevertheless, the record for openhandedness clearly belonged to Nigeria. It was rumored at the time that the Nigerian federal government had set aside £10 million, including £1,000 allowances for ministers, but these reports were ridiculed by the Nigerian minister of information. The figure was £1,75 million, he insisted, and much of this was recoverable in the form of permanent improvements such as the Lagos streetlighting or through the sale of cars and buses used during the festivities.

Soon thereafter the used car market must have sagged, for each guest—politicians, scholars, members of the professions, and multifarious public figures invited by the score from the world over—was provided on arrival with a driver and a new Chevrolet or Jaguar for as long as his visit lasted, all vehicles, incidentally, painted the independence colors of green and white and given license plates beginning with "IND." Flown in first-class, the arrivals were put up at the new and expensive Federal Palace Hotel and treated to the usual round of receptions and dinners. On independence night a mammoth crowd attended the state ball, refreshments for the occasion provided without stint at government expense.

Such openhanded hospitality seemed more than appropriate to those who were about to be free. No Nigerian was heard to complain of the cost, not even in the slum shacks where the faces filling the doorways shone back only amused pleasure as the independence spectacles and the notables flowed past. For them there was street dancing into the late hours, parades, exhibition halls, and the suddenly popular national museum with its spectacular art treasures. For them also was the unique artistry of Louis Armstrong, brought over for the occasion not by the government but by Pepsi-Cola—"Pepsi brings you Satchmo" the posters announced—and his concerts could be attended by anyone with the admission fee of two shillings sixpence and five bottle tops. Most of all, for them there was the understanding that here was a moment in history. "Time doesn't matter today," was one comment. "We can spend anything we like. We can spend time, we can spend money."

Independence, however, carried more profound implications—more than an individual, or even a national, triumph. Nkrumah's exultation was tempered by the knowledge that Ghana was an example for all the people of Africa. "If we . . . succeed," he informed his countrymen, "we shall aid . . . other territories . . . the sooner to reach conditions under which they [too] may become independent." Similarly, in Tanganyika, the great day was marked by the lighting of a beacon on the summit of Mount Kilimanjaro, a flame to shine symbolically for all who sought freedom. Julius Nyerere had some years earlier given the simple explanation: "We, the people of Tanganyika, would like to light a candle and put it on top of Mount Kilimanjaro which would shine beyond our borders giving hope where there was despair, love where there was hate and dignity where before there was only humiliation."[3]

In Tanganyika, as elsewhere in Africa, independence meant more than freedom from colonial rule. It meant the freedom to build a new life, a better world.

# 1

*The Crisis of Independence*

# 1
## Colonial Legacies

*The Ambiguities of Colonialism*

After seventy-five years of colonial rule African independence in the 1960s was for most a new experience, but the quest for freedom was as old as colonialism itself. During the nineteenth century Europeans had occupied vast sections of the African continent—Boer and Briton in South Africa, the Portuguese holding Mozambique and Angola, French and English interests nibbling at enclaves along the western coast from Cape Verde to the Niger Delta, then the final rush of occupation that followed the Berlin Conference of 1884–1885. African resistance had been various, sometimes intense, sometimes confused, and ultimately impotent in the face of superior Western military technology. With the eventual establishment of colonial administrations, opposition was forced into such refinements as independent African churches, political movements masquerading as cultural organizations, or token representation in colonial legislative bodies. At the same time there were Africans who welcomed colonialism or at least resigned themselves to foreign domination, arguing that Africa could learn much from the outsiders, modernizing their economic and political institutions in preparation for the time when African societies might take their place in the world community of nations.

Thus, during the colonial era, an ambivalence developed among many Africans, particularly those familiar with the West, an ambivalence in which an admiration for Western ideas and institutions clashed with traditional African ethical and social standards. If this raised confusion and uncertainty in the minds of those Africans who regarded the worlds of Europe and Africa as antithetical, to others it promised a happy integration of complementary cultures, brought into being by those Africans familiar with both worlds. When political independence arrived in mid-twentieth-century Africa, the ambivalence of colonial times remained to complicate the pressing problems of new nations— how to convert the artificial geography of European colonies into stable, cohesive nations, how to turn the benefits of economic growth from Western profit to African advantage, how to assert a genuinely African culture in the modern world.

## Antecedents[1]

Ambivalence was not the hallmark of the Europeans who came to Africa. Portuguese clerics along the coasts of Kongo and Angola baptized slaves bound for the Americas, serene in the conviction that the outward-bound chattels had been rescued from the eternal damnation of their seeming barbarism. Dutch settlers arriving in South Africa during the seventeenth and eighteenth centuries felt no remorse as they decimated indigenous hunters and herdsmen while appropriating the lands of those they regarded as inferior beings. In West Africa the nineteenth century opened as European, chiefly British, humanitarians mounted a major attack on the Atlantic slave trade, an essential component of which was the replacement of pagan, slave-trading societies with Christianized cultivators of those agricultural commodities in growing demand in the West. The coastal towns of Freetown, Monrovia, and Libreville were all founded as rehabilitation centers for former slaves, but the reforming impulse extended well beyond resettlement, involving no less than a new look for the whole of West Africa's traditional civilizations.

In communities like Saint-Louis at the mouth of the Senegal River, the dominant French presence was marked by what came to be called assimilation, that is, the total conversion of indigenous peoples to European culture, at least in its Gallic variation. Africans who came under British influence were subjected, like the former slaves of Freetown, to Anglican Christianity and the ethical, cultural, and social standards of Victorian England. The objective was not colonies but the establishment of independent communities directed by an African middle class of farmers, artisans, and traders—a clearly superior alternative, it was argued, to economies based primarily on the sale of surplus population. As with the French, the British effort was essentially assimilationist, an early instance of Western technical assistance, and a genuine effort to remake indigenous societies in the image of what was regarded without question in Europe as the most advanced civilization the world had yet achieved.

As exercises in cultural persuasion these efforts were not an immediate success. Tropical disease took a heavy toll among the missionaries and government officials posted to West Africa, while local populations remained largely indifferent to alien ways and religious beliefs. Nevertheless, small and significant gains were made. European ideas and institutions took root gradually in coastal points like Goree, Cape Coast, Accra, and Lagos, these cosmopolitan centers serving as seed ground for the dissemination of Western values and standards that percolated into the interior, carried by the shifting African population migrating ceaselessly between town and country.

Some Africans actively sought to acquire and master the elements of Western culture. There were those attracted by European technology, not only the evident advantages of mechanical contrivances but scientific, mathematical, and linguistic skills as well. These inroads led naturally to other imports such as personal dress, housing, and, of course, religion. In Senegal a small *métis*, or mulatto, population—descendants of European-African alliances—embraced the language and culture that France had hoped to implant in her African holdings. At Freetown the liberated slaves who poured in during the first half of the nineteenth century were quickly attracted to the Western culture they found in their new home. Torn loose from familiar surroundings, the new arrivals accepted Christian conversion, sent their children to be educated in the mission schools, mastered English, adopted forms of European dress, and settled down as aspirant bourgeois tradesmen, clergy, or schoolteachers. If the transformation was not as complete as among the métis of Senegal, the movement was clearly in the direction of a Western way of life.

The growing influence of European culture was exemplified in the careers of a number of West Africans, some self-made men sympathetic to the drive of Western enterprise and acquisitiveness, others singled out by European missionaries for special training in such fields as education, medicine, or the ministry. These acolytes helped staff a network of mission stations established at points throughout the African interior; more than that, they reached beyond their function of Christian conversion, advocating the civilization of the West as a means of revitalizing and modernizing traditional African societies. Such an individual was the Abbé P. D. Boilat, a young mulatto cleric, who set himself the task of encouraging the assimilation of French culture in Senegal as priest, educator, and publicist. Another was James Africanus Beale Horton, son of a Sierra Leone liberated slave, who spent an active career urging the establishment of modern, Westernized, independent states throughout West Africa. Perhaps the most celebrated of all, Bishop Samuel Ajayi Crowther, survived the agonies of enslavement through rehabilitation at Freetown and eventually emerged as a leading exponent for the assimilation of the bourgeois Victorianism espoused by his British missionary sponsors.

Boilat left Africa to live in France long before the era of colonial control, and Horton died prematurely on the eve of the Berlin Conference, perhaps already partially disillusioned by the racial prejudice and the increasing economic and political interference that preceded the onset of overt colonial occupation. Crowther's long life extended from the early years when Freetown meant personal liberty to the days of protectorates and crown colonies. He had begun his career as cleric and missionary for the Anglican Church Missionary Society, working both in Sierra Leone and Yorubaland. He then assisted in the establishment of missions on the Niger before being chosen by the Society in 1864 as bishop of a vast West African diocese that included those river establishments and stretched from Senegal to the equator.

Significantly, existing British-directed c.m.s. missions and colonies like Lagos and Sierra Leone were excluded from Crowther's jurisdiction as there was resistance to the prospect of white missionaries serving under a black bishop. Crowther nevertheless pressed on with a vigorous program, stressing the development of a prosperous commercial agriculture that exported cotton, groundnuts, arrowroot, indigo, and other crops to the European markets, produced by communities of sober Christian farmers based on Western models. In his propagation of Christian doctrine, however, Crowther did not ignore local custom. Traditional fables, proverbs, and songs were adapted to support and strengthen Christ's message, along with appropriate indigenous ceremonies and religious terms. In order more effectively to broadcast the faith, Crowther urged preaching in the vernacular, a practice that he supported by publishing grammars in Yoruba, Nupe, and Ibo, as well as Yoruba translations of several of the Scriptures.

Crowther remained as bishop for over a quarter century, but his later years were beset with problems of mission efficiency and the resistance to change by the people he had sought to convert. Hindsight sees the folly of trying to redesign a whole culture in a few short decades, but beyond parochial African complications lay difficulties originating in Europe. Gradually the early nineteenth century humanitarian enthusiasm faded, to be replaced eventually with full-blown imperialism, as imperialism reflected in missionary programs as much as in the policies of their European governments. Crowther's control over his own diocese was gradually circumscribed, and by the time of his death in 1891, he had been effectively superseded as bishop. But by that time the affairs of West Africans were no longer self-directed. Europeans had taken control. The colonial era had begun.

## The Shock of Colonialism

It would be a mistake to assume that Africans automatically turned away from European colonialism, sickened by the brutality of arbitrary force, repelled by the finality of alien power. Some did, of course, but these were usually leaders of traditional states under attack by invading armies—for example, the Mandinka empire builder, Samouri Touré, or Jaja, the mercantile opportunist of the Niger Delta who defied none less than imperial Britain at the height of her imperial glory.

Among Africans who had been schooled in the ways of the West, the reaction was complex. There were throwbacks to the Abbé Boilat, looking forward to the day when assimilation would be complete and a black European replica would take his place in the world. Another few rebelled, urging their people to cleave to their time-honored traditions and customs. Most, however, reflected the inconsistencies and opportunities of their anomalous position. Educated in the West, they sought the advantages of modernization for their own people; yet, as Africans, they were dismayed by the consolidation of foreign power and sensed the danger that important traditional institutions and values might be contaminated and destroyed.

Many members of the small but crucial group of educated Africans saw a special role for themselves as men of two worlds. As sympathetic advocates of European culture, they felt themselves particularly well suited to explain the advantages of the modern world to their own countrymen. Equally, they saw their African heritage as an inestimable asset to foreign rulers whose unfamiliarity with local customs and institutions frequently confounded effective administration. In this special role as mutual interpreter, it must be added, they glimpsed the opportunity to share in the exercise of power.

The authority wielded by Blaise Diagne, Senegal's deputy to the French chamber from 1914 to 1934, may go a long way to explain his warm support of French domination in Africa. Other Africans similarly favored showed a like regard for French colonialism; throughout the British colonies, by contrast, official suspicion of educated Africans circumscribed the sharing of power and converted potential collaborators into early nationalist opponents. In Nigeria, for example, Herbert Macaulay may well have been propelled on his career as a violent, British-baiting patriot by the early rebuff to his hopes for advancement in the colonial administration. On the Gold Coast the nationalist leader J. E. Casely Hayford reversed the process, abandoning his initial role as administration gadfly in favor of subsequent cooperation as he searched for concessions and influence.

There were principles involved as well. Clergymen and publicists like Edward Blyden of Liberia, Majola Agbebi and James Johnson of Nigeria, or S. R. B. Attoh Ahuma on the Gold Coast were variously concerned with the assertion of African independence in the face of colonial authority. Overt political resistance was out of the question; the alternative was cultural affirmation, in divine worship, or through use of local dress and language, indices that signified deeply felt distinctions between the cultures of Africa and Europe. Attoh Ahuma heaped scorn on the black white man as "a creature, a freak, and a monstrosity." Blyden urged African Christians to throw off missionary controls, those "foreign props and supports," and establish their own independent, self-governing churches. James Johnson baptized babies with African names and endorsed polygamy and household slavery as not incompatible with Christianity. Agbebi supported the word with the deed, helping found the first independent church in Nigeria, wearing African dress even while traveling in the West, marrying his daughter in a traditional ceremony, even publicly defending odious anachronisms like human sacrifice and cannibalism.

Such behavior belied a fundamental seriousness, a profound misgiving that widespread, uncritical acceptance of European ways could lead to destruction of the essential African civilization. Johnson pointed to the rise of drunkenness and adultery that followed exposure to European custom; Agbebi complained of social anarchy and moral deterioration among Africans who had been taught contempt for their own institutions. Blyden insisted on the unique qualities of black culture—a divine gift, he called it, the destruction of which would deprive mankind of its spiritual completeness and perfectibility.

In practice, however, ethnocentrism proved elusive. Attoh Ahuma preferred the noble African plowman to pen-pushing counterfeit Europeans but admitted that Western civilization had important contributions to make in Africa. James Johnson inveighed against Western dress but wore none other himself. Blyden, the racial exclusivist, kept his European name, cultivated a wide acquaintanceship among political, religious, and intellectual leaders in England, and entertained a lifelong admiration for Western letters, including the classical languages of Greek and Latin. For all their advocacy of an independent church movement, neither Blyden nor Johnson followed Agbebi in supporting conviction with action, Johnson remaining to the end a loyal cleric of the Anglican church. Blyden flirted with Islam, which he declared was well adapted to the spiritual needs of blacks, but, interestingly, he called Mohammedanism a "form of Christianity."

These inconsistencies were not hypocrisy but ambivalence, not faltering devotion to Africa but recognition of European strength, less weakness of character than clarity of vision. They were men of two worlds, true cultural hybrids. They understood the values of Western civilization and yearned for their benefits in Africa as much as had predecessors like Bishop Crowther and Africanus Horton. More than that, they appreciated the advantages to be gained from access to the sources of power. Blyden was drawn to William Gladstone by a mutual interest in classical literature, but Blyden employed that acquaintance to urge favors for Africa from an all-powerful British statesman.

In like fashion, familiarity with Europe by the Gold Coast barristers, John Mensah Sarbah and J. E. Casely Hayford, helped their country-men to deal with the constraints of imperial power. Trained in English law, both were able to challenge the authority of British colonialism on the Gold Coast and on occasion to help block legislation regarded as objectionable and contrary to African custom. In Nigeria Herbert Macaulay played an analogous role, leading a twenty-year campaign of embarrassing the colonial authorities and defending traditional institutions through adroit employment of such Anglo-Saxon fundamentals as freedom of speech and the constitutional guarantee of petition and rule of law.

### Neocolonial Influences

The euphoria that accompanied independence in Africa was under-standable and predictable. Colonialism was ended. The African was free henceforth to determine his own destiny. Yet, the more thoughtful were already pondering the morning after. Formal, nominal sover-eignty, they feared, might yet prove the easier part. Genuine freedom, leading to stable, prosperous, purposeful African societies, could be more elusive.

Did the old ambivalence linger? What of the acceptance and rejec-tion of Europe that had marked the careers of the Hortons and the Crowthers, the Blydens and the Casely Hayfords? Would a similar love–hate attitude blur the objectives and hamper the performance of a new generation of African leaders? More than that, did the marks of colonialism dissolve at a stroke of the pen? Could long decades of alien administration vanish with the departing colonial proconsuls? Indeed, was it necessary, or even desirable, to rid Africa of the institutions and their guiding principles that Europe had left behind?

There seemed to be a triad of holdovers from colonialism that re-mained to complicate what had been gained on independence day. First, political complexities threatened national stability. Second, eco-nomic impediments obstructed the quest for material social develop-ment. Finally, and for many most profoundly, a disturbing confusion of cultural objectives, both African and European, threatened to com-promise the full realization of new-won independence.

Perhaps the political legacies of colonialism were most obvious. In

Nigeria, as airliners left bulging with former rulers, it was less their departure than an empty craft standing to one side, almost unnoticed, that embodied the moment's true significance—the plane that was to carry Prime Minister Abubakar Tafawa Balewa to New York, where Nigeria would take its place as the ninety-ninth member state in the United Nations Organization. Balewa's maiden speech at the United Nations dwelt in large measure on the growing crisis in the former Belgian Congo, a crisis that eventually brought civil war and almost shattered the country beyond repair. Many Africans blamed European colonialism. The colonial system, they said, had made improbable unities of disparate peoples solely in the name of administrative efficiency; then, as with the Belgians, the victims had been cast loose to fend for themselves with little sense of nationhood, with few facilities or the trained leadership needed for success.

Nigeria itself was a case in point. At independence, *Time* magazine had voiced skepticism regarding the cohesiveness of a "land made up of 250 bickering tribal groups . . . with little in common but mutual suspicion and jealousy." With more charity, London's *Economist* wondered if independence had come too easily to fashion the bonds of unity, and there were Nigerians who agreed. "To some of us, it's been too smooth in Nigeria. Nigeria is a colony where no leader has been in jail. We consider this a stigma, really. We wish there had been a struggle . . . that would unite us with a purpose."

These comments by a Nigerian official might as easily have been voiced in a dozen other countries—in Rwanda and Burundi, in Chad or the Sudan, all destined to face savage, wasting civil wars. Kenya and Uganda were to find their freedom sorely tried by tribal regionalism; even in Ghana, with its martyred "prison graduates," there were serious divisive forces based upon ethnic and parochial antipathies. Perhaps most striking of all was Cameroon, the first of seventeen states to reach independence during 1960, its solemnities conducted under tight security in the face of terrorist attacks that had shortly before claimed forty lives and caused much destruction of property in Douala.[2]

Such fratricidal behavior was compounded by another political legacy of colonialism, the institution of legislative democracy. France, Belgium, and particularly Britain had been at pains to install parliamentary systems of government in former colonies, systems patterned after metropolitan models and designed particularly to insure political stability.

These two-party transplants did not long survive in lands where the idea of organized legislative dissent was strange, even threatening. The Ibo have no word for "opposition," Africans pointed out, only "those who always disagree," or "those who mean no good." In Ghana the loyal opposition was looked on as anything but loyal, more fitly described as the enemy. Government knows best, one minister explained, as an opposition politician was deported, branded an alien though he had been born and reared in Ghana. "If a person is acquitted in court," the minister continued, "that does not mean he is innocent. . . . The government is in a better position to judge. . . . Should I wait until I am assassinated before I defend myself?"[3]

A second form of colonial legacy was the threat of continued economic vassalage to onetime European political masters. The former French colonies, in particular, seemed locked into a parental mercantilism that had survived and transcended political freedom. At independence, Ivory Coast President Félix Houphouët-Boigny, among others, paid elaborate compliment to the wisdom and bounty of France, and, indeed, he had much to be thankful for. Two years earlier at Abidjan, Houphouët had opened a $6 million bridge paid for by France, and with independence, it was said, the departing gift of former rulers was an elegant presidential palace raised at a cost of $17 million. Along with other former French colonies, the Ivory Coast was granted entrée into the European Economic Community, a preferential status secured by a French government that continued to lavish direct aid as had been the case during colonial times. In 1961, for example, the Ivory Coast received $150 million in technical assistance, along with support for the Ivorian coffee crop, equaling one-third of its annual exports.[4]

Citing the insufficiencies of African economies, Houphouët welcomed Europe's assistance, a sentiment clearly echoed among many of Britain's former colonies. In Nigeria, Prime Minister Balewa made no secret of his desire for British capital and trade. "If the Government and the commercial interests of Great Britain will have the courage and . . . the good sense to invest in Nigeria," he asserted, "we for our part will guarantee a fair return. . . . We appreciate what has been done in the past . . . and we look for further financial expression in the future of Nigeria."[5]

Even Kwame Nkrumah's Ghana seemed at least momentarily overwhelmed by Europe's economic ascendancy. Guests attending indepen-

dence festivities in Accra included Lord Portall, resplendent in his
R.A.F. air marshal uniform though now a director of Barclay's Bank,
and many other representatives of European and American financial or
industrial concerns. Nkrumah's personal guest list contained the chairman of the association of British cocoa merchants and brokers, as well
as John Cadbury, who was responsible for the cocoa purchases of his
giant firm. Such a gesture, understandable in light of Ghana's position
as a major world cocoa producer, nonetheless clashed queerly with the
prime minister's views on nonalignment.[6]

Nkrumah's position had long been well known. Like Guinea's forceful leader, Sékou Touré, Nkrumah felt that true independence involved
sovereign states free alike from economic dependency or political entanglements. He could point out, as many did, that the Ivory Coast's
prosperity came at a price. Three-quarters of her imports and almost
two-thirds of her exports moved exclusively within the franc zone. Encouraged by tax holidays and the easy repatriation of profits, capital
from abroad was quick to invest in the country's light industries such
as food and timber processing, and soon foreign control of local manu-
facturing took its place alongside longtime domination of the Ivory
Coast's international trade. Shopkeepers, craftsmen, clerks, government
workers, and industrial managers poured in from France to monopolize
the economy. By 1964 one of every ten persons in the capital city of
Abidjan was European. It was to be no temporary influx. "Make no
mistake about it," was the word, "we are here to stay." And they did.[7]

In neighboring Ghana, Kwame Nkrumah struggled to avoid similar
involvement and warned darkly of the consequences of what he and
others were already describing as neocolonialism. Internally, Ghana
sought economic independence through large-scale investment in heavy
industry and modern port facilities as well as in service industries that
included hotels, a shipping line, and the national airline, Ghana Air-
ways, which had come into being along with a modern airport at Accra.
Such expensive moves cut deeply into the country's financial reserves
and soon led to extensive borrowing from public and private sources
in the West. Economic involvement was further intensified as foreign
capital moved quickly to establish a wide range of consumer industries
in Ghana that included breweries, textile and flour mills, vehicle assembly plants, and manufactories of aluminum, utensils, and soap.[8]

Nkrumah was certainly sensitive to the dangers of soliciting Western assistance as a means to freedom from Western entanglements. In just such a way France has maintained economic control over former colonies, he warned. Newly independent, these nations "remain suppliers of cheap raw materials and tropical foodstuffs while continuing to serve as closed markets for French products." The inclusion of French-speaking Africa into the European Common Market, Nkrumah continued, merely perpetuates the status of protected markets for European manufactured goods, a process that can only retard economic growth and retain a colonial character for Africa, while the cost of illusory technical assistance is defrayed by profits gained from exchanging expensive finished goods against Africa's cheap raw materials.

Nkrumah saw the solution in continental unity, an African unity that could counterpose its own strength to that of Europe. For the pragmatic Houphouët, an African economic community was premature, if not utopian. For Nkrumah it promised economic emancipation—the efficiency of pooled manpower, land, and capital resources across the continent, the economies of a common currency and uniform trade regulations, and the strength of a united Africa in lieu of the feeble individual efforts of some two-score weak and impecunious nations. More than that, Nkrumah concluded, "a Union of African States will raise the dignity of Africa and strengthen its impact on world affairs. It will make possible the full expression of the African personality."[9]

### The Urge for Cultural Independence

Nkrumah's "African Personality" was no empty slogan. Though subject to varying definitions, the term embodied a desire for the liberation of Africa from the cultural entanglements of the West. Herein lay the third impediment to true independence. Nkrumah, along with many other Africans, felt the need to go beyond political or economic freedom, to achieve as well an independence from the ethical and aesthetic standards of the West, to affirm age-old indigenous traditions, customs, and values in a modern world. It was a natural impulse, a desire to be rid of alien, colonial ways with their foreign educational, linguistic, artistic, and philosophical measurement, a desire to introduce an authentic African idiom into the mainstream of contemporary world civilization.

Once again, however, achievement proved elusive; cultural independence would not come by royal decree or legislative statute. For one thing, there were African traditions that seemed dated in a modern world, while foreign ideas and institutions—long resident in Africa— refused to disappear, remaining occasionally to be misinterpreted or misused, sometimes in bizarre fashion. In the Akwapim district of Ghana, for example, the paramount chief entertained friends with a sherry party given about the time of Ghana's independence. The old chief presided in his traditional robes and medallions of state, seated on a leopard skin, surrounded by retainers, his golden staff and official linguist close at hand, his talking drums singing the royal praises. The chief's nephew, British educated, lounged nearby, viewing the proceedings through his monocle, his flannel blazer sporting the gold crest of a soccer club. His grandson was there too, garbed in the latest fashion from abroad—pointed shoes and a wide-shouldered suit. The young man was asked if he aspired to the stool one day. He shook his head firmly. Heavens no! He had higher hopes. "What, me be a chief? Fifty pounds a month and no expense account?" He much preferred his present position, he explained. What was that? Why, traveling salesman for a European schnapps distiller.[10]

Many Africans recoiled from such vulgar incongruities, yet they did not wish to deny the outside world or seek isolation within a narrow past. Political freedom, achieved with the departure of colonial governments, still left residual complications. Economic independence remained elusive, awaiting in part a loosening of external economic constraints. Cultural independence appeared no less important; indeed, during the early independence years there was growing conviction that a vigorous African culture was an essential prerequisite to political health and economic prosperity. For cultural independence, however, first there would have to be a corresponding intellectual decolonization. Traditional African values and institutions could then revive with fresh vigor, developing and adapting to the exigencies of a modern world.

# 2

## Présence Africaine *and the* Expression *of* Cultural Freedom

*The Meaning of Independence: Julius Nyerere and Sékou Touré*

One obstacle to achievement of cultural independence was the overwhelming desire among Africans for quick economic development. To many, independence meant self-direction for the purpose of self-benefit. No longer would the assets of the nation accrue to others, to outsiders, to colonial masters. Africans, particularly those educated in the West, had long expressed their grievances over discrimination by colonial governments in such matters as job placement and career advancement, scholarship appointments and educational accessibility, or the opportunity to build businesses based on the resources of the country. Independence would put an end to such discrimination.

The pent-up desire for material advancement was reflected at once in the policies of new governments, which moved not only to modernize their economies and raise living standards but to do so with all possible haste. The latest advances in Western technology were to be introduced without delay. There was no time to be wasted, no time for transition, no reflection over questions of appropriateness and adaptability to African conditions. Little attention was paid to the possibility that the machines and procedures introduced might not suit African needs, that there was scant experience in dealing with these imports, that the rush to modernization might intensify Europe's grip on African economies, or that much of African life still reflected traditional standards and institutions that satisfied and worked. Among the planners the old ways were momentarily forgotten.

There were, of course, exceptions—those who recognized the complexities of independence, who welcomed Western innovations but who saw the need for psychological and cultural emancipation from Europe and the importance that lay in a reaffirmation of traditional African civilization. Many were those individuals concerned with ethical, aesthetic, or philosophical judgments—artists, writers, educators, and other humanists—but some, as well, were members of the new political leadership of independent Africa, Léopold Sédar Senghor of Senegal was an obvious example, but no less concerned were others like Kwame Nkrumah of Ghana, Sékou Touré—who precipitated the independence of Guinea in 1958—and Julius Nyerere, the thoughtful president of Tanzania.

Nyerere's view of independence was certainly forward-looking, and many of his ideas were rooted in Western liberal thinking; yet, he turned to the African past for justification of the democratic, egalitarian socialist society he envisioned for his Tanzanian people. Nyerere reasoned that political independence would have to be followed by quick material development, which, in turn, rested heavily on Western aid. What Nyerere did not wish to import from the West was the individualistic, self-seeking, acquisitive character of its capitalism, and, like Senghor, he rejected the socialism of Europe for he could not, in Africa, accept the socialist doctrine of class conflict. Nyerere, therefore, turned to the communal socialism that he perceived in traditional African society, urging a reassertion of the community solidarity of a way of life in which wealth was produced and shared by all.

Nyerere's personalized view of a modern Africa emerged as a mix of old and new, Africa and Europe. From Europe he looked primarily for technology and financial investment; from Africa he sought a state of mind that would unify a nation of citizens committed to the common good. "Our first step," said Nyerere, "must be to reeducate ourselves; to regain our former attitude of mind. In our traditional African society we were individuals within a community. We took care of the community and the community took care of us. We neither needed nor wished to exploit our fellow men."

Colonialism introduced different and wrongheaded attitudes, continued Nyerere, such as the principle of private land ownership, which led to inequality and the creation of a class of social parasites. We must therefore return to traditional customs of landholding based not on ownership but utility, he pointed out. We must create an African socialism, an ethic by which each individual places social welfare ahead of personal profit. Nyerere called this attitude the spirit of *ujamaa*— "familyhood," in the traditional meaning of the term, "African socialism" as a modern free translation. In either sense, he noted, it was an African tradition to be applied in a new mutation.

> We, in Africa have no more need for being "converted" to socialism than we have of being "taught" democracy. Both are rooted in our own past—in the traditional society which produced us. Modern African socialism can draw from its traditional heritage the recognition of "society" as an extension of the basic family unit. . . . It was in the struggle to break the grip of colonialism that we learnt the need for unity. We came to recognize that the same socialist attitude of mind which, in the tribal days, gave to every individual the security that comes of belonging to a widely extended family, must be preserved within the still wider society of the nation.[1]

Nyerere's humanism may have reflected a somewhat idealized image of traditional African society as well as a utopian view of human perfectibility in any age; at all events, within a few years of independence he found it imperative to intensify the drive for African socialism in his young nation through the celebrated Arusha Declaration of 1967. The declaration was a change in emphasis that stressed self-reliance and attempted to proscribe what Nyerere perceived as an incipient acquisitiveness among Tanzanian leadership. What remained unchanged, however, was his conviction that the morality of a modern African socialism rested in those tenets of social behavior inherited from traditional African society.

Across the continent in West Africa, Sékou Touré voiced similar sentiments, albeit under different circumstances. There was the same ambivalence toward Europe and Western culture, the same devotion to the need for a declaration of African independence that went beyond political freedom to affirm the importance of African culture. Like other political figures in France's former colonies, Touré had professed a genuine desire for a Franco-African community, conceding France as the first among equals. Nevertheless, in urging rejection by Guinea of General de Gaulle's constitution of the Fifth Republic, Touré denounced colonialism in stinging terms and asserted the need for all peoples to express their own qualities, to establish their sense of dignity through national liberty. "Step by step," Touré stated, "societies and their people extend and consolidate their right to happiness, their claims to greatness, and develop their contribution to the economic and cultural wealth of all mankind. We Africans are no different. . . . According to our ways we seek fulfillment."

On independence, therefore, Touré urged the people of Guinea to decolonize in thought and deed. He meant more than such obvious moves as the renaming of streets and the substitution of Guinean for French personnel. He meant an end to the servility of colonialism. He meant the fusing of Guinea's diverse peoples into a unity of Guinean citizens. Most of all he meant the establishment of a Guinean mentality alive to the implications of independence—the self-respect that came with self-government, the pride and contentment that followed in the expression of African culture and values.

Response to Touré's message was immediate and enthusiastic as both government and the population at large moved to reshape the nation; yet, despite the strong rhetoric of Touré and others, the emphasis centered more on Africanization than on an obliteration of French colonial institutions. Some were abandoned as irrelevant, but others were adapted to local conditions and still others retained virtually unchanged. At the same time there was no unreflective withdrawal into an archaic African past, whatever its emotional appeal. For example, Sékou Touré, like Kwame Nkrumah, had recognized that traditional chiefs were an anachronism in modern Africa and so the chieftaincy was not permitted to revive.

For most of the citizens of independent Guinea, the transition from colonial times was minimal; French influence had touched them lightly. For the small number of westernized elite, however, it was more difficult to abandon standards and values assimilated along with the French language and education; yet it was this very leadership that was charged with the task of bringing to fruition the social and cultural revolution implicit in political independence. As in Tanzania, the shortfall between achievement and conception was manifest not only in the inefficiency and corruption that have shown themselves in all of Africa's newly developing societies but perhaps as well due to a certain ambivalance among the elite of Guinea as to wherein lay the most productive inheritance from the past to insure a prosperous African future.[2]

Sékou Touré's assessment of the responsibilities of government lacked any such equivocation. The true political leaders of Africa, he stated, are those whose efforts on behalf of national liberation are marked by basic support of an African culture. Colonialism, he continued, tried to destroy that culture in order to dominate. If we are to succeed, he said, the process must be reversed:

> Our unceasing efforts will reveal our own road to development, bringing our evolution and emancipation without a change in our personality. Each time we adopt an African solution, authentic in nature and conception, we ease our problems because those participating are not confused or surprised by what they set out to achieve. They grasp without difficulty the way they must work, act, or think. Our own qualities will be fully utilized and in so doing we will accelerate our historic evolution.[3]

### The First International Congress of Black Writers and Artists

These last sentiments by Sékou Touré were expressed at Rome in 1959 at the Second Congress of Black Writers and Artists. The first of these two conferences had taken place three years earlier in Paris, but the objective was the same in each case, and was the same that motivated Africans during the years that brought political independence: how to match newly won sovereignty with a propelling cultural emancipation. Coming as it did before much of Africa had gained political independence, the Paris meeting became a crucial early attempt to establish and define the need for cultural affirmation in Africa.

Both congresses were sponsored by the black cultural revue, *Présence Africaine*, and were inspired by that journal's editor and founder, Alioune Diop. Diop's idea for the 1956 congress had been germinating for some time, a meeting that would bring together leading black intellectuals—*"les hommes de culture"*—partly so that those long separated by colonialism might at last become acquainted, but mainly to liberate and reaffirm the civilization of the black man, so long oppressed under the weight of slavery and alien control. With conscious purpose, if not irony, the chosen conference site was the Sorbonne Ampitheatre Descartes, named for France's great apostle of human reason and understanding.

The conference met in late September. The weather was warm and the auditorium often stifling. On the afternoon of the second day, however, the hall was filled to capacity. At the front was the speaker's table, from which the seats rose in semicircles, containing not only the delegates but also many visitors—newsmen, scholars, students, and others with amateur or professional concern for Africa. There was much interest in the speaker about to be introduced. He was Aimé Césaire, they were told, distinguished poet and Martiniquan deputy to the French national assembly, longtime advocate of the movement known as Negritude, to which he had contributed much substance as well as the very name by which it was known. That day he would talk on the theme of black culture and colonialism.

Sitting quietly during the introduction, Césaire seemed to young James Baldwin as bland and benign in manner, vaguely like a middle-aged schoolteacher. All that changed once Césaire began to speak, said Baldwin, who was reporting on the conference proceedings as a journalist. With speech there came into focus a sharp intelligence and the strength to give it force and direction.[4]

Césaire began without equivocation. What do we delegates have in common, he asked rhetorically? It is not our common color but our common experience as a colonial people. And what has colonialism meant to us, but a denial of our own self, a refusal to admit the humanity of the black, an unwillingness to allow him his presence in the world as a human being, as a man? We are united by this colonialist oppression, and we are united by our common culture, which that oppression has sought to destroy.

This common culture, Césaire continued, is a product of social forces, including language, but its health relies on freedom of expression; a colonial regime that suppresses the self-determination of a people will surely kill that people's creative power and with it the people's culture. Moreover, said Césaire, in order to flourish, culture needs some form of organization, an organization that is political. Freely given by a colonial administration, political organization becomes part of the culture that it helps to condition.

They were beginning to get what they had come to hear, these black delegates from Africa, from the Americas, from other parts of the world. These were the words that were in all hearts, now given eloquent expression by one of their own. The hall was silent in concentration, Baldwin recalled, as all were caught up by the speaker's words. European colonialism masquerades as many things, Césaire went on, his phrases taking on a new intensity. Colonialism called itself the mark of a higher civilization—a superiority in philosophy, in language, in technology, in social organization—and it would impose this upon others in the world considered less fortunate, Césaire informed his listeners. That is the colonial process. At best, the colonialists claim, this higher civilization can be assimilated and with felicitous results; after all, they like to point out, was there not the historical precedent of the Gauls finally welcoming the civilizing impact of Rome's legions?

Let us not be deceived by such self-serving egotism and hypocrisy, Césaire warned. We are not offered a genuine gift, some abundant cornucopia of Western culture. What is thrust upon us is naked oppression through a system that ignores human dignity and intellectual rigor in its pursuit of economic advantage. Money is the foundation of this Western culture, said Césaire, and for profit it will eliminate everything in its path—culture, philosophy, religion—all that might impede or paralyze the march toward enrichment by a group of privileged men.

It stands to reason, Césaire insisted, that the colonial system cannot give what it has of value. If the colonized were to receive the benefits of Western economic, political, and social riches, the transformation would be quick and complete. A truly mixed culture would emerge, like that of Japan, based upon the selectivity of need, but such a situation requires self-expression for subject peoples that cannot survive under colonialism. Instead we have a hodgepodge of cultural traits, scraps drawn from here and there, a kaleidoscope lacking harmony and unity practiced by an indigenous elite that is isolated from its sources, a marginal mutation that endures while the true culture of the people rots away. Small wonder there is an inferiority complex among us, a complex not accidental but induced. Make no mistake about it, concluded Césaire, the imposition of a colonial civilization has but one end in view, and that is the complete subordination of the subject people. This is barbarism achieved through cultural anarchy. And it is death for the colonized society.[5]

Such ringing declarations could not fail to bring down the house.

The applause was long and enthusiastic. The speaker was surrounded with ecstatic well-wishers, James Baldwin reported, joyful in their shared enthusiasm for words that had so powerfully expressed both their frustrations and their convictions. In his address a day earlier, Alioune Diop had said much the same things, but Diop's discourse was more restrained, less volatile, and in the end less compelling.

Not all were persuaded, however. The American writer, Richard Wright, longtime supporter of *Présence Africaine* and long concerned with relations between the Western and non-Western worlds, felt himself nonplussed by Césaire's words, so different from what he, Wright, planned to say when he addressed the conference. Baldwin, too, was disturbed. Swept along by Césaire's eloquent indictment, he nevertheless felt that there was an emptiness about the argument. A brilliant speech had played skillfully on emotions and expectations but had said nothing about the basic issue. The European impact was no philosophical toy, a mere set of words. It was a reality. What, indeed, had colonialism made of the African, his culture, his dreams? Baldwin wanted to know. What of the fact that it had created men of two worlds, men like the speaker? At this conference, of all places, why had not Césaire addressed this central question?[6]

Coming before the delegates the next day, Richard Wright moved to confront the issue of African civilization, its validity, and its relationship to the West. He did this with some diffidence, he said, because of the considerable void between his own thoughts and what he had heard during the preceding discussions. Wright protested that his convictions were as strong as ever. Moreover, he was uncomfortable with a seeming lack of objectivity within the conference, and a tendency to avoid basic issues.

For Wright the main point was not the evils of colonialism; these were evident enough. Rather, the question was what validity African culture had in a modern world, and what had been the impact of European civilization on Africa, whether for good or for evil. Was Europe to be rejected out of hand merely because it was foreign and colonial? Should ignorance and superstition be sustained purely out of support for the traditions of African civilization? Wright's own experience and background, he explained, was unequivocally Western; despite the immorality of racial prejudice in America, he had inherited and assimilated a whole set of Western values that had entered the world of Asia and Africa in the train of colonialism. Were they to be denied because of the evident stupidity and barrenness of colonialism, or were they to be accepted on the strength of their own intrinsic merits?

What he was talking about, said Wright, were such concepts as rational thought and pragmatic action, the autonomy of art and the power of science, free circulation of ideas in a secular state, and humanity as an end in itself. These values came from the West but they are not exclusively Western, insisted Wright. They belong to us all. What matter if they arrived in the company of a clumsy and cruel colonialism? "I . . . say 'Bravo' to the consequences of Western plundering . . . that created . . . the possible rise of rational societies. . . . Thank you, Mr. White Man, for freeing me from the rot of my irrational traditions and customs, though you are still the victim of your own."[7]

The issue seemed drawn between these two culturally assimilated black men. Césaire, the French-educated, évolué, argued that colonialism crushed indigenous culture precisely in order to rule politically. Freedom, political or otherwise, therefore seemed possible only through a vigorous assertion of cultural autonomy. Wright, from his American background, was no less critical of either cultural or political imperialism, but he also supported the validity of Western values and institutions in a modern world, to be applied wherever they appeared useful for man's universal benefit. Thus, for Wright, rational thought would be better exemplified by an African protesting racism than by a European racial bigot.

Was there no reconciliation of these two antithetical positions? In pressing his case for westernization, Wright seemed to rebuff any surviving anachronisms of African culture, however romantic or appealing. Césaire's defense of black culture did not rule out selective utilization of Western institutions; nevertheless, his was a clear call for a renascent African civilization and with it the implication of political independence. In the supercharged atmosphere touched off by Césaire's words, there was little sympathy for the kind of doubts expressed by Wright and Baldwin. Only later, as the congress closed its proceedings, were the delegates able to agree on resolutions that affirmed the brotherhood of all men while demanding the rehabilitation of black cultures in order that they might be appropriately integrated into the general body of world civilization.[8]

## Negritude

The major differences of opinion that emerged from the dialogue between Aimé Césaire and Richard Wright were not the only ones that separated those attending the Paris congress, and they were related to other disagreements associated with Cesaire's doctrine of Negritude. Scarcely known at the time outside France and her possessions, Negritude, among French-speaking Africans, had long been a passionate belief or a target of criticism, and always a point of contention. In Anglophone Africa people were hardly aware of the dispute, Davidson Nicol of Sierra Leone later recalled. For us, he pointed out, Negritude was a new thing. For Césaire, for Alioune Diop, and *Présence Africaine*, however, Negritude was an article of faith, its affirmation a chief reason for arranging the congress. For Léopold Senghor, already a celebrated poet as well as political leader and Senegalese representative in the French Chamber of Deputies, it was no less than the expression of unity that bound black men together the world over.

Senghor, then, regarded the cohesion and endurance of African culture as the ideological heart of the Sorbonne conference, the objective of which was to serve notice on the world that an African way of life possessed a validity that contributed to the totality of world civilization, the Civilization of the Universal, as he termed it. In his formal remarks, Senghor described and explained the culture of the black man, a discourse that in effect reviewed many of the main tenets of Negritude.

It was a vivid and effective analysis, familiar to most of the French-speaking delegates, interesting, even arresting, if not yet controversial, to the others. The African mind, said Senghor, is sympathetic rather than antagonistic, African reason intuitive in contrast to the white man's analytic logic. Negro-African metaphysics stresses unity of the natural and the supernatural, the seamless continuity of existence from the ancestors to the living toward the yet unborn. In such a scheme, art is not, as with the European, the imitation of life; rather, it is life itself as well as the expression of life's essential character, life's surrealism.

Negro-African culture, Senghor continued, is best traced through its basic traits of image and rhythm. In the West an artistic image is the representation of some other thing. In Africa the image does more—it suggests, it symbolizes, it embodies. Thus, the elephant is strength and the spider prudence, the horn is moon and the moon fertility. Rhythm plays a similar role, said Senghor. Music is not for listening. It accompanies the spoken word and the dance, converting in its rhythmic insistence prose into poetry and body movement into surreal revelation. Rhythm expresses life's vital force, Senghor concluded. Through concrete, material, sensual means, it moves from body to spirit. As the dancer's limbs describe the most sensual of movements, his mind moves to the serene beauty of the mask, of death.[9]

"Much of this made great sense to me," acknowledged James Baldwin, although he admitted that a good deal of what he heard was beyond his experience; the only example he could think of that resembled the joyful communion of artistic expression described by Senghor was the frenetic, sometimes neurotic, spirit of American jazz. Richard Wright, poised between his own black consciousness and the inflexible conditioning of the Western world, was also greatly attracted by Senghor's philosophy but felt bound to question its relevance for modern Africa. After all, said Wright, this beautiful culture of Africa, with its poetic richness, was never a match for the guns of Europe's imperialists. For five hundred years militant, white, Christian Europe dominated Africa and its cult of ancestral religion in a "morally foul relationship." Did that ancient religion help the people in resistance or did it actually aid the alien guns? Wright wanted to know. Was it not time for Africa to grasp some of the West's most powerful values in order to defend itself?

Wright's own doubts over Negritude sprang partly from convictions tempered during long debates conducted in the cafés of Paris, and partly from his own disillusionment with contemporary African culture as he had lately found it during a journey to Ghana. His skepticism was not isolated, however, for there were many others present highly critical of Senghor's views and doubtful about the congress that had been called in part to express and promote them.

Criticism came from various, often antithetical, quarters. There were Marxists and there were nationalists. There were Europeans and there were Africans. There were scholars and there were polemicists. And there were different generations of all of these. Small wonder the doctrine of Negritude clashed with a host of preconceptions. Frenchmen, beset with liberation movements in Vietnam and Algeria and emotionally committed to the continuation of a France overseas, tended to be put off by a point of view that stressed cultural, if not political, independence. When Alioune Diop first launched the idea of a congress of black artists and writers, most of France's Africanists were horrified. This smacked of racism, they argued; but, more than that, it separated France and those people to whom France had given so much. Perhaps there was also apprehension among French geographers, historians, anthropologists, or sociologists that their own professional work in Africa might be jeopardized.

French Marxists were likewise disturbed, citing Negritude's potential for racial cleavage, but actually dreaded a defection from their oft-proclaimed proletarian struggle against international capitalism. Among Westernized Africans there were many who held dear this image of world revolution and feared a break in the ranks based upon that most un-Marxist standard of skin color. Such a feeling was particularly acute among most young Africans studying abroad in France.

For a number of years Diop had solicited opinions concerning his idea of a congress as well as for other expressions of an African presence in the world. His encouragement stimulated a series of lively responses from young students that *Présence Africaine* published in 1953 in a special issue, *Les Étudiants Noirs Parlent.* At about the same time a heated literary debate burst forth over the validity of Negro-African writing as separate from Western literary forms. Diop himself editorialized continuously in his revue on these and allied themes—for instance, in 1955 he published an article entitled "Colonialism and Cultural Nationalism" in which he stressed the need for cultural freedom in Africa, that modern African societies might thrive through the nourishment of their own traditions, history, and culture.

Diop's views on African independence came close to Senghor's Negritude, and Negritude fell under particularly heavy fire from the leftists, black as well as white. As early as 1949 the African Marxist, Gabriel d'Arboussier, had attacked Negritude as a "diversion from the class struggle." The controversy over black literature appeared first in 1955 when *Les Lettres Françaises,* the cultural journal of French communists, featured an attack by René Depestre, a Haitian poet living in Brazil. Depestre argued that a natural African quality in

Antillian poetry should not obscure the reliance of social realism on the French literary heritage; in other words, a little Negritude was permissible provided it did not interfere with the literature of Marxist revolution. This contention was seized upon by Aimé Césaire, who accused Depestre of cleaving to Western literary forms while allowing only occasional scraps of material from his African heritage. True poetry, said Césaire, need not be self-conscious of origins. Good poetry cannot help but reflect the poet's being; in a racist world the African poet can scarcely forget his blackness, can scarcely fail to express his Negritude.

The indictment of Negritude by young African students was more powerfully reasoned. From the first appearance of *Présence Africaine* in 1947, students had devoured each new issue, feeding their growing sense of national and cultural pride, and responding to Diop's assertion that the new journal was especially aimed at the intellectual refreshment of the youth of Africa. In time, however, differences of opinion emerged over the doctrine of Negritude, especially after the appearance of Jean-Paul Sartre's celebrated exegesis, *Black Orpheus*, which was published in 1948 as a preface to Senghor's anthology of new black poetry written in French.

If Negritude were a consistent philosophy, the students argued, it would forge a firm link between cultural independence and political freedom; yet they were convinced that both Senghor and Alioune Diop held back from this logical step. Basically, therefore, student opposition to Negritude and the Sorbonne congress of black writers and artists was based upon the issue of political independence, which the students felt was opposed by the leading voices of the Negritude movement. Their most articulate attack came from the pen of the Togolese, Albert Franklin, who aimed primarily at the arguments contained in Sartre's *Black Orpheus*.

Writing in *Les Étudiants Noirs Parlent*, Franklin firmly rejected Sartre's defense of Negritude, terming much of it a myth and a fiction. To begin with, said Franklin, the collectivism, the sexuality, the sense of rhythm, the closeness to nature attributed to the black man occur in one form or another in all the races of the world. With an insight beyond his years, Franklin argued that it was economic sophistication, not vaguely drawn character traits, that determined the nature of societies, and he then went on to demolish Sartre's assertion that the African intellect was intuitive by contrast to the European's rationalism. This would presuppose that Africans were incapable of abstract thinking and generalization from particulars, that they had no empirical science or scientific methodology—all belied, said Franklin, by African medicine, mineralogy, or widely admired techniques of West African bronze casting.

As for Sartre's antiracist racism, Franklin went on, this foundation stone of Negritude is pure negation—white racism is to be combated by an equal and opposite black racism. Leaving aside the scientific fact that white is the fusion of all color and black its absence, Franklin observed mischievously, racial differences are once again to be explained by economic factors. The white man has progressed scientifically far beyond the black, it is true, but this progress is explained not by skin color but by educational and social achievement, by technological superiority.

Franklin singled out Aimé Césaire as a good communist whose own militant Negritude gave massive support to millions of oppressed people but which could easily be confused with the dreamy, contemplative brand of that philosophy that favors irrational over rational thought. Sartre's dialectic posing the thesis of white racism against the antithesis of black racism is even more dangerous, warned Franklin, because it separates the oppressed of the world along lines of color. This division must not be endured, Franklin concluded. Negritude cannot be allowed to drive a wedge into proletarian solidarity in the name of a national liberation that would ask the oppressed of Africa to fight against their European brothers. For this reason alone, Negritude must be opposed, left to its "withdrawal, anguish, despair."[10]

*Présence Américaine*

One of Alioune Diop's chief activities during the Paris conference was to keep conflicting views under control, to head off ideological disputes that might split the delegates and thereby destroy a show of unity, so necessary for the concluding resolutions of the congress. This was no easy task, for there were many tensions in the hall, variations on the major theme of the relative merits of African and Western culture.

On the second day, an outburst of irritation from the spectators forced Thomas Ekello, a clergyman from Cameroon, to abandon his talk on the influence of Christianity on African culture. The animosity toward Pastor Ekello, and other clerics who followed, was based on the conviction among many Africans that Christianity had played a devastating role in European conquest and colonization. Ekello and Reverend Marcus James of Jamaica, tried to draw a distinction between Christ's message and the subsequent shortcomings of his priests, but this did little to dissipate the hostile atmosphere in the hall. In conclusion, Reverend James was bound to concede that Christian practice in Africa had been a cruel travesty, that European failures had come from an insecure morality and a confusion between technical and spiritual superiority.[11]

Another area of difference if not dispute arose among delegates who had experienced diverse colonial regimes, more particularly between those from the British and French colonies. Most of those attending the conference were from the French areas, and with them came not only the French language but also the intense reaction to Gallic culture that an uncompromising French assimilation had engendered. "There were not enough English-speaking people there to make a mark," Davidson Nicol recalled, adding somewhat ruefully that many of the Francophone Africans sooner or later were swept into power because, unlike the British, the French made a policy of recruiting an elite leadership into positions of importance. Possibly British cultural insouciance accounts for the lack of a passionate literature of protest from British Africa, as Nicol reported in his conference paper; perhaps a relaxed manner was only the simulated casualness learned by Africans from residence at English universities.

To be sure, those from the British territories fully supported the conference commitment to black African culture, but generally their support was less fervent and tempered with self-scrutiny. In counterpoint to Césaire's discourse on colonization and African culture, the West Indian writer, George Lamming, was able to draw attention to inner weaknesses, pointing out that there were many Africans successfully exploiting their blackness in a white world, "doing extremely well in the skin trade," as he put it. "The enemy is not only on the outside, he is on the inside as well," said Lamming, who went on to enunciate another point that may not have been fully appreciated by the more sanguine exponents of Negritude. The black writer, he said, must survive the limitations that white labels put on him, for he is in reality the voice of all men in the contemporary world. He speaks to his own people, of course, but ultimately his search for the meaning of his personal destiny is a search on behalf of all mankind. This he must do with all his strength, judgment, and good faith.[12]

Alioune Diop found his diplomatic powers tested to their fullest by strains that quickly developed around the delegation from the United States. Here again, the essential issue was the conflict in values between Africa and the West, although other points of contention may have been at work—questions of political ideology or cultural pride, for example. To begin with, the Americans were present almost by chance, chosen only a few months before the congress at the urging of Richard Wright. Wright, moreover, though nominally a member of the American group, stood somewhat apart from his colleagues by consequence of his self-exile in Paris and his literary reputation, which attracted blacks from all quarters. This ambivalent position caused him some anxiety, but this was a minor embarrassment soon overshadowed by events at the opening session.

The meeting began with a welcoming address by Alioune Diop, and this was followed immediately by the reading of several messages from absent well-wishers. Among these was a characteristically crusty statement from the American black leader, W. E. B. Du Bois, announcing that he had not come to Paris because he had not been granted a passport, adding, "Any American Negro travelling abroad today must either not care about Negroes or say what the State Department wishes him to say." The attentive James Baldwin reported the waves of derisive laughter that greeted these words, to the intense embarrassment of the American delegates, an embarrassment Baldwin doubtless shared.

The Americans were a distinguished group, including Horace Mann Bond, president of Lincoln University, three university professors—Mercer Cook, William T. Fontaine, and the delegation chief, John A. Davis—along with James W. Ivey, editor of *The Crisis*, the journal of the National Association for the Advancement of Colored People, which Du Bois himself had helped found many years earlier. Distinguished they were and generally middle of the road in political and social outlook; certainly they were not in tune with the known communist sympathies of Du Bois, nor were they close to the largely

Marxist orientation of many of the congress delegates. Certainly, too, they supported the right of American citizens to travel abroad, but the absence of Du Bois seriously weakened their position and made their task of explaining the conditions and position of blacks in America extremely difficult. They brought with them as well the constraints of the McCarthy era that had weighed so heavily on Americans irrespective of race.

In his remarks Du Bois went on to urge that Africans take the road of socialism already traveled by Russia and China, not the backward betrayal into colonialism represented by the United States. These were bitter words to the American blacks who had devoted their lives to ending discrimination in their own country, and their dismay was compounded by the expressed approval of Du Bois's indictment by delegates, who, despite their socialist leanings, made no complaint of the French colonialism that still controlled their lives.

The contretemps of the morning were only a beginning. During the noon recess John Davis was asked why he considered himself a Negro. He certainly did not look like one, he was told, and there was an implication that he did not act like one either. Davis responded that he was a Negro by choice; given the racial imperatives of American society, he could want to be nothing else. His explanation was clear to James Baldwin, who had joined the discussion, but Baldwin was certain that the experience of blacks in America could have scant meaning for Africans emerging from colonialism. Invasion, occupation, and oppression invited overthrow and expulsion of the oppressor, Baldwin thought, but blacks in America were part of their own society, however badly, however unfairly it treated them. America was their home; moreover, they were needed there. They did not want to overthrow their society; they only wanted to change it, to reform it, to join it, so that they too might benefit from its many advantages.

Such a point of view was difficult to express, but Davis and his colleagues were bound to try. When Thomas Ekello was shouted down, Horace Mann Bond protested this discourtesy in open session, and the American delegation secured for Ekello the opportunity to finish his remarks. "We feel strongly about freedom of religion and separation of church and state," Davis explained. "In the area of religion, all Americans are members of a minority group."

As for Marxism, Davis pointed out that the Communist party in America had long used blacks for its own ends, that blacks in the United States supported constitutional reform to iron out the inequalities in American society. He emphasized the anticolonial commitment of American blacks, a viewpoint Davis said was shared by all his countrymen and practiced by their government since the days of George Washington. In addition, Davis explained to the assembled delegates, blacks in the United States are sensitive to their African background and culture, as the survival of spirituals and the development of jazz attests. To all this, Davis concluded, the Negro in America would like to add a positive note, not to contribute merely to another condemnation of colonialism, but to affirm the growth of new societies in Africa and elsewhere, societies free of oppression and discrimination.

To some Africans in the hall, Davis seemed to be saying that African culture was primitive, that colonialism should end, but not in order to perpetuate a picturesque cultural backwardness. In their remarks on the floor and during informal conversations, the American delegates spoke repeatedly of the advances made in American society, of the rehabilitation of Europe after the Second World War through Marshall Plan aid, of the progress taking place in the United States, particularly the constitutional and statutory changes that enabled blacks to share equally with others the fruits of American civilization.

For the delegation from the United States it was a particular shock, therefore, when Aimé Césaire, in his address on culture and colonialism, included Americans among the blacks of the world laboring under the yoke of colonialism. The colonial situation is our common denominator, said Césaire, who then went on: "And our American brothers, through racial discrimination in a great modern nation, are placed in an artificial situation incomprehensible except in terms of a colonialism that still endures."

This was too much. It was too much for John Davis, for all the others. It was especially offensive to Mercer Cook, specialist in French literature, longtime Paris resident and Sorbonne student, friend of Senghor, Césaire, and the other adherents of Negritude. How could they regard him and his colleagues as colonial subjects, rowing in the same galley, as he put it, with the colonial people of Africa? Was all this talk of black culture only some sort of ruse, a trap? Was the Paris congress only a device to ring the changes on colonialism, in the United States as elsewhere?

Cook raised these questions on the conference floor, but Césaire held firm, with some assistance from Senghor. He did not mean that American blacks were literally in the same colonial condition as Africans, said Césaire. He did mean, however, that the circumstances in which black Americans found themselves were directly attributable to their history, first of all a history of slavery, and later a history of social and cultural discrimination that was a direct consequence of that slavery. For his part, Senghor insisted that Americans, like Haitians, were laboring under the constraints of international capitalism, just as Africans labored under colonialism. None could give free expression to their cultures while those conditions endured.

The Americans might well have felt alienated, misunderstood, and rejected by the other black men in the hall. Indeed, there were those present who accepted the charge of Du Bois and regarded John Davis and his colleagues as no more than creatures of the American State Department; but there were also others who saw them in a different light, something more akin to their own self-image.

To the Senegalese historian, Cheikh Anta Diop, Marxist and staunch adherent of Negritude, the United States delegates were faithful representatives of the society that had produced them. They fully supported the so-called American way and they were firmly anticommunist. While they were wholeheartedly behind the aspirations of Africans for freedom from colonialism, said Diop, they regarded modernization through high technology as the most effective means for African social and economic advancement. Their support of American society was a form of self-support, for they were firmly committed to achieving equal status for blacks in America. Change would come through peaceful, lawful steps, through consensus by all Americans, white and black.

"I remember Davis well," Cheikh Anta Diop recalled, "a good man, levelheaded. He and the others were typical Americans. Davis was always talking about the importance of American foreign aid. They all sounded like Americans, not like blacks. Later, at the time of the civil rights movement, I thought of Davis and his insistence of racial integration through persuasion, through assent, through legal means. This was the position of the American delegation."

The views of Richard Wright were somewhat different, Diop went on. Wright was of a more philosophic turn of mind. He saw Western ideas and values working their way into the policies of developing nations through Western-educated leadership. Men like Nehru, Sukarno, and Nkrumah were to be the vehicles for grafting a clearly superior Western rationalism onto the traditional beliefs of their people. In any case, concluded Cheikh Anta Diop, neither Wright nor the other Americans at Paris showed any of the militancy that developed in the United States later, during the 1960s, a movement more inspired by the belligerent philosophy of Frantz Fanon than by the Negritude of Senghor and Césaire.

Indeed, it was Senghor who was chiefly responsible for softening the tensions that had begun to isolate the American delegation at Paris. Senghor brought the Americans and their critics together, initiating discussions that led to mutual understanding and respect, and, incidentally, launching the Americans into an active promotion of the ideas of Negritude through the American Society of African Culture (AMSAC), which they founded shortly after the conclusion of the Paris congress. Following the precepts of Negritude, AMSAC presented performances, publications, seminars, and lectures to develop a heightened sense of pride and accomplishment among American blacks and to educate all Americans concerning black achievement, their goal mutual esteem among Americans, black and white. That this essay in moderation failed is more a reflection of the temper of the times than of any intrinsic weakness. During the 1960s, the more militant views of Frantz Fanon prevailed in America, as the black nationalism of Malcolm X progressed through the black power exemplified by Stokely Carmichael to the ultimate violence and self-destruction of the Black Panther movement. But by that time AMSAC had also expired, its temperate policies unwanted in an era of extremism, its usefulness destroyed by an unwitting connection with the Central Intelligence Agency, from which it had received financial support through a number of philanthropic foundations.[13]

## Pan-Africanism or Communism?

There was yet another aspect of the basic schism within the congress between African and European values. This was the conflict between

Pan-Africanism, a concept of worldwide black solidarity, and international communism, a major objective of which was the unification of the world's workers irrespective of race. That the Paris congress was divided on this issue was exemplified repeatedly—in the sharp differences expressed by W. E. B. Du Bois and John Davis, in the shocked horror of French Marxists, black and white, over the mere existence of an international congress that united blacks, by implication against their white fellow workers, in the personal paradox of Aimé Césaire, at once the poet of Negritude and prominent member of the French Communist party.

The contradiction between communism and Pan-Africanism had long been the subject of widespread debate among blacks, certainly among nationalists in Africa, particularly in South Africa, where African leadership had largely come to reject communism as an aid in their struggles against official racial discrimination. While many Africans subscribed to socialist principles regarding public control of the means of production and distribution, they also suspected international communism of utilizing misery, poverty, ignorance, and want in Africa on behalf of Soviet foreign policy objectives. African Marxists, therefore, were often ambivalent, poised between their socialist beliefs and their desire for domestic economic and political advances. Only one month before the Paris meeting, an influential black writer from the West Indies, George Padmore, had published *Pan-Africanism or Communism?*, a history of past and recent black movements, the thesis of which was that advances by blacks in Africa and elsewhere had always come primarily through self-help. Those who hoped for future reform, said Padmore, a former communist and Comintern member, had best forget the blandishments of self-serving communists and place their faith in Pan-African solidarity.[14]

Padmore had planned to attend the Paris conference but was prevented from doing so by illness. His Pan-African views were present, however, and in no less a person than Aimé Césaire, the architect of Negritude. Padmore had resolved his dilemma by resigning his Comintern post many years earlier, devoting himself thenceforth to Pan-African solidarity. At the congress, Césaire may have also reached similar conclusions. He did not speak out at the time, but one month later, in October 1956, his convictions were given public expression in a well-publicized letter to Maurice Thorez, Secretary General of the French Communist party.

It was a letter of resignation, said Césaire, a reaction to the excesses of Russian communism and the acquiescence thereto by the French communists. But, there is more, Césaire continued. There is the black man, his needs and his aspirations. He will no longer be bound in allegiance to the workingman of France if that alliance means divorce from his black brothers in the Antilles, in America, in Africa. As Padmore had before him, Césaire was turning from the illusion of communist unity and equality toward the promise of Pan-African cohesion. "I . . . believe that the dark-skinned peoples are rich in energy, and in passion; that they want neither in vigor, nor in imagination; but that these potentials cannot but sicken and fade in organizations that are not their own; not constructed for them; not built by them and adapted to ends only they themselves can fix."[15]

### A Congress Cultural or a Congress Political?

There was a final paradox, if not schism, that emerged from the Paris congress, and it was identified at once by Mercer Cook of the American delegation. On arrival in Paris, Cook had asked Alioune Diop if the congress was cultural or political. Diop's response was unequivocal. "It is purely a cultural congress," he stated. Cook's experience did not seem to bear this out. "Evidently it is not always easy," he later observed, "to separate the cultural from the political."[16]

The comment was more than justified by the proceedings of the congress, perhaps no more so than in the words and actions of its three leading sponsors: Alioune Diop, Léopold Senghor, and Aimé Césaire. In his speech Césaire had rung the changes on colonialism and held up for scorn the hypocrisy of French assimilation. In demonstrating that indigenous culture could not flourish under colonial restraints, he reached a seemingly inescapable conclusion—political factors shaped culture and were part of it; self-determination was a necessary prerequisite to the creative power of a people; hence, political independence and cultural freedom went hand in hand.

In his Sorbonne comments on colonialism, however, Césaire was bound to avoid an unambiguous call for independence, and the reasons were clearly more political than cultural. In 1946 France's Fourth Republic had brought civil rights and citizenship to large numbers of her overseas populations, but had done so within the context of the French Union. France was considered an indivisible republic at the time; there could be no independence for associated territories; even talk of independence was regarded as subversive. In 1956, only a few months before the Sorbonne congress, the French community of overseas possessions had undergone a fundamental change in structure, but this shift did not affect the basic relationship between France and her territories. A large measure of local autonomy had been granted, but this was regarded not as a step toward independence but as its substitute.

It was a difficult position for blacks in the French regions, particularly as political independence was in the air—already established in North Africa and on its way in Ghana and other parts of the subsaharan continent. For Césaire it was particularly awkward because Martinique was a French department, considered as much a part of France as Burgundy or the Touraine. Hence Césaire tended to stress cultural nationalism, leaving the more explicit demands for political autonomy to nationalists from the African territories.

For Léopold Senghor there were similar difficulties. Through long-standing personal and cultural ties, and as a member of the French government, Senghor was deeply committed to close relations between France and her African territories. Small wonder his Negritude came under attack from African students who charged him with inconsistency in supporting cultural freedom but opposing the natural consequences of political independence. In fact, this judgment was not entirely fair.

As early as 1946 Senghor had stated publicly that France would have to consider independence for her colonies. Later he backed off from this position, partly because of the terrible losses suffered during the liberation wars in Madagascar, Vietnam, and Algeria, and partly because he came to believe that reform could be gained by constitutional means through pressure by the African bloc in the French Chamber of Deputies. By 1956 Senghor seemed to be moving uncertainly toward some formula that would maintain a link between metropolitan and overseas France, something that might permit cultural liberation without political divorce. Later he went so far as to invent euphemisms for independence, suggesting such locutions as *autodétermination* and *autonomie*.

With the advent of the Fifth Republic and President de Gaulle's alternatives of autonomy within the new French Community or total independence, Senghor's ambivalence deepened. For a time he advocated independence within a multinational confederation of states, then urged his supporters to vote for de Gaulle's community and its constitution; but he purposely absented himself from Senegal during the moment when the vote was cast. He seems to have been caught between two loyalties. He wanted to remain close to a France intent on holding her overseas connections whatever the tactical details. Equally, he hoped for a form of independence that would permit Africa to act as a powerful counterpoise to metropolitan France within some form of French federation, a position on federation similar to that of Sékou Touré. Thus, at the time of the 1956 Paris congress, Senghor was engaged in a political activity that might lend authority to the cultural affirmation of Negritude.[17]

Political action also accompanied the Negritude of Alioune Diop, and on two distinct levels. One of Diop's major concerns at Paris was to unify worldwide cultural assertion by blacks, and to do this under the leadership of *Présence Africaine*, while emphasizing the primacy of Africa. Diop felt that black civilization in the Americas had been diluted by large infusions from the West. The essential black culture was to be found in Africa, he insisted; at the same time African civilizations needed special support since so much remained in fragile oral forms. Reconciling conflicting ideological positions, soothing ruffled feelings, playing down parochial loyalties, Diop was able to persuade the congress to unite in a declaration of black cultural independence. At the same time he moved to establish the Society of African Culture under the aegis of *Présence Africaine*, an organization for the propagation and dissemination of black culture.[18]

Diop secured Césaire's acquiescence in African cultural leadership although he remained uneasy over the subsequent creation of the American-based AMSAC as a possible rival to his Society of African Culture. As to political relations between Africa and France, however, Diop appeared less uncertain than Senghor. By the time of the Sorbonne congress, Alioune Diop had concluded that cultural independence was wholly dependent upon political freedom and he said so, both in *Pré-*

*sence Africaine* and elsewhere. His statement, "Colonialism and Cultural Nationalism," issued one year before the congress, made the point explicitly. Colonialism can never bring peaceful and constructive collaboration, said Diop. Assimilation leads only to the destruction of cultural initiative. "Spiritual health rests on culture which in turn springs from the freedom of a people's political and social institutions."[19]

With all its stresses and divisions, the First Congress of Black Writers and Artists was able to reach important conclusions. There was at least an implicit concession that aspects of European culture were essential in the development of a modern Africa. Next, there was the unequivocal assertion of the importance of African culture, and black culture more generally, to a healthy world civilization. Finally, the congress inextricably linked cultural expression to political independence and economic growth. If, as Césaire and others had insisted, culture could not thrive without political liberty, was not the reverse also true? Did it not follow that political independence, along with economic advance, was equally reliant upon the assertion of a genuine cultural freedom? From the delegates attending the Sorbonne congress, there came forceful affirmation.

# 2

*The Arts and Cultural Independence*

# 3

## The Visual Arts
## and African Independence

### The Humanist and the Intangibles of Independence

In asserting the validity of black culture, the Paris and Rome congresses of *Présence Africaine* turned naturally to the black humanists of Africa and the Americas. Clearly it was the practicing writer or artist, critic or scholar, educator or historian, philosopher or theologian who was best qualified to comment on the qualities of black culture. In this narrow sense it was obvious to call on the specialist to testify concerning his specialty. In a larger sense, however, the humanist in Africa was particularly well qualified to assess the quality and direction of independence, political as well as cultural. The independence that came to Africa in the 1950s and 1960s was first expressed in political and economic terms, but important areas of social and intellectual activity were also involved, and the preoccupations of the African humanist often brought him into contact with basic questions of national development and purpose.

As with individuals, the health of nations often depends upon intangibles—axioms governing standards of national behavior; the desire to create a saner, safer, healthier world; definitions of agreed-upon ethical or aesthetic principles; the reconciliation of material with spiritual needs. Here the African humanist was on his own ground. Here, as in past times, he expressed himself in his poems and histories, his dramas, his dances, and his art. In so doing he was observing and judging, admonishing and exhorting, assessing the quality and character of the world in which he lived. The *Présence Africaine* conferences, therefore, were part of a larger movement that stretched back to the early nineteenth century and before, and took as a major function the identification of essential human values in an African context, their application to the world from which they sprang and which they helped create.

## The Decline of Excellence

Of the various art forms of Africa, it is probably the visual, or better still, the plastic, that is best known outside the continent itself. It was the sculpture of Africa that attracted Picasso, Modigliani, and other early twentieth-century European modernists, lending them important assistance in their search for new means of expression. The traditional carvings and castings of Africa have since become substantial additions to museum collections in the West, while periodic exhibitions have awakened growing interest and appreciation for the artistic accomplishments of traditional Africa. Small wonder. Who could fail to be moved by the mystery of the Luba figurine, the dynamism in a Senufo mask, the dignity of Ife's royal bronzes, or the grace that infuses a Bambara antelope headdress?

Best known outside Africa, traditional African sculpture has probably been the least understood of Africa's arts, both inside and outside the continent, by the general public and sometimes by the experts as well. At first traditional carving was regarded as primitive, the product of unsophisticated workers unable to handle their medium, incapable of mature expression. This misconception has now been largely laid to rest. Nevertheless, as recently as 1958 it was deemed appropriate for a major book on African sculpture to contain an introductory essay explaining the true nature of "primitive" art. At the time of independence many Africans still shunned their own artistic heritage, regarding it as the product of barbarous, idolatrous worship.[1]

Praised or damned, the art of traditional Africa has been the victim of another misconception—that it is a thing of the past. "We are in at the death of all that is best in African art" was the epitaph of William Fagg, longtime curator for African art at the British Museum, suggesting that the traditional carver has become an anachronism in modern,

Western-oriented African society. "The modern African artist is being fatally reactionary," announced the art critic of the *New York Times* in 1970, "when he attempts to follow sculptural traditions that expressed a society now dead." An art can scarcely exist outside the concepts and institutions of its own society, he went on, and modern Africa is moving steadily away from its old precepts toward fusion with the modern international world.[2]

There is validity in this point of view. The old way of life has been seriously, probably irrevocably, disturbed by foreign ideas, economic modernization, and the rise of national states. The old patrons—the shrines, the religious societies, the traditional rulers—no longer commission works, and those artifacts already created are slowly vanishing before the ravages of collectors and white ants. Artists have abandoned their craft for other occupations or have turned to newer markets, chiefly in the tourist trade, which they supply with effete, poorly fashioned replicas of their former handiwork. Essentially functional, traditional African sculpture has become decorative, therefore meaningless—meaningless, therefore insipid. Little thought is given to aesthetic merit. Art for art's sake had no place in traditional African society.

Nevertheless a requiem for traditional African culture is premature, if not misdirected. Traditional society, village life, its customs, its arts—all these are changing, but dead they are not, nor even dying. More properly they may be described as evolving under pressure from new circumstances, a condition that all arts must achieve to escape atrophy and an end to life. Age-old ceremonies, for instance, an Ewe funeral in an Accra suburb, an Egungun masquerade from Yorubaland, or a Kalabari festival of the Niger Delta region, still are to be found, though their function may be shifting from ritual to entertainment. At the international black festival of the arts held in Lagos in 1977, the most exciting activity did not occur at the stadium, with its formal schedule of events, but at the festival living quarters, where the performers engaged in extemporaneous traditional dancing and drumming, an exuberant display that prompted one observer to speak of an "African Woodstock."[3]

The virility and adaptability of traditional society and its arts may be seen from another perspective. For many years the bronze workers of Benin have been discounted for the poor quality of their craft—

repetitive in design, wanting in imagination, coarse in execution, fit only for the tourist trade to which it chiefly caters. Countless copies of Ife busts and other African classics come forth from the Benin furnaces, feeble caricatures of a once noble art, stamped out like the shoddy souvenirs they are. Nevertheless, presented with a commission that has importance and meaning, the craftsmen of Benin reveal capabilities reminiscent of their forebears, who produced the bronzes that once marked the glory days of a great kingdom.

In 1981 the occasion was an investiture for the obi, or prince, of a small farming community about sixty miles east of Benin. Traditionally the bronze casters were forbidden to work for any but the ruler of Benin. Now that is all changed, and they had a commission, a staff, and a stool, akin to their traditional function. The town was Idumuje Ugboko, lying in the hilly rain forest near the Niger River. The obi was Nwoko III, recently returned home to assume his chiefly functions, but there was a new element added. The designs for stool and scepter were created by Demas Nwoko, brother of the obi and an artist and architect of renown with training and experience in Western artistic methods and traditions. Demas Nwoko supplied the drawings from which the Benin workers made their clay and plaster casts. Long and intense discussions ensued between Nwoko and the compound leaders. The artist explained his needs, insisting, demanding. The artisans pointed out technical complications and made counter suggestions. A creative collaboration emerged that acted out in modern form an ancient, universal process, producing in the end imaginative designs executed with crisp technical proficiency. It was a far cry from souvenir art, and it indicated that purpose and understanding could still inspire the traditional artist of Africa.

Demas Nwoko and the Benin bronze workers joined in searching out new directions for an old art form, but this is only one particular facet of the contemporary arts in Africa. There is also a folk art, found chiefly in the towns and concerned with commercial advertising in the form of fanciful slogans rendered with embellishments on trucks and buses or illustrated signboards for local retailers. Most commercial art, however, remains in the hands of foreign corporations using familiar Western billboard or television advertising, as much an import as the products it promotes.[4]

A nontraditional, Western-inspired art has also developed, largely through the impetus supplied by outsiders. Some Christian missions, for example, have attempted to utilize classic African motifs to decorate their churches, while numerous art schools and ateliers have encouraged and trained cadres of painters, sculptors, weavers, and potters. The formal schools, for the most part initiated during the colonial era, have offered a standard Western curriculum and have produced artists who work in the conventional media of Western painting and sculpture, employing academic color, perspective, and composition, but with an African subject matter.

Some graduates of these schools have shown genuine talent—Demas Nwoko studied at the fine-arts division of Zaria's Nigerian College, and there were others. Kumasi's Technical College provided early training for the Ghanaian sculptor, Vincent Kofi, who produced powerful, massive wood carvings in his creative years during the fifties and sixties. At the same time, in the Sudan, where the Islamic injunction against representational art had limited expression to calligraphy and geometric design, a Khartoum Technical College graduate, Ibrahim el Salahi, breached the interdiction with remarkable paintings and drawings that managed to be both representational and stylized, giving deep manifestation of the Islamic way while in the process of violating its ban on figurative expression. As in the West, few of these artists have been able to gain a livelihood from their work, which has appeared occasionally on public buildings or in private collections, mainly of foreigners.

The ateliers have been more eclectic and more interesting, but have tended to project the artistic predelictions of their founders. The results have included some impressive and colorful works—the artistic flowering at the Rhodesian National Gallery in Salisbury during the sixties comes readily to mind. Nevertheless, close observation has revealed attributes that convert apparent innovation into a reflection of ideas and movements originated elsewhere: for example, the well-known Poto Poto stick figures so suggestive of Paleolithic cave drawings, or the expressionism and surrealism found in the work of Nigeria's Oshogbo artists. Like the products of the art schools, these efforts have found greatest encouragement among expatriate collectors, but little support or understanding among the African population at large.

*Oku Ampofo and the Akwapim Six*

While outsiders have often been responsible for initiating and encouraging the arts in modern Africa, Africans themselves have been greatly concerned with developing a cultural growth to accompany newly gained political independence. Failure and ambivalence have been common, but essentially the effort involves a rediscovery of the cultural values of the past, presenting traditional modes of expression in some new mutation that seems appropriate to the exigencies of the modern world.

This process of guiding tradition into new channels has not been restricted solely to the independence years, as can be seen in the efforts of such men as Edward Blyden or Africanus Horton. In more recent times others, like the Ewe composer, Ephraim Amu, or his Nigerian counterpart, Fela Sowande, have sought an artistic renascence, but their work began well before the onset of the Second World War and the appearance of serious movements for political independence in Africa. There have been early innovators in the fine arts as well—the Nigerian, Ben Enwonwu, for example. None, however, has produced a body of work and a career that better exemplifies the process than Oku Ampofo, the sculptor and physician from the Ghanaian town of Mampong.

Ampofo has been both innovator and catalyst, his influence felt through the example of his work as well as through encouragement of other artists and the development of arts institutions designed for public appreciation and instruction. As instigator, Ampofo followed and built upon the work of another, a South African, H. V. Meyerowitz, who came to the Gold Coast in 1936 to teach art at Achimota College and whose exertions bestirred and encouraged a whole generation of Ghanaian artists and craftsmen. The times were ripe, Ampofo has since insisted. There were many in the Gold Coast with a thirst to know more about their own culture and arts, but they were hampered by an enervating timidity during the interwar years of total European colonial domination. Meyerowitz stimulated the curiosity of those who came to know him, introducing them to various techniques, but particularly urging them to appreciate their artistic heritage and infusing them with the determination to learn and create.

Ampofo had received a scholarship for medical study at Edinburgh, but he did not take easily to medicine, with its emphasis on illness, pain, and the less-aesthetic aspects of the human body. At the same time he brought with him a long-standing love of art, which was stimulated by visits to museums and attendance at lectures dealing particularly with the traditional arts of Africa. Medical studies were neglected, so much so that Ampofo's bursary was canceled and at one point he was on the verge of being sent home. In fact, he had simultaneously enrolled with a sculptor in Edinburgh, and it was here that he concentrated much of his time and energies. The crisis was survived, however. Ampofo now applied himself to his medical training and finished his course with the loss of only one year's time, returning to the Gold Coast during the early years of the Second World War, there to take up his medical practice.

Nevertheless, artwork was never far from mind or hand. Ampofo had finished his stay in Europe with a continental tour of the great collections of African art, including Tervuren, the British Museum, and the Musée de l'Homme. On coming home, he established an art studio as well as a clinic; moreover, he took an immediate and active interest in the work of others, and bent his efforts toward their encouragement. Ampofo's medical practice caused him to travel far into the countryside, and he soon became aware of a paradox—changing social and economic conditions caused by modernization were spelling the end of the traditional way of life, yet there was an abiding popular interest in the old ways in dance and music, in quasi-religious customs and their artifacts, and in the continued respect for chiefs and elders. The energy and desire were there; what was lacking was a sense of direction, new strategies to meet new conditions. The small quiet doctor, self-effacing and soft-spoken, was determined to find a way.

H. V. Meyerowitz had already made a start by scouring the country for traditional craftsmen, bringing them to Achimota, and suggesting new uses for the old crafts. When Meyerowitz died in 1948, Ampofo became the chief proselytizer for the arts in the Gold Coast. On his return home in 1940 he circulated among the schools, looking for new talent, and talked with other practicing artists who were also searching for a renascence in the arts. Gradually Ampofo brought together a group representing a number of different art forms. There was J. C. Okyere, the painter, John Cobblah in ceramics, the weaver E. Asare, F. A. Gympo, a painter and sculptor, as well as a number of others. In 1944 they determined to have an exhibition, which was entitled significantly, "New African Art," the first presentation of its kind in the country. The showing was a success and soon prompted others, for the original group was highly productive and was steadily augmented by new members. Two exhibitions followed in 1946 and 1948; then, in 1950, Ampofo and his chief collaborators formed the Gold Coast Arts Society, with assistance from the British Council. When the Gold Coast became the independent nation of Ghana, the society's name was converted to the Ghana Arts Council, with Ampofo as its vice-president.

They were busy years. Some of the founders of the Arts Society came to be known as the Akwapim Six—Okyere, Asare, Gympo, and Cobblah, along with the sculptor A. A. Opoku, the painter J. D. Okae, and, of course, there was Ampofo himself. Ampofo was deeply immersed in his medical work as he was but one of two physicians resident in the whole of Akwapim. He toured the district two days each week and spent three more at his clinic in Mampong. Somehow he also managed to find time for his sculpture and to press forward with this organizational and promotional work. Periodically he was tempted to abandon his practice and devote full time to his beloved artwork, but wiser counsel prevailed. Having refused a position with the colonial administration because of the shortage of doctors in the field, he felt bound to continue his medical labors. Characteristically, Ampofo's medical work also generated a modern adaptation of the old ways as he began to study and utilize the pharmacopoeia of traditional African medicine, applying it to his Western medical training.

Ampofo's home in Mampong became the center of activity for the Akwapim Six and for others who were soon attracted, raising the number of active associates to some two dozen. Like the doctor, the others had jobs to attend to—their art was avocation. Most of the time they worked individually but came to Ampofo's when they could, chiefly during vacation periods. At these times they worked and studied together, learning from each other, borrowing techniques or stylistic details, but the basic concept that informed their work was always clearly in mind. Like the artists of the Italian Renaissance they returned to classical sources for inspiration, but in the process the motifs of traditional African arts were metamorphosed by those seeking not the rediscovery of the past but its restatement in support of a living present. Each artist made his own discovery through his personal idiom. For the painter, Kofi Antubam, for example, it became a development of the mural; for some of the weavers, experimental new applications of the old *kente* cloth patterns; for Ampofo an interest in wood grain and coloration.

Beyond this there was a basic premise and a revolutionary change. The premise stated simply that African art should reflect and serve the ways of African life. "That is the way our art should go," said Ampofo. "It should go according to how we live." It definitely should not follow European models, he continued, for these are foreign and unsuitable. It was much better, Ampofo insisted, to draw on indigenous society, which has great vitality and enables the artist to produce things that are recognized and appreciated. To be sure, Ampofo concluded, techniques and tools can be borrowed from the West, but even here, as a sculptor, he noted that the African adz and chisel usually gave him all he needed, as did the traditional method of cutting sculptures out of solid blocks, measuring the proportions with the naked eye, then freeing the form—a statue or a stool—by chipping away the imprisoning wood as Michelangelo had once freed his figures from their confining marble.

The change introduced by the Akwapim Six was a major concession to what modernity had done to traditional Africa. Traditional art had always been functional, but Ampofo and his colleagues were prepared to go beyond function toward more purely aesthetic objectives. In employing a traditional design or pattern, they felt, an additional purpose might be served. Thus a fabric could be used as a robe but it also might appeal as a wall hanging. A sculpture need no longer be a fetish figure; it could be decorative as well, embellishing domestic or public buildings, existing perhaps principally for the visual pleasure it provided.

Ampofo neglected no opportunity. After Meyerowitz's death, he approached several of the craftsmen who had been working at Achimota and brought them to Mampong at his own expense. Like an African Medici, he gave them work so that what they had learned would not be wasted. And it was not. When, for example, the weaver, Asare, produced designs for the hanging that was Ghana's gift to the United Nations, it was Ampofo's weavers who produced the cloth.

A tireless persistence was also behind the successful exhibitions. Ampofo drove throughout the country, visiting schools, seeking out individual artists, inquiring about new production, purchasing examples, framing canvases, mounting sculpture, and preparing ceramics and textiles for eventual showing. In 1955 he proposed an exhibition of the Akwapim Six; thereafter there were annual shows to take account of the growing quantity of artwork. Ampofo developed an extensive private collection of examples he hoped would form the nucleus of a permanent museum or archive representing the best modern work in the country. A new African government could not be expected to interest itself in collection and preservation, Ampofo felt, yet he wanted to assure the survival of contemporary production. His home soon held a large sampling, many of the pieces given freely, for the contributing artists understood and sympathized with what he was trying to accomplish.

Ampofo's travels sometimes took him outside his own country. On one occasion, he drove to Togo and then on to Dahomey, where he visited the city of Abomey and acquired examples of Dahomean bronzes and wall hangings. There were times when collecting became more than the acquisition of a new work, however. While in Dahomey, Ampofo drove to a remote village because he had heard of a very old traditional carver who lived there. When he arrived, Ampofo found that the carver had died but the work was being continued by his son. Unfortunately most of the carvings were uninteresting, done for the tourist trade. Disappointed, Ampofo turned to leave, but then noticed a carved figure of an old man smoking a pipe set off to one side and partly obscured by weeds. It was just what the doctor was looking for, but the carver refused to sell. The carving was a representation of his father, he said, and the old man had habitually sat in that spot when he smoked. The son had sculpted the likeness, thus enabling his father still to enjoy his accustomed place. He would not sell the statue, he said; that would be selling his own father. The doctor had expressed such interest in the work, however, that the carver insisted Ampofo take the figure as a gift. He would carve another, he insisted. His father would then be in two places with people who loved him, and thus his peace could spread through two households. Ampofo took the figure home and placed it in a special corner of his sitting room, where it still resides today.

Ampofo's own sculptures have a characteristic idiom although they are faithful to the principles he and his Ghanaian associates have laid down. Most of his pieces are sculpted in wood, and on occasion, he has used a conglomerate of marble and cement built up with armatures. His figures are large, sometimes slightly smaller than life-size, sometimes considerably bigger. For the most part they are modeled in the round—busts or full figures—each representing an expressed emotion or characteristic gesture, something recognizable to a Ghanaian, something "according to how we live." The bodies are anatomically distorted, although not radically so, and there is usually tension in the posture, representing reaction to some situation or condition. Thus, one large stone sculpture with twisted legs and arms thrown dramatically over the head is a response to tragedy, a gesture immediately identifiable locally. Another wooden figure shows a woman bather startled in her nudity, shielding herself with her arms, this time in a movement that is universal. It is the modesty of bucolic simplicity, the doctor adds, in contradistinction to the flaunted sexuality of the city dweller.

Ampofo's use of wood as a medium and his emphasis on female subjects are calculated. The wood comes from trees, which are revered in traditional African society as natural objects, but Ampofo has added a personal touch by utilizing grains and varying colors as an integral part of the design and composition. Indeed, Ampofo spent much time in his travels seeking out unusual woods with which he might experiment. Many of his carvings supplement basic sculpted form with a mosaic of contrasting hues—light browns, yellows, and mahogany—that accentuate anatomical features or emphasize a striking line of movement.

The rounded figures—fluid, sleek, smoothly finished and highly polished, voluptuous in some cases but essentially cylindrical—do indeed suggest the tree. Others are elongated with high headdresses and slender, extended necks banded in rings, a mark of beauty that has traditionally been induced by rubbing a preparation into the skin. The female figure may be a personal preference for the doctor, but Ampofo insists that it is primarily the influence of women in African society that has dictated his choice. He cites the traditional wealth and political power of the market women, whose support was so actively solicited by Kwame Nkrumah and so instrumental in establishing the Convention People's party cells throughout the country on which the strength of Nkrumah's regime was founded.

Like his fellow countryman, Ephraim Amu, Oku Ampofo long predated the upsurge of political nationalism that began to accelerate at the end of the Second World War, leading to the eventual emergence of independent African nations some fifteen years later. Both men sought to declare independence from European influence in the arts by reasserting traditional values and motifs in a modern idiom. There were good reasons, says Ampofo, why the drive for cultural freedom antedated political action. In the first place, a repressive colonialism prior to the outbreak of hostilities in 1939 encouraged African response, but not in political form. Nationalist reaction could be safely diverted into cultural channels without arousing an administration as insensitive to the potentialities of cultural expression as it was suspicious of more direct political motivation. A cultural renascence at the time was analogous to the independent church movement that had emerged in West Africa a half century earlier.

Secondly, Ampofo continues, there was much frustration among Africans who had been educated in the West only to be denied any role in the development of their own societies. Like the woman scorned, the rejected *évolué* became a natural center of disaffection, often expressed in cultural terms. On the Gold Coast, for example, the activities of J. B. Danquah, the nationalist leader, were as much cultural as political; he emphasized a consistent demand for the importance of traditional institutions and conventions in the developing modern state. Finally, says Ampofo, young Africans were greatly aroused during the 1930s by Haile Selassie's resistance to the Italian invasion of Ethiopia, even as they were impressed with the traditionalism and opposition to British rule conducted by Mohandas Gandhi in India.[5]

For Ghana, therefore, the desire for freedom of cultural expression long anticipated political action. When political nationalism burst forth after the Second World War, Nkrumah and other leaders were quick to employ aesthetic and artistic achievements for political advantage. And by that time Ghana's cultural renascence was in full flower, lending support to the independence so eagerly sought.

# 4

## The Independent African Theater

### African Theatrics

**T**heater has always been the essential African art. Its broad reach embraces supporting activities in dance, music, and the plastic and decorative arts. It entertains with saga, romance, farce, or fable. It initiates youth into adulthood and instructs all, its narratives preserving the wisdom of a people. It is concerned with expressions of social proprieties and moral verities. Ultimately, the theater of traditional Africa was the place where man searched out the meaning of his existence and the location of his being in a cosmic infinity. Crowded into the ritual arena of the stage was the immensity of the universe, inhabited by man and his gods, a magic microcosm in which man could identify himself through hallowed rites and signal the triumph of the human spirit in the epic tales of hero-gods.[1]

Clearly there was much that was sacred in the traditional theater of Africa. Religious festivals often contained dramatic reenactments of historical or mythological events. Initiation rites were typically accompanied by music, its cadences underscoring the movements of dancing maskers. Secret societies relied on theatrical mystery and spectacle to provide them with much of their power. Among the Yoruba, for example, the Gelede society of the women and the men's Egungun order combined both ritual enactment and public entertainment through processions of masqueraders. The Gelede was concerned with the conciliation of witches, the Egungun's function was worship and appeasement of the ancestors. Witches were powerful and dangerous, their propitiation a serious business. They were placated by sacrifice and prayer, but they were also entertained with a public processional that included dancing, which also served to hold the attention and interest of the populace at large. The great masks of the Egungun represented the ancestors. To watch was to experience the fascination and awe of the mysterious. To touch was sacrilege and could result in death.[2]

In traditional Africa, theater also reflected the many facets of everyday existence. What village was there that did not have its festival of the earth's fertility, the celebration of planting and the harvest? Which could not enact dance-dramas depicting such essentials as the tribulations of marriage or the vicissitudes of the hunt? In parts of West Africa there were performances of plays in the early twentieth century that were quite free of European influence—but complete with plot, unity, theme, and cast—dealing with universal themes of human frailty and everyday living. One can only speculate as to the temporal origin of such productions; it is known, however, that five hundred years ago, in the ancient empire of Mali, there flourished a great variety of skilled entertainers—mummers and magicians, storytellers and puppeteers, jugglers, conjurers, acrobats, and animal charmers.[3]

Little of this activity fits the Western definition of theater, with its emphasis on dramatic text and rehearsed performers, its special stages and properties, and its sometime willing suspension of disbelief by a segregated audience. No doubt there is always a blurred line between differing interpretations of what constitutes theater. No doubt, too, a European definition has little relevance for Africa. Nevertheless there appears to be one basic distinction between drama in the West and theater in Africa, a distinction involving the role of the audience. Although there are experimental exceptions, the Western theatrical tradition carefully separates audience and performer. The proscenium is more barrier than entryway, the stage a bejeweled box, its interior inhabited by actors who imitate humans for the entertainment or instruction of segregated spectators, whose divorce from the action emphasizes an essential noninvolvement.

The African audience is quite the opposite. There has been some adulteration through the importation of Western plays and theater architecture, but, by and large, audiences in Africa regard themselves not as passive spectators but, at the very least, as active commentators and at best as integrated participants. By the same token, the actor never loses sight of his true identity, which he maintains by exchanging asides with the audience as he plays his part. Basically he regards himself as a storyteller. An American critic, commenting on contemporary theater in Ghana during that nation's early years of independence, remarked on the informal atmosphere and the demonstrative character of the audience. Spectators shouted instructions and occasionally shook hands with actors during a performance. They laughed at false emotion or hammy convention; it made no difference if the moment were climactic or the matter serious, the audience seemed happily comfortable in its dual role of spectator and critic.[4]

In Nigeria the propensity for audience participation was utilized on occasion to heighten dramatic effect, as illustrated in a 1962 production of *The Taming of the Shrew* by the traveling theater of the University of Ibadan. At the outset the audience was left waiting in growing impatience, the bare hall empty of action, only a porter slowly sweeping the stage, an old "highlife" phonograph record playing tinnily in the distance. At last the manager appeared, full of apologies, explaining that the touring company had been held up; alas, the performance was cancelled. Actors already sprinkled through the audience at once charged the stage, heckling the manager, and demanding he provide props and costumes for an impromptu performance by the audience itself. The manager reluctantly agreed, explaining the plot and characters, and passing out costumes to actors posing as spectators who began a halting rendition, reading from scripts. Gradually the pretense was dropped, and the audience finally became aware that the actors were no longer reading their parts. Geoffrey Axworthy, first director of the University Arts Theatre and School of Drama, reported the climax of this amiable spoof:

A whisper passes around the hall, growing into an overwhelming wave of laughter, which stops the play. Such audiences love a practical joke and by this time are truly hooked. They even carry on the pretense. When Katherina, in the closing scene, drops back into her original character of an emancipated Nigerian girl . . . and refuses to do the submission speech, the actors, and then perhaps the whole audience, may beg her to carry on, for the sake of the show. She agrees, it being understood that no self-respecting Nigerian woman would behave like this nowadays.

"It took some courage," Axworthy concluded, "for the girl to make this point before an all-male Muslim audience in Northern Nigeria."[5]

For the Nigerian playwright, Wole Soyinka, there are deeper implications than a mere West African ebullience or fondness for audience participation. In the West, he says, drama has abandoned its function of fixing man's place in the universe and in society in favor of an "esoteric enterprise spied upon by fee-paying strangers." By contrast, the traditional drama of Africa has concerned itself with such essential themes as the symbolic struggle between man and those spiritual presences that seek to prevent harmony and well-being for the community. In such drama, says Soyinka, the audience is not an audience but an integral part of the drama, defining the arena of conflict and supporting the protagonist with offering and incantation in his struggle with the powers of the nether world. Thus, with Soyinka, differences in dramatic style reflect a profound divergence in spirituality—the splintered individualism of the West against the communal harmony of an African worldview.[6]

## Ibadan University and the Eclectic Theater of Nigeria

"The real roots of the modern African theater are firmly . . . in the schools." So states Geoffrey Axworthy, he having been himself an important factor in the growth of drama at Nigeria's first university at Ibadan. The Nigerian playwright, Wole Soyinka, has quite a different opinion. "I would definitely contest Axworthy's view," he has said. "Drama has always been part of our philosophy, of the lives of people in my country. In various forms." Soyinka receives stout support from Ebun Clark, whose study of the Nigerian playwright-actor-impresario Hubert Ogunde emphasizes the influence of traditional Yoruba theater on Ogunde's own work, which, in any case, owed nothing to the schools.

Such an unequivocal difference of opinion scarcely seems reconcilable. Nonetheless, "they are both correct," remarks Dapo Adelugba, a student under Axworthy and an eventual successor to both Axworthy and Soyinka as director of the Ibadan University Arts Theatre. "The

Ogunde tradition," Adelugba continues, ". . . is a modern version of . . . an even older tradition of travelling players." This conclusion is expanded by Abiola Irele, now a university professor and specialist in African Francophone literature, and in Axworthy's time an active participant in student dramatics at Ibadan. "We are dealing with different kinds of drama," says Irele.

> Ogunde's was a popular drama and it was very very important. . . . I remember in the 'forties . . . going to see one of his plays in Lagos and the songs were popular hits. . . . He touched a very very large public. It's professional . . . self-sustaining . . . really popular theater which has merged or fused aspects of traditional theater with his own. . . . But in terms of intellectual theater . . . the university theater . . . with a prepared text and . . . a definite intellectual content . . . played a prominent role.[7]

The issue becomes a matter of definition, of emphasis. Like many African peoples, the Yoruba had strong traditions of drama involving not only religious solemnities but also a theater of entertainment that has been traced back some four hundred years. This tradition has survived in metamorphosed form in the popular works of Hubert Ogunde, but there was also another tradition that developed in the schools during the colonial era, not only in Nigeria but throughout the English and French possessions in West Africa. While this second tradition took shape as a European import, it came to play a central role in resisting the cultural erosion of Westernization, adopting and encouraging elements of traditional theater, and moving toward a modern but increasingly African form of theatrical expression.

The schools began with European productions—Shakespeare, Molière, Gilbert and Sullivan, for example—then gradually began to stage plays with African themes and settings. The William Ponty School in Dakar became widely known for its dramatic works based on folktales and traditions. Among its graduates were individuals like Bernard Dadié and Coffi Gadeau of the Ivory Coast, Bakary Traoré from Senegal, and Keita Fodeba of Guinea, all of whom concerned themselves with the growth of a modern African theater in the postindependence era. Similar developments at schools in the British colonies produced a generation of theatrically minded university undergraduates, and these were particularly active at the new university college of Ibadan in Nigeria.

During its early years Ibadan was attended by a number of Nigerians who subsequently embarked on important literary careers. Wole Soyinka was one, but there were also the novelist Chinua Achebe and the poets J. P. Clark and Christopher Okigbo. In 1957 the Ibadan students founded their own literary journal, *The Horn*, a modest publication of hand-stapled mimeograph sheets, but a vehicle for aspiring poets and critics and doubtless an encouragement to the literary effervescence that characterized the exciting years just prior to national independence. *The Horn* regularly provided critical reviews of campus theater presentations, a necessary service in view of the numerous plays that were mounted by the student dramatic society.

Student writing for *The Horn* frequently combined alien European influences with an indigenous African inspiration, but the dramatic presentations were at first exclusively Western. For example, lighter works like *Outward Bound* or *The Man from the Ministry* were presented along with the more substantial *The Devil's Disciple* of George Bernard Shaw, which featured Wole Soyinka as Dick Dudgeon. Other productions brought faculty and students together, but the orientation remained European. One ambitious evening offered the *Antigone* of both Sophocles and Jean Anouilh. Brecht was represented by *The Caucasian Chalk Circle*, Shakespeare with *A Midsummer Night's Dream*.

Axworthy arrived at Ibadan in 1956, recruited as a member of the English department to encourage practical work in drama at the new Arts Theatre located on campus. In addition to the student dramatic society, he discovered a number of expatriate amateur groups, like the students, concerned exclusively with European theater. Moreover, although serious plays were presented, too much time was devoted, in Axworthy's judgment, to trivial "West End hits," plays that in many cases were totally irrelevant and incomprehensible in a Nigerian context. Axworthy recalls the example of one melodrama concerning a girl who attempted suicide by turning on the gas, a cultural displacement in a tropical African setting that was compounded by the plot resolution—the heroine surviving because the coin-operated gas meter ran out.

To offset such incongruities and to introduce professional productions of world theater that spoke to Africans, Axworthy established an Arts Theatre Group, open to everyone. He began with plays like Go-

gol's *The Inspector General,* chosen for its relevance in a colonial situation, and Ibsen's *An Enemy of the People* that could be shared easily
by Africans and Europeans alike. While Axworthy's innovations were
received with enthusiasm, the student dramatic society continued an
active program. At Axworthy's suggestion the society staged after-
dinner plays in the dormitory dining halls, some original, some adapted.
These offerings, which were toured from hall to hall, gave rise to the
idea of a special student play for 1960, one to be put on tour throughout the country as a university contribution to national independence.
The after-dinner entertainments were not only successful but provided
invaluable practical experience in staging under difficult circumstances,
an experience that proved most helpful when the independence play
went on the road in the spring of 1961.

This student decision was a conscious attempt to bring the university
to the people. At a conference of the National Union of Nigerian Students held in the summer of 1960, it was felt, said Adelugba, "that
the time had come for the university to play an important part in nation building, and that we should get away from the ivory tower image . . . and reach out to the general community." After much de-
liberation, an African adaptation of Molière's *Scapin, the Trickster*
was chosen with Axworthy ultimately directing and Adelugba playing
the lead. As *That Scoundrel Suberu* it toured all the way from Ibadan
to Calabar, several hundred miles of one-night stands that brought the
traveling show variously to a town hall on one evening, a law court on
the next, then an open-air cinema, or a television studio. They played
on dining hall tabletops, and in auditoriums lighted with bush lamps
against a background featuring flyblown portraits of local dignitaries.
They played to audiences who had never seen a dramatic production
as such but whose sense of theater was acute, having been shaped by
experience with indigenous spectacle and ceremony. The adaptation
of *Scapin, the Trickster* must have hit the mark. Axworthy reports
that during a television broadcast in Enugu, there were calls from angry lawyers threatening to take legal action against an author who had
so insulted their profession![8]

The idea of a university traveling theater had caught on. Other
productions subsequently went on tour, and, like *Suberu,* were designed
to fit an African setting. Shakespeare's *The Taming of the Shrew*
commented on the emancipation of women in Africa and made good

use of an interplay between classical and Pidgin English. *The Comedy of Errors* was staged as if produced by one of Nigeria's indigenous theater troupes. The 1965 production of *Danda*, written by a Nigerian, portrayed the escapades of an African Till Eulenspiegel, prompting a local official to congratulate the touring company as a unifying force during the difficult early years of Nigerian independence.

The University Travelling Theatre was only one aspect of the burgeoning Arts Theatre program, however. In 1963 the original Arts Theatre Group had been developed into a School of Drama with Axworthy as director. One of its first projects involved an attempt to bring together in cooperation with the Ogunmola company the two traditions of Nigerian theater—the school production and the popular entertainer. In this fashion the tradition of ritual festival and drama was exposed to European influences just at a time of intense nationalism, vigorous tribalism, and severe political stress.

Although Hubert Ogunde and his professional players dated back to the period of the Second World War, other groups had subsequently appeared in Yorubaland, presenting plays and "folk opera" on tour, most notably the players of Kola Ogunmola, a teacher turned impresario from the Yoruba farming community of Oshogbo. Ogunmola had begun his career in a church school where he staged short plays, some involving biblical themes done in modern versions idiomatic with local language and culture. These innovations were ill received by the church authorities and cost Ogunmola his job, but he persisted in his theater interests, forming a troupe of traveling players from his students and presenting works of his own composition. It was a vernacular theater reaching far into the heart of local culture, dealing with matters unknown at the university. It dramatized local history, myth, and social problems, exploiting a colorful language rich in proverb, subtle in nuance.

Ogunde had perfected an original style that mixed traditional Yoruba theatrical forms with borrowings from Europe and America, including jazz from New York's Harlem. Ogunmola took Ogunde's dramatic structure as his own model but eliminated the foreign accretions, relying on his acting skills, an African musical idiom, and the popularity of his moralistic themes to gain a widespread following. Axworthy arranged for the Ogunmola group to stay in residence at the drama school during 1962, a collaboration he hoped would be mutually beneficial. "I thought while he could learn something from us about the technical side of theater," Axworthy later observed, "we had a tremendous amount to learn from him about the rapport with the audience and the way the [performance] was structured."[9] The reciprocity was a great success. A year of respite from the demands of traveling enabled Ogunmola to rehearse his repertoire at leisure and to learn additional technical skills that improved the pace of his productions. For Axworthy and the university players there was the opportunity to observe the work of a professional company and its talented director.

Ogunmola had borrowed from Hubert Ogunde the concept of an opening glee in which the whole company participated. This dramatic overture, which in fact is an adaptation from the traditional theater of the Yoruba,[10] was subsequently utilized by the University Travelling Theatre in its production of Shakespeare's *The Comedy of Errors*, while Ogunmola's gaily painted "mammy wagon" with its generator, control board, and lights helped shape the design for the Travelling Theatre's own physical properties and equipment. When the university "theater on wheels" toured the country in 1964, its Grand Shakespeare Festival was seen by more than 100,000 in only a few weeks. Nonetheless, the most striking result of the collaboration was Ogunmola's production in 1963 of Amos Tutuola's celebrated novel, *The Palm-Wine Drinkard.*

The play, *Palmwine Drinkard,* emerged from the efforts of many people, but its great success may be traced chiefly to what Ogunmola and the Nigerian designer, Demas Nwoko, were able to do with Tutuola's script. At Axworthy's urging, Tutuola reworked his text for the stage, and the edited version was given to Ogunmola, who sketched out the scenes in cooperation with Tutuola. Nwoko's contribution was visual, the sets and costumes, but his original creations were so strongly designed that they influenced the choreography and ultimately the direction of the play itself. In the end it became a mutual production, one with a brilliance that realized the potentialities of a modern African theater. Axworthy was jubilant. "It was extremely well received by town and school audiences," he wrote. "I think it is the most exciting production ever seen in the country." Wole Soyinka's program notes reflected the prevailing mood.

A bold experiment in theatre has just succeeded. . . . Ogunmola's sojourn with the School has culminated in a first-rate evening of theatre, proving in the only effective way possible that,
with the right and sensitive kind of guidance, the 'people's theatre' of folk opera can rise to an appreciable level of professional-
ism. . . . One's veins fairly thump with joy at evenings such as
the Ogunmola–Nwoko team has provided. . . . It promises or-
gies of theatre for the future.[11]

Indeed, it was Soyinka who was to provide the major impetus of
new production. The *Palmwine Drinkard* had brought together European and African theater by applying Western stage techniques to an
indigenous company presenting an African story in the Yoruba language. Soyinka sought the same result but proposed to create a modern African theater in English, expressing the authentic idiom of
traditional drama in a form comprehensible to an international audience. "The great merit of Mr. Soyinka's work," said a contemporary
critic, "is that while he handles English sensitively and with an awareness of the European dramatic tradition, he at the same time brings
African themes to life . . . trying to evolve a peculiarly African
dramatic form based on the indigenous dance drama."[12]

During the 1950s, Soyinka had completed his undergraduate studies
in England, then became attached to the Royal Court Theatre in London, where he wrote a number of pieces for the stage. Chief among
these were two plays with an African setting, *The Swamp Dwellers*
and *The Lion and the Jewel.* Toward the end of his London residence
he also began to develop ideas for an ambitious work, *A Dance of the
Forests,* created expressly to mark Nigerian national independence in
1960. That same year Soyinka returned home, ending a six-year absence, nominally to pursue a study of traditional drama in West Africa,
but more pointedly to reestablish contact with his own people and
culture at a signal moment in Nigerian history.

The return of Wole Soyinka was a catalytic charge in an already
spirited atmosphere. The student dramatic society had produced *The
Swamp Dwellers* and *The Lion and the Jewel* in 1959 to great popular
acclaim, but the true importance of these productions was not in an
evening of good theater, but in the demonstration that an African had

written plays worthy of public presentation, that an African nation on the eve of political independence was capable of a concurrent cultural freedom. A wave of enthusiasm swept over the Ibadan student body. There was much discussion surrounding the plays and the prospect that they held out for a healthy local theater. There was also a harvest of imitative output. Aspirant student dramatists labored into the night, and *The Horn* was engulfed with literary and critical contributions.

At the time Soyinka saw his return chiefly as an opportunity to establish a local company for the performance of non-Western drama, coincidentally continuing his own exploration of traditional African drama in modern form. Later he came to realize that he had been engaged in something larger: the freeing of the theater at Ibadan from alien control just as Nigeria was throwing off the political constraints of colonialism. "We took the arts away from the expatriates," said Soyinka.

> The drama groups which existed among . . . the middle class, the intelligentsia . . . were largely expatriate groups who were performing Galsworthy, Priestley, Shaw, Shakespeare. . . . What we did with the formation of the troupes which we started about that time was to introduce, first of all, fully black theater companies performing in English . . . performing plays from the Third World.
>
> I just wanted to set up a company. . . . When I came I found that both the human material I needed and the space were in the hands of the expatriates so then I set about seducing the actors who were performing . . . with the expatriate groups. . . . They joined us because they saw that something more exciting was happening.[13]

While Axworthy was part of the expatriate monopoly, Soyinka continued, the young Nigerian was grateful when Axworthy introduced him to Nigerian audiences. "He took *The Lion and the Jewel* . . . to Nigeria and staged it . . . which then became a sort of eye opener for a number of would-be playwrights. . . . A lot was contributed by far-sighted people like Geoffrey Axworthy," Soyinka concluded, but he felt that one production was only a gesture, however useful, and it was necessary to go outside the university and establish independent theater companies.

Soyinka probably underestimated the influence of the initial presentation; in Adelugba's judgment, "It pushed the university theater strongly in the direction of the African theater." In any event, Soyinka founded his own company, 1960 Masks, a group of recent university graduates working in theater-related jobs, and it was the Masks who presented *A Dance of the Forests* in Lagos as part of the independence celebrations in October 1960. It is probably fortunate that this big allegorical work was as obscure as it was irreverent, for the jaundiced commentary it contained on aspects of the African past, present, and future would surely have caused anger and resentment had it been better understood at the time.

During the early independence years, Soyinka's many activities as playwright, producer, and student of traditional African theater did not prevent him from maintaining contact with the university. He played a leading part in Axworthy's production of Brecht's *The Caucasian Chalk Circle,* completed his own *Trials of Brother Jero* for a production by the student dramatic society, and directed a Masks staging of *Song of a Goat* by J. P. Clark, a recent university graduate and fellow dramatist-poet. When the Ogunmola company took up residence at Ibadan, Soyinka seems at last to have been persuaded that the expatriate influence was waning, a judgment reflected in his enthusiastic reception of the *Palmwine Drinkard.*[14]

Soyinka's African theater was a theater of commitment. He regarded the writer as the conscience of his society, functioning "as the record of mores and experience . . . and as the voice of vision in his own time." There was no time for romantic tales of an idealized past, Soyinka insisted, no need to pose as savior of the materialistic West, no refuge in the "futile token twitches" of counterfeit reforms. Earlier than most he perceived the self-serving and arbitrary character of many new African governments. Virtually alone he raised his voice in protest.[15]

Plays like *The Lion and the Jewel* and *The Swamp Dwellers* were humorous or sober comments on the quality of African civilization, but *A Dance of the Forests* was something more, presenting an image of African life that reflected a profound skepticism, if not rejection, of African leadership at the very moment that independence was sweeping the continent. Subsequent works like *The Strong Breed* and *The Road,* produced in 1964 and 1965, were more concerned with metaphysical speculations unrelated to any particular society; nevertheless, at the same moment, Soyinka was employing his talents to comment on contemporary affairs through the medium of political satire, accompanying the word with an active personal involvement that came to be a Soyinka trademark.

By 1964 the political climate in Nigeria had turned ugly, marked by corruption, rigged elections, and a profound and growing public unrest. Into this atmosphere Soyinka introduced a series of humorous reviews—culminating with *Before the Blackout* at the University Arts Theatre in 1965—that served as a vehicle for his new quasiprofessional company, The Orisun Theatre. The performances were well attended and enthusiastically received, the material full of bite, its targets clearly recognizable by a knowing audience. Soyinka caricatured public figures, taking particular delight in the foibles of politicians, his favorite targets Kwame Nkrumah and Dr. Hastings Banda, the president of Malawi. It was broad but effective slapstick—for example, in a characteristic skit commenting on the highly suspect Nigerian census of 1963, Soyinka portrayed officials counting with fine impartiality livestock along with the human population.

The name of Wole Soyinka, however, was soon to be associated with a piece of political theater of a different sort. The regional government of Western Nigeria had been in a state of crisis since 1962. By the autumn of 1965, it was near collapse, the incumbent premier, S. I. Akintola, widely regarded as holding office through election fraud, public outrage showing itself in physical violence and property destruction that was mounting to the point of open rebellion. Akintola attempted to calm public sentiment. It was announced that he would broadcast from Ibadan a defense of his administration and justification for the accuracy of the election results. He never made it. Just as it was beginning the broadcast was interrupted. A masked intruder had appeared in the studio, commandeering Akintola's tapes at gunpoint, and substituting one of his own. Briefly listeners heard a squeaky voice in imitation of Akintola, shouting party slogans, and inviting the premier to resign. The incident was over in a moment, as the gunman quickly disappeared, but Soyinka was later arrested and charged. The evidence at trial was conflicting and inconclusive and the defendant was ultimately acquitted.[16]

Whatever Soyinka's connection with the radio station antics, he soon became directly involved in the civil war that broke out in Nigeria in 1967. Soyinka traveled to Benin and Enugu, attempting a reconciliation between seceding Biafra and the Nigerian military government headed by General Yakubu Gowon. He went with no official sanction. It was a quixotic, personal effort, faintly reminiscent in character of the Akintola episode, but in this instance the consequences were far more serious. Shortly after his return home, Soyinka was taken into custody by the federal government, remaining imprisoned without charge or trial until his release over two years later, in October 1969.

Imprisonment put an end to Soyinka's theater activities, but not before he had been able to stage his important political play, *Kongi's Harvest*, in 1965. Like the revues, *Kongi's Harvest* dealt with contemporary events, making a particular target of Ghana's President Nkrumah, whose increasingly dictatorial government had outraged Soyinka's populism. It was good theater—full of life, humor, and movement that cloaked a deadly serious commentary on the pretensions and obscenities of tyranny. If some of the topical material appears dated today, the basic indictment of arbitrary government, both traditional and modern, makes *Kongi's Harvest* germane to any age. When Soyinka dismisses Kongi and his kind, the humor quickly darkens into bitterness: "Imprecations then, curses on all inventors of agonies, on all Messiahs of pain and false burdens, on all who fashion chains, on farmers of terror, on builders of walls, on all who guard against the night but breed darkness by day, on all whose feet are heavy and yet stand upon the world, on all who see, not with the eyes of the dead, but with eyes of Death."

It was ironic that *Kongi's Harvest* was chosen to inaugurate the Dakar Festival of Negro Art in 1966. The Festival was designed to demonstrate African unity and was attended by many high-ranking African dignitaries. Nkrumah had fallen from power only two weeks earlier, and Soyinka was genuinely troubled. "I don't feel like putting on this play," he said. "It's like kicking a man when he's down." More than that, while the play was to launch a new theater in Dakar before a distinguished audience, it had a particularly disrespectful message for those political figures in attendance. Not surprisingly it was cooly received. Those who did not understand English were bored, and those who did were offended. It was a play of words, wit, and satire, a marvelous piece of theater; but in this instance it was performed in the wrong place at the wrong time.

*Kongi's Harvest* represented development of another sort. Soyinka's earlier plays had contained a measure of African dancing and drumming but also reflected strong European influences. Back in Nigeria his work took on a more typically African character, in form as well as content; then, as Abiola Irele observed, Soyinka made his breakthrough with *Kongi's Harvest,* which contained a full measure of the dancing, music, and pageantry of traditional African theater, thereby achieving the objective of a genuinely African theatrical idiom in English. Indeed, *Kongi's Harvest* went further, since along with elements reminiscent of Ogunde and Ogunmola, there were echoes of Brecht as well as Soyinka's own maturing talent.[17]

### The Pedagogical Theater of Efua Sutherland

It was a small structure, unpretentious but handsome, traditional in inspiration yet modern in design. The dazzling whitewashed walls with their dark trim resembled a village compound and were meant to. Inside, at one end, a platform stage was covered by an overhanging roof; but the auditorium, with its seats of carved Ghanaian stools, was open to the night sky. It stood in a rough, weedy place approached by dusty footpaths, its simplicity contrasting sharply with the gaudy grandeur of Accra's nearby Ambassador Hotel.

The crowds were gathering at the entrance that was shaped like a huge traditional stool and flanked by two massive Akuaba dolls, sculpted male and female symbols of fertility. These carvings were the work of Oku Ampofo, who had created them for the Ghana Drama Studio in time for its inaugural in October 1961. It was an invited audience for the first night, something of a diplomatic event attended by ambassadors and university professors, rich market women and party officials, even some nuns and, said one observer, graced by "pretty girls precariously swathed in brilliant prints, lightly turbaned, loaded with gold, anciently elegant in a manner that Europe would not dare." The international press was there, as was a local chief, wearing his crown and attended by three retainers.

The audience was finally settled, filling the 350-seat theater to capacity, but it was not yet time for the performance. The spectators waited and chatted, then there was a wail of sirens in the distance that rapidly grew louder, accompanied by the growling of motorcycles, and finally from beyond the wall the sound of slamming car doors. A moment of pause and in strode *Osagyefo*, Kwame Nkrumah, with his Egyptian wife and a retinue. On the stage a tall slim girl waited. It was Efua Sutherland, a leading Ghanaian writer and founder of the Drama Studio. Amidst steady applause Nkrumah made his way to the platform and was welcomed and introduced by Mrs. Sutherland. Nkrumah spoke briefly, but touched on many things—the popular need for education and entertainment, the desire that a network of theaters be established throughout the land, the hope for renascence of the arts in Africa—most of all, Nkrumah's recurrent dream of pan-African unity, aided in this instance by the universal language of art. Concluding, he pointed to Africa's long-standing reliance on outsiders for its material and cultural growth. "From now on Africa must look inwards," he said. "It is only by our own exertions that our . . . endeavours can bring about the progress, unity and strength of Africa."[18]

It was a sentiment that Efua Sutherland might well have echoed, for it was such thoughts that had launched her several years earlier on the course that led to the founding of the Ghana Experimental Theatre and the construction of its building, the Drama Studio, designed in the shape of a domestic courtyard. At first Mrs. Sutherland had been the young Fante girl, educated in mission schools and in England, interested in Greek drama and hankering to try her hand at writing poetry, then settling down to a career as a small-town schoolteacher. That was in the early 1950s, as events forever changed the Gold Coast colony and Nkrumah simultaneously inspired his countrymen and goaded the British government into an accelerated drive toward national independence.

To the young teacher, political independence suggested cultural autonomy. School texts, literary works, church and school plays were all Western; traditional African ideas were seldom in print, having been transmitted through oral traditions. "I saw something that pushed me," Mrs. Sutherland said, ". . . children's books in schools which I objected to. I didn't like what was going on. And then independence itself," she added. "I was terribly excited about independence." In 1957, with the encouragement of established public figures—J. B. Danquah, Kofi Busia, and Michael Dei-Anang in particular—Mrs. Sutherland founded the Ghana Society of Writers and launched the literary revue, *Okyeame*. That autumn she had attended the Afro-Asian Writers' Conference at Tashkent, where she was shocked by the emptiness of the book exhibit shelves representing the writing from Africa. "That hit me," she confessed. "I said to myself then that I would help to fill those shelves."

More specifically, Efua Sutherland was determined to develop play writing, to create a body of dramatic literature written by Africans, to be enjoyed by Africans, both schoolchildren and the public at large. Realizing the need for organization, she set out to develop a systematic program, and in 1958 the Ghana Experimental Theatre made its appearance alongside the Society of Writers. A place to work was found when the Boy Scouts allowed her to use a small aluminum shed near the seashore, and a group was recruited by scouring the city of Accra for people interested in drama and possessing practical skills such as carpentry, tailoring, mechanics, or house painting.

At its inception Mrs. Sutherland's program sought to link modern theater to the dramatic traditions of the country. People living in the cities were familiar with the rites and ceremonies that were part of traditional village life, but their circumstances rarely permitted them to participate. Storytelling could come close, however, especially if it were developed in dramatic form through the addition of mime, dance, and music. Mrs. Sutherland began, therefore, by writing short plays based upon the stories about Ananse, the spider, a familiar character loved by all. These she staged successfully, then moved on to the next problem, that of writing plays appealing to a people who had been schooled only in the theater of the West.

Efua Sutherland sought something both new and familiar, something that drew on knowledge of Shakespeare, Shaw, or Molière but spoke in an African idiom. She decided to make use of the Ghanaian interest in religion, which led her first to choose the Everyman theme—Christian but universal. She called her play *Odasani*, an Akan word meaning "man." "It offered opportunities," Mrs. Sutherland recalled, "to speak to Ghanaians in terms that were important to them. . . . I developed a play in which you have very Ghanaian characters and Everyman's problems . . . living carelessly . . . finding out the complications . . . the conversion . . . the confrontation with Death."

Other like scenarios were explored; then, in 1960, the Drama Studio moved to a new site and work went forward in earnest, not only writing and production but in the design for a new theater. Mrs. Sutherland was struck by the need for a place, something palpable and tangible, to represent what she and her group were trying to achieve. "I needed it at that time," she said, "not just to provide a space for this program but also to stand as a symbol . . . something . . . that people could point their fingers at and say, 'that's a place where experiments in African drama are going on.' "

As a symbol, it was important as well that the new theater be more than just another new building. "You could have just . . . got a design from a book and designed one of these model theaters. . . . I didn't want that," she insisted. Like the plays, it had to be something new but familiar.

> I designed it as a Ghanaian courtyard. Once again the importance of people being able to identify with it. The actors . . . and the audience could walk into this place and feel at home. . . . It was terribly important that the building itself be in consonance with the idea. . . . As a Ghanaian courtyard because everything that happens dramatically in life in this country usually happens in the courtyard. The naming ceremony, the puberty rites, all those things. . . . The courtyard of a house, an ordinary house. . . . It would be familiar.[19]

Nkrumah took an interest in the work at the Drama Studio. Mrs. Sutherland had written to him describing what she and her colleagues were trying to achieve and requested assistance with construction costs. She had raised some funds abroad, and Nkrumah responded with assistance from the Ghana government to make up the needed balance. His interest was more than perfunctory, for he visited the studio when construction was still under way, arriving unannounced one day and expressing his delight with the zeal and dedication of the group.[20]

Nkrumah's visit came on a Sunday morning, a day when the company was hard at work, for time was precious and the members of the Drama Studio were jobholders and could come together only in their spare moments. Efua Sutherland had recruited them from various quarters—the university, schools, the department of works, the army barracks—searching for individuals with a love of theater, finally bringing together a group of forty, many of whom revealed a genuine talent for acting, staging, and designing. By 1961, as the theater building neared completion, the production of the Ghanaian Everyman, *Odasani,* was ready. It was *Odasani,* therefore, that inaugurated the Drama Studio on that warm October evening in 1961.

There followed a period of growth and experiment, a period in which education in playwriting and production of a new African drama paralleled the development and education of an African audience. Efua Sutherland persuaded Joe deGraft, a university lecturer in English, to join her in running the studio. New scripts went into production, deGraft and Mrs. Sutherland producing the bulk. Two companies rehearsed simultaneously, supplemented by art classes and special sessions in playwriting. Rehearsals took place evenings, and performances were scheduled on weekends, except during the spring and autumn rains, when the studio was temporarily shut down. Occasional tours brought the players as far as Cape Coast, where they were well received.

The audiences slowly expanded, both in number and variety. The nearby Ambassador Hotel contributed its share of visitors from abroad, but Efua Sutherland was primarily interested in home audiences and a homegrown theater—acknowledging a debt to the West but basically seeking an idiomatic African expression. One visitor remarked on the problems of drilling eager but inexperienced recruits. "During the time when the actors danced or moved without dialogue," she noted, "the rhythm and flow of action was smooth. However, the moment they opened their mouths to speak they seemed to descend with a jolt into an invisible box that limited their movements and caused their actions to be stiff as well as stilted." Mrs. Sutherland was determined not to yield to Western traditions of acting, and her more-experienced players showed the results. "They move with ease, spontaneity, and naturalness that one sees but rarely," the same observer remarked. "An ingenious acting coach can improve their work by teaching techniques and yet retain the individuality that someday will develop into the Ghanaian style of acting."[21]

For Mrs. Sutherland, creation of authentic African theater was one of two major objectives; the other was continuity. The recruitment of Joe deGraft was meant to serve this purpose, but there was also the matter of systematic training in the theater arts and an institutional base that would insure the permanence of the studio. The need was widely felt and, indeed, the impulse, when it came, was from the government and the national university at Legon, located just outside Accra. In 1962 a drama section was instituted at the School of Music and Drama, which was part of the Institute of African Studies at the University of Ghana. Courses were inaugurated and most of the students in the initial class came from the Drama Studio company. DeGraft was selected to head the new drama program, and Mrs. Sutherland herself joined the university faculty in 1963.

Her program launched and apparently secure, Mrs. Sutherland next turned to the creation of a syllabus in drama, a task that gradually brought awareness of the need for fresh material, drawn once again, from traditional African sources. Before long the university-based program began to reveal its limitations. It was too academic, too exam-oriented, too reliant on students of uncertain talent. "The syllabus . . . was a sort of omnibus thing without a focus," Mrs. Sutherland recalled. "I could see what are called 'dry outs' in creativity. . . . I saw the need for research to develop an African dimension in the program. . . . I went straight back to my original thoughts on African sources."[22]

The return to sources was literal. Mrs. Sutherland went to the villages, where the storytelling tradition was still virile, and in 1965, at Atwia, a small Fante farming community, she found what she was seeking. Atwia was poor, its resources slim, its population only a few hundred, but it had a reputation for storytelling that reached as far as Accra, some seventy-five miles away. In Atwia Mrs. Sutherland discovered not only the right storytelling tradition but also an oral literature thriving amidst a population that had transcended its material poverty with a spirit of self-help guided by its chief, Madame Nana Okoampa and the elders of her court. Efua Sutherland had known Nana Okoampa in Accra before she returned home to assume her chieftaincy. When Mrs. Sutherland arrived in the village she found the chief participating in a procession, a visual impression for the visitor that was soon reinforced by the literary riches she found. "After that first visit," Mrs. Sutherland remarked, "I was so struck with that village . . . I couldn't rest. I thought, now what do you do about this mine of sources?"

Atwia had already raised funds and contributed communal labor to build its own school, and Mrs. Sutherland saw the possibility of constructing a community center that would reinforce the literary traditions of the village. She utilized research funds to purchase blocks, cement, roofing, and other materials—designing a building somewhat reminiscent of the Drama Studio in Accra. The house went up in 1966; the village contributed the labor, the women carrying cement, children gathering gravel, young people returning home on weekends to participate in the construction. The villagers selected the site, located at the center of the village near important shrines. Only later did Mrs. Sutherland discover the reason for that particular choice. During a ceremony involving the pouring of libations at major clan houses, some were also poured at the community center. Why, she wanted to know. It was the site, they told her, where an important clan house had once stood.

Mrs. Sutherland thought of the building essentially as a theater, but for the villagers it had many functions of theatrical or dramatic content. It was a place for storytelling, for wake keeping and church services, for official meetings, and the greeting of guests. It was a kind of New England town-meeting house, the emotional nerve center of the village. There was no Fante word for "theater," and for a time Efua Sutherland was puzzled as to how the house might be named. One day, as she watched the construction, she heard a woman calling to another. The woman was saying, "Go to the house and tell them the baby is crying, that I am in the House of Stories. *Kodzidan.*" Thus was it named, and as Efua Sutherland remarked with satisfaction, "That's what we ought to try and call the theater buildings we are building, by a name that really means something to the people." From Accra's Drama Studio, with its form of a traditional courtyard, she had come to *Kodzidan,* the House of Stories of Atwia.

The development at Atwia, then, combined local custom and usage with theatrical techniques brought by Mrs. Sutherland through her plays based upon the Ghanaian storytelling tradition. Continuity has been provided through the exertions both of the village and Mrs. Sutherland herself. For example, a young man who had grown up at the time of the initial construction returned home later as a teacher at his own request; he now directs a children's drama workshop for the Atwia district organized by Mrs. Sutherland through the Ministry of Education. There have been numerous performances organized at the House of

Stories—some by children, others by high-life groups that began at Atwia then toured the countryside. On one occasion the whole village participated in a television film that was created for broadcast in the United States.

Efua Sutherland wanted to capitalize on the start of the Drama Studio and the success of Atwia to bring the results of these efforts to a wider audience. In 1968 she inaugurated a professional touring company, naming it, *Kusum Agoromba,* "those who perform the right things." Based at the Drama Studio, these players had a repertoire of ten works, most written in the Akan language by Mrs. Sutherland, for she well understood that the widest dissemination would come not through English but by means of local languages. The inaugural performance took place in the Holy Spirit cathedral in Accra, and subsequent presentations in other towns were often held in churches, sometimes in lieu of the usual sermon. *Kusum* extended its performances to include Ghana television along with its tours, which eventually covered all corners of the country.

Sometimes there was initial skepticism. People from the countryside tended to distrust Westernized Africans, those educated, university-trained city dwellers who come to study village life, much like Europeans, but rarely remain to build and create. At Atwia Efua Sutherland at first encountered resistance, even prejudice. "What is this fine lady doing walking on our pebbles?" an important village elder wanted to know, watching developments with dark suspicion. Resistance usually faded with accomplishment, however—at Atwia and elsewhere. On one occasion the *Kusum* players presented *Odasani,* Everyman, at a Sunday evening service in a provincial town. At the end of the performance an older member of the congregation remarked, "I thought when they started, what is this!" Then he turned to Mrs. Sutherland, who was standing anxiously to one side. His stern features broke into a smile. "You have fed us," he said.[23]

With *Kusum* established, Mrs. Sutherland turned to other devices. Continuity had to be preserved. She organized workshops in children's drama and in playwriting for children, taking the seminars on tour when possible, bringing the drama out of the city into the countryside. By the 1970s, some ten years after the inauguration of the Drama Studio, emphasis had shifted subtly from drama to education. Drama became the vehicle for learning, the means rather than the end. "The education process is going on," Efua Sutherland asserted, calling her work an informal interdisciplinary seminar. "It is working beautifully. The kids will learn anything. You can't stop them."

The problem of continuity still remains. Mrs. Sutherland has long been convinced of two things. First, she knows that a younger generation, the generation of her own children, contains many talented individuals ready to carry on the task of social and cultural development, able to perform as well as or better than their elders. Second, she is certain that the local community is better equipped for the work than the larger national institutions—governmental agencies, universities, the sophisticated establishments in the large cities. "The state has a role today, sure, but there is more," she says, her voice vibrating with the conviction she feels: "I have seen what communities can do and there is no doubt in my mind that communities do it better than hired labor. . . . A pride. Their own unconscious awareness of who they are and how they want their community to be. . . . It's beautiful the way they do it. . . . Pride and joy. . . . And it's still possible to do that in Ghana because most of Ghana is these village communities."[24]

# 5

## *Africans Dance*

### *Africa Still Dances*

It is a half century since Geoffrey Gorer wrote *Africa Dances*, his vivid account of a journey through West Africa. He spoke of many things—the landscapes and the villages, the customs and the culture, the colonial administrators and the people they governed. Most of all he wrote about the dance. "Africans dance," he said. "They dance for joy, and they dance for grief; they dance for love and they dance for hate; they dance to bring prosperity and they dance to avert calamity; they dance for religion and they dance to pass the time. Far more exotic than their skin and their features is this characteristic of dancing; the West African negro is not so much the blackish man . . . as he is the man who expresses every emotion with rhythmical bodily movement."

In 1962 Gorer reissued his book with a new introduction in which he took account of the vast changes that had come over the African continent in the interval, changes culminating in the end of the indignities and miseries of colonialism and the emergence of an independent Africa. He also speculated as to the future of African dance, whether it would survive the changes of modernization. He concluded, somewhat ruefully, that it probably would not.

Gorer was too pessimistic. Africa still dances.

Dancing may occur in an Ewe hamlet or the streets of Treichville. It can be found in an Ibadan nightclub or a disco in Mombasa. It will be performed by cattlemen or farmers, by plainsmen and forest dwellers. It will be different in form and purpose from what Gorer described, for the vast changes in Africa have affected dance as they have everything else. Nonetheless, the dance, and the music it dances to—these abide. They remain embedded deep in the life and heart of Africa.

Two observations, a score of years apart, may help illustrate the point. In the spring of 1958 a visitor crossed the broad surface of the Congo River at Stanley Pool to reach Brazzaville from Leopoldville. One of his objectives was the atelier of Pierre Lods, a young French artist who had come to Equatorial Africa after the Second World War and had remained to encourage a style of local painting that eventually gained wide recognition as the Poto Poto school, named after the Brazzaville suburb where these artists worked. After meeting the Poto Poto painters, the visitor was taken by Lods to a nearby café. It was a warm Sunday afternoon, suitable for a drowsing siesta, but there were no siestas in Poto Poto that day. On Sundays there was street dancing among the Bakongo residents, and the participants were gathering, already attempting some preliminary flourishes. Gradually the group settled into a rhythm, and the dance began. "A group of young men and women dance to drum music in a circle roughly like the Big Apple," the visitor reported:

but no Big Apple ever resembled this. The movements don't appear to change and the drumbeats repeat and repeat, but the whole thing has an hypnotic effect and seems to gather intensity to the point of abandonment. Most of the dancers or musicians have tin cans half filled with small stones which sound a bit like Caribbean gourds. Formerly they danced in full paint and feathered costume, but now they wear ordinary street clothes. This is an unfortunate loss but the effect is still powerful. . . . Most of the people here are at least nominally Christian and many are Catholic, yet here they were abandoned in a pagan rite that wouldn't pass muster in a Harlem nightclub let alone Saint Patrick's Cathedral. . . . Lods says that virtually all the old art forms have disappeared in the past ten years. This one exercise per week is all that is left of traditional dance in this area, and no traditional sculpture is now practiced. Clearly the dance is the central art here as it is in West Africa. . . . It is a puzzle as to how this can be made to grow and prosper.

Another spring, this one in 1979, found the same visitor attending the opening of an art exhibition at the Legon Institute of African Studies, a ceremony that was part of the thirtieth anniversary marking the founding of the University of Ghana. The exhibition was an interesting mix of traditional and modern works, but as the midafternoon heat closed in, the formalities sagged under a series of speeches by assembled dignitaries. The steadily sweating audience was mesmerized, seated stiffly on folding wooden chairs, uncomfortable in their coats and ties or flowered frocks reserved for such occasions. Then, all at once, a group of drummers to one side came into action. There were six or eight musicians, the orchestra of the Institute's School of Music and Drama, but their rhythms were particularly marked by the authoritative baritone of the big drums set against the nervous staccato of the talking drums. The audience stirred, still seated, moving sympathetically to the compulsions of the orchestra. It was a brief recital but suddenly the atmosphere had changed. Gone was the boredom, the correctness, the sleepiness. Soon everyone moved to an adjacent open-air quadrangle where groups of dancers had assembled, ordinary citizens recruited from nearby Accra for the ceremony and ready to give spontaneous performances of their traditional dances. "There were two groups," the visitor reported, "one from the north and featuring muscular dancing accompanied by drum, two xylophones, and hand and foot gongs by the dancers. The other group was Ewe from the Volta region with its own drums and a circle of female dancers with handkerchiefs. It was very good and infectious, and when they broke out the beer, it wouldn't have taken much to get the thing going all-night. . . . This sort of affair has great appeal, and it has much life in it."[1]

### The Musician

The performances at Legon did not just happen. Rhythm may be innate in the African psyche, but the erosion of traditional loyalties and beliefs resulting from modernizing trends has brought communal and individual memory loss. Gorer's fears were justified. The old dances were dying out, in Ghana as in the Congo; positive affirmation was needed to revive the old, and, more, to reshape its character to meet new demands under new circumstances. Fortunately there were those like the Ghanaian composer, Ephraim Amu, who recognized the problem and set out to do something about it.

Ephraim Amu was born in the Ewe-speaking Volta region of the Gold Coast in September 1899. The month may be more important than the year; according to local belief, Amu, as a child of August and September, "vibrated powerfully with music right from infancy." The boy's schooling prepared him for a career as teacher and Presbyterian catechist, but his central passion certainly was music. He took work in theory, harmony, and composition, and learned to play the harmonium, studying in his spare time to supplement regular lessons. When in 1920 he returned to teach at his old school at Peki, he introduced musical instruction and tried his hand at composition—at this early stage only in Western musical modes.

There was more to the young man than an academic passion for music, however. At Peki and later at Akropong, where he joined the faculty of the Presbyterian Teacher Training College, Amu was struck by the silent bafflement of the parishioners reacting to the European hymns that were regular Sunday fare at the Presbyterian church where he served as a sometime preacher. Amu thought he knew the reason: many were illiterate, and, in any case, not having attended school, were unfamiliar with European songs and hymns. To the young schoolteacher this was an unhealthy situation and he determined to do something about it. Amu began by gathering examples of the indigenous music of the region, his own musical interests and training facilitating this initial search. There followed several original compositions, which Amu rehearsed with his students at the college. He realized that there might be opposition by those who did not feel that African musical forms were appropriate to the requirements of holy service. At the same time a musical idiom that the members of the congregation knew and loved seemed ideally designed to bring them more fully into the spirit of Christian worship.

In 1928 Amu was ready to introduce an original hymn as part of the Sunday service of the Akropong Presbyterian Church. Uncertain over the reception of his work, Amu prudently placed his podium near a handy exit before leading his student choir through three verses. As the singing began, Amu searched the congregation for a reaction. "I noticed there was absolute quiet," he later observed. "Nobody moved at all. We sang the second verse and it was just the same. Then we sang the third verse and it was still absolute quiet. I didn't know what the reaction was. So we finished and sat down." Fearful, Amu awaited the explosion, but the explosion never came. Immediately after the service, while standing outside the chapel, Amu was approached by the senior minister, a fellow Ghanaian whose disapproval he had most dreaded. As he came near, the clergyman broke into a smile and extended his hand in congratulation. "I have never heard such beautiful music as this," he said.

Such favorable initial reaction was misleading. The congregation was enthusiastic over Amu's innovation, but most of the church fathers, though Ghanaian, were troubled by his iconoclasm. The interval between the two world wars was the high-water mark of colonialism and many Africans joined Europeans in discounting their own culture. Amu's strange uncouth sounds were inappropriate to Christian worship, it was argued, and he was urged to abandon foolish ideas and be guided by his superiors in pursuit of a promising career in the ministry. Far from yielding, Amu's resolve hardened in the face of opposition. "I was convinced I was moving in the right direction," he later recalled. "I felt encouraged by the resistance they gave."

Another controversy soon arose. Increasingly impatient with inappropriate European cultural accretions, Amu devoted himself to the renascence of African custom. He used calabashes for drinking, and spoke local languages in preference to English. His marriage ceremony was conducted in traditional form, and he abandoned European dress in favor of the robes and sandals of the region. Such conduct, Amu insisted, was practical as well as cultural, reflecting time-tested adjustments to land and climate. Abruptly, Amu began conducting his Sunday services in African dress. In those years sermons were invariably delivered in heavy broadcloth suit, collar, and tie, the congregation similarly clad, similarly suffering. "I felt that the attire in which we preached was ridiculous," said Amu. "In this hot country it was grueling on us to wear a black suit with vest and everything, which I did wear for some time. . . . By the time one went through all that one was fully wet with perspiration. . . . So without asking their opinion or their permission I appeared in the pulpit one Sunday morning . . .

in cloth. Immediately after the service, the ministers called me into their presence." Once again Amu refused to yield. The ministry ceased to interest him, while his preoccupation with local culture grew. Amu was ordered to discontinue his activities. He declined, and in 1933 he lost his post at the teacher training college.

Though the dismissal was disappointing at the time, hindsight must view it as a liberation, an affirmation of past achievement and future commitment. During the five years that had passed since Amu presented his first song to the parishioners at the Akropong Presbyterian church, his musical interests had greatly broadened and deepened. In 1934 he moved to Achimota College, a much more encouraging atmosphere for experimentation. There he remained until 1951, taking a degree in music at the Royal College of Music in London during the war years, but for the rest teaching languages, music, agriculture, and scriptures at Achimota. In 1949 a college of music was established at Achimota; two years later it was moved to the Kumasi College of Technology and Amu went north to be its director.[2]

Throughout his career Amu's musical activities involved teaching, collecting, and composition, but to a large extent the first two were meant to serve the last. The collection of traditional music was a necessary source of form and content to the aspiring composer, while teaching provided the performers as well as a more knowledgeable audience. Not long after Amu's first ventures into song literature, he realized that he would have to study drumming, for it was evident that rhythm was central to all African music, and in Africa, rhythm was the province of the drum. This posed complications for vocal literature. On the one hand, an orchestra of three, four, or five drums typically combined a pattern of distinct rhythms, each instrument playing its own, and all coming together in counterpoint. Traditional songs, however, had their own melodic line and harmony, their intonations and rhythms governed by the speech rhythm of the text. Arranged for part singing, such songs could well involve a series of consecutive intervals that were unacceptably dissonant. Amu solved this problem by relating each part of his songs to a particular drum rhythm, bringing them all together in a polyphonic structure that maintained interest and tension while avoiding the progression of unacceptable intervals.

It was an elegant resolution that retrieved old modes and reshaped them in new ways, but it proved complicated in performance. "It is difficult for most Africans to perform my music correctly," Amu admitted, "because their knowledge of drumming is very little." Perhaps, however, the results were worth the effort. "The art of counterpoint . . . makes the music very interesting," Amu went on, "because when you have to listen to one part doing something and another part doing another thing it creates great interest. . . . And I am glad to say," he concluded, "it is enjoyed by both literate and illiterate in this country. It means something to them."

Amu employed the drum to give shape to his songs, but his interest in traditional African instruments was concentrated in particular on the reeds or flutes indigenous to his own native soil. There was, for example, the six-note bamboo flute, played transversely, which Amu had listened to as a child. "When I grew up I heard nothing more about it," he recalled. "There were not many players in this part of the country, but I always had very clear memories of the things I had heard when I was a boy." Amu set about to find players and finally located a few—one, in fact, in his own hometown. "I went to him," said Amu, "and he played it for me and showed me how to make it and then I started learning."

Amu soon discovered more examples of this flute—some with slightly different intervals—along with a number of other reed instruments of different design. Most were difficult to play because of technical limitations, like the length of the column of air or the placement of stops. Since Ghanaian music in the southern districts was based with minor variations on the same diatonic scale as that of the West, musicians there had made an easy transition to the European fife during colonial times, and the traditional flutes fell into disuse. Amu set about redesigning several of these instruments, and, again, considerations were part practical and part aesthetic. The bamboo flute, called *Atenteben,* played transversely, was difficult for many students; consequently Amu converted it into an end-blown recorder that facilitated performance without losing the special character of its sound. Another woodwind, the cane flute, *Odurugya,* had a lovely tone but was limited to five notes because its great length inhibited additional fingering. Amu bent the flute at an angle, thereby facilitating reach, which in turn made possible a full scale that extended through two and one-half octaves. The original or traditional *Odurugya* was retained, but was reduced both in size and length and given a wooden mouthpiece. It was considerably longer than the *Antenteben* but approximately half the length of the *Odurugya* and was therefore named *Odurugyaba* or "small *Odurugya*." Efficiency was improved and variety increased, while the unique tonal quality of each instrument was preserved.

It was not long before Amu's explorations extended into other parts of the Gold Coast. He traveled north to Kwahuland in search of one particular flute; on another occasion he persuaded the *asantehene*, Prempeh II, to allow him to learn to play the Ashanti *Odurugya*. As he mastered these instruments and made his technical improvements, he graded them into voices from soprano to bass and in varying keys, organizing the components into orchestras formed from his students. These groups were then combined with drum ensembles that, along with Amu's voice choirs, gave him a rich outlet for performing his compositions, which were also a combination of new and old.

Ghana's tonal languages offered wide latitude for experiment in melody, while the flutes and "talking" drums could be made to produce sounds that had literal meaning. Amu's song literature was antiphonal; that is, parts were sung and played by different choirs responding to one another in counterpoint. His music was traditional and recognizable, but it was also modern and forward-looking. The melodies were simple, the harmonies elementary and therefore accessible to all. The complexities lay in the performance, which wedded the harmonies of tonal languages with African drum rhythms. Beyond this there was a genuine synthesis of indigenous materials from different regions.

Amu wrote his songs in both the Ewe and Twi languages. Since much of his career was spent in Twi-speaking areas, he wrote in Twi for immediate utility. There was no problem of communication. "The Twi-speaking people considered my Ewe songs more interesting than those I did in Twi," Amu recalled. "They learned them with every interest and enthusiasm. And my Ewe people learned the Twi songs in exactly the same way. In the institutions where I taught for so many years, I composed in both Twi and Ewe, taught these to all the students from the various tribes, even including Nigerians who all sang in these languages quite happily."

When a new secondary school was opened in Ashanti, Amu composed a song commemorating the occasion. When King Prempeh heard the song he was greatly moved. "Who wrote it?" he wanted to know. "It was Amu," was the reply. "Ah," said Prempeh proudly. "Our own

Amu." What was coming into being was not only something old in new form but something that reached out beyond the limits of parochial custom to forms that could be appreciated on a national scale and beyond.

At the end of 1960 Amu retired from his post at Kumasi but not from his work. He was immediately appointed senior research fellow at the newly formed School of Music and Drama at Legon and there was able to continue his work of collecting and recording traditional music, of composing, and of instructing students both at Legon and at Peki, where he visited regularly. He prepared materials for use in schools and churches, and trained a chorus with a flute and drum orchestra that performed throughout the country, and which eventually toured overseas. In 1969 his performers visited the United States and received much public acclaim. In Washington one critic reported, "The highest drama of the evening came with Ghana Choir's folk-like songs, written by their director, E. Amu, and sung in their own language." In New York the audience rose and applauded, unwilling in its enthusiasm to wait for the last piece to end. "That was a great moment in my life," Amu recalled.

Like many innovators, Ephraim Amu at first outran his times, but he soon discovered that he was not alone in his convictions, that his sense of direction was as impeccable as his determination. By the end of the Second World War profound changes in world opinion and conditions had set colonial peoples on the road to an independence that was cultural as well as political. In 1949 the Presbyterian church held a synod in Accra, and Amu was now invited to address the assembled clerics on the subject of African music. Those who had opposed his efforts asked him to produce a book of hymns for church service. Here was vindication indeed that was perhaps even more satisfying than the honors that ensued. An honorary degree from the University of Ghana was followed by a medal from the Ghana government, and finally, in 1972, by a citation from the Ghana Arts Council. "You had foreseen the cultural revolution which we are witnessing today," the commendation stated. "You did not only speak about it, you lived it, and sang about it. . . . You persisted all through the struggle and won in the end."

Stirring words. Yet possibly the citation came closer to the essential artist when it spoke of the composer's songs, the early creations with their "charm, imagery, vividness, gaity, confidence, and the determination of youth," the later works exhibiting the "experience and patience of maturity."[3]

## The Catalyst

In the early years of Ghana's independence, visitors from America were struck by the widespread appearances of modernity—the new buildings rising all over Accra, the finely paved roads with their new cars and trucks, the high-tension power lines marching across country on spidery steel stilts. Whatever a newcomer's preconceptions, nothing seemed very much like Africa; rather, the image of an American suburban landscape came more readily to mind.

The alien un-African atmosphere was even more pronounced on the campus of the University College at Legon, with its handsome buildings of vaguely oriental design, its crisply starched British faculty, and its Western curriculum that seemed to contain little more than an occasional gesture toward the Africa it was meant to serve. There were a few Ghanaian instructors—after ten years some nine in a faculty of 130—but the rate of change seemed glacial despite protests that Africanization was basic to all staff planning. Visitors asking to meet Africans often encountered disinterest if not difficulty. There was Kofi Busia, the professor of sociology, but he was busy with many affairs and, in any case, leaving the university for politics. There was Reverend Baeta of the divinity department but unfortunately away on a visit to Japan. There were some junior people, most of them absent on study leave in Britain. Questions of an Africanized curriculum tended to be diverted to discussions of academic standards or the need for research to prepare new materials, sometimes ending with a supercilious dismissal to the effect that there was, after all, nothing "African" about philosophy or physics or mathematics.

One exception, mentioned almost as an afterthought to a visitor who came to the university college in 1958, was a young Ghanaian musicologist attached to the department of sociology as a research fellow. His name was J. H. Kwabena Nketia and he worked alone in a small laboratory tucked away in an out-of-the-way corner where he was engaged in the classification of traditional African musical forms collected on many field trips throughout Ghana. He had been appointed by Busia some years earlier, and since that time had been left largely to himself. He had no teaching responsibilities; indeed, there was no place in the syllabus where he might function, so he had busied himself copying, transcribing, and organizing the musical information he had gathered with the objective of developing materials that might eventually serve a department of music with particular reference to the music of Africa.

On the far edge of the world of Legon, Nketia nevertheless was much in the mainstream of the renascence of traditional arts and culture in Ghana. Not surprisingly, he turned out to be a student and protégé of Ephraim Amu. Nketia had studied music in London, like Amu, he had taught at the training college at Akropong and served as church organist, like Amu he had written vocal and instrumental music that employed African modes and rhythms, like Amu he was interested in both accumulating and creating materials that might be suitable for church services and for instruction in the country's expanding school system.

While in London, at the close of the Second World War, Nketia had also studied linguistics at London University's School of Oriental and African Studies, a step that had distressed Amu, who feared a creative musician might be lost to scholarship. Amu need not have concerned himself. Nketia combined his work in linguistics with generous portions of musical study; his interest in the word was primarily poetic, and since African poetry was largely sung, he remained well anchored in the field of music. Nketia's musical interests concentrated on composition, theory, and analysis. When he returned home to resume his post at Akropong and later at Legon, Nketia was able to combine his own composition with research and analysis of indigenous forms. In 1955 he published a monograph on Akan funeral dirges, and over the years he produced a steady stream of scholarly books and articles dealing with the traditional music of Ghana, writings that brought an international recognition that may for a time have transcended his reputation on his own campus.

In 1958 Nketia came to the United States where he worked under Henry Cowell, a composer particularly interested in the fusion of Western and non-Western music. He also studied at The Julliard School, Northwestern University, and the University of California at Los Angeles, the last of which offered a program in the study and performance of non-Western music. The benefits at UCLA were mutual, for the program had previously been exclusively Asian; hence Nketia was able to bring attention for the first time to the music of Africa while expanding his own experience and interests. When he returned to Ghana, Nketia was ideally grounded to develop a wide range of musical activities that would encourage research, teaching, and creative composition in the music of Africa.[4]

Nketia's return in 1960 coincided with the establishment of the independent University of Ghana. The following year an Institute of African Studies was inaugurated to which Nketia moved his base, at the same time laying plans for an augmented music program that emerged in 1962 as the institute's School of Music and Drama, with himself as its head. Subsequently he also served as deputy director of the institute and in 1965 succeeded Thomas Hodgkin as director. Fortune had changed and earlier frustrations were converted to the opportunity for the concrete realization of ideas that had long germinated in the crowded music laboratory of the sociology department.[5]

There was much to be done. As with so-called primitive art, non-European music had long been regarded in the West as picturesque or barbaric, frequently both, often the subject for humorous commentary by untrained observers like explorers or colonial officials; not the stuff of serious study, certainly not in schools of music, but if anywhere then among the more esoteric branches of anthropology. To begin with, then, said Nketia, any purposeful exploration of ethnomusicology—the study of non-Western music—had to rid itself of those cultural prejudices that measured everything foreign by a domestic, ethnocentric yardstick. Genuine musicianship would have to be a prerequisite to scholarship, and emphasis would certainly be required on "the study of music in culture."

Such a study began with collection and analysis of field research, said Nketia. Analysis involved examination of tuning and scales, tonal and rhythmic structure, the relation of sounds to speech and vocal style, and, of great importance, the kinship of musical production within the context of the society from which it sprang. "It is here," said Nketia, "that we look at the . . . values associated with the music and the cultural and historical dimensions which are needed for the understanding of these traditions and values."

This must not be a theoretical exercise, Nketia continued. There must also be performance and new composition. This was the great contribution of Amu, a pioneer who had begun the creation of the old music in new forms a generation earlier, Nketia remarked, and who was joined at the School of Music and Drama by the dancer A. M. Opoku, for "African music and dance are inseparable and no African ethnomusicologial programme can afford to neglect the visual dimension of this music which influences its conception as well as its interpretation and function."

Performance of African music involved more than mastery of an instrument, vocal style, or dance maneuver, Nketia warned. It must be accompanied as well by a thorough familiarity with the unnotated repertory that is part of the oral tradition, by an ability to improvise within the prescribed limits of that tradition, and by a grounding in the parts of other instruments in the ensemble. "A good knowledge of the songs which are combined with the drums is also essential," Nketia concluded.

Such activities must not be limited to their academic manifestations, Nketia pointed out, scholars functioning merely for the edification of other scholars. There would have to be points of dissemination throughout the community at large, an outreach to children and adults to refresh their memories of the traditional arts of Africa, to offer the opportunity of participation as performer and observer. This was the reason for the Ghana Music Society, founded in 1958, for the Ghana Dance Ensemble, which was instituted four years later as an active arm of the Institute of African Studies, and for the encouragement that the Institute was able to lend to Efua Sutherland and her Drama Studio.

It was a large order, breathing new life into old songs, and Nketia knew it. African communities were in the full flux of change. There was much that survived from the traditional ways but there were also new groups—Christians, Muslims, industrial laborers, professional cadres, civil servants, urban dwellers—whose training, background, and consequent tastes were vastly different from what had existed before. Far from harboring sympathy toward traditional forms of artistic expression, such groups were estranged and frequently hostile. What need could they possibly have, Nketia asked rhetorically, for fertility dolls or wooden combs? Why should they want to collect useless, seemingly crude, artifacts from a bygone time, or perform dances and attend Ananse plays that seemed quaint in comparison to the Gilbert and Sullivan, the Handel, or the Shaw and Shakespeare they had learned at school? Why not carry on with these time-tested imports? If they were not digestible, there was always "highlife" or the popular music of the West that came in liberal doses through radio and gramophone.

Still, there were those who were more receptive, if not more knowledgeable. Politicians were quick to call for a renewed appreciation of the African cultural past, but their appeal was based upon extra-artistic considerations and their understanding was usually negligible. There was danger in such neotraditionalism, Nketia warned. It could easily degenerate into cultural shows remarkable only for their quaintness, ephemeral manifestations no better understood by their own people than by the outsiders who found titillation in exoticism.

Yet Nketia was convinced that there was something important, indeed profoundly essential, in the retrieval of traditional African culture and its metamorphosis into modern forms. It had to succeed, but how? First of all, said Nketia, there had to be a genuine love and appreciation for the arts. This could be developed through education, he felt—through knowledge and understanding directed at all levels of the educational system and at the public at large. And education would have to work both ways, Nketia went on. New social groups presupposed a new sociology of the arts, requiring new approaches that would attract citizens to an enjoyment and appreciation of Africa's rich artistic heritage. The basic human attraction to music, the urge to dance, the desire for aesthetic enjoyment was there as strong as ever. It just needed to be nurtured and guided.

For Kwabena Nketia, then, responsibility lay with the community of intellectual leadership, those "knowledgeable men (who may be preliterate), scholars, writers and artists who play a critical role in different facets of national life." This group extended beyond the arts to politics, administration, the sciences, and other fields of endeavor; its main qualification was the capacity to identify contemporary development in the arts that reflected new and socially germane intellectual and cultural values. As Nketia noted,

It is very easy for an intellectual community of any kind to stay aloof and be satisfied with its own activities, ideas and modes of thought instead of acting as a leaven in society. It is certainly my hope that in the creative arts there will be interaction between the narrow circle of intellectuals and the community at large so that the gap between the past and the present, between the traditional and the contemporary can be bridged. It is only then that we can restore, through the media now available to us, the African concept of the arts as a form of community experience.[6]

## The Dancer

Here indeed was a large order for Legon's new African Studies Institute and its School of Music and Drama. Nketia, nevertheless, was confident that he had the necessary resources. Amu's presence assured the quality of composition and performance, while Efua Sutherland's associate at the Drama Studio, Joe deGraft, was ready to prepare programs of study in drama production, speech, acting, play analysis, and the technical aspects of staging. Nketia himself would give overall direction while organizing research concerned largely with field recording and the collection of instruments. Programs of study for individuals, from performers to schoolteachers, would be provided at various levels leading to certificates, diplomas, degrees, and eventually to graduate study. Music courses would also be available to ordinary baccalaureate students from other divisions within the university. Much of the emphasis was on creative work and performance. There were to be choral ensembles, orchestras for traditional music, dance-study companies, and playacting groups. Public performances would be part of the curriculum—concerts, dance recitals, and dramatic presentations.[7]

The focus on performance had always been basic to Nketia's concept of a center for the living arts, and it certainly fitted the predilections of Albert M. Opoku, who came to the institute in 1962 as a senior research associate to take charge of the dance programs. In background, experience, and personal inclinations, Opoku was ideally suited for the work assigned. Descended on both sides from chiefly families in Ashanti, Opoku had as a youth been exposed to a traditional education that was standard training for those who might one day occupy a stool—that is, succeed to one of the many chieftaincies in and near the Ashanti center of Kumasi. More particularly, some of Opoku's forebears had been responsible for protection of the Golden Stool, the great emblem of the Ashanti people; others were related to the office of *okyeamehene*, the chief linguist or spokesman for the *asantehene*, king

of the Ashanti nation. While these offices had been stripped of their political authority during the years of colonialism, they still retained importance in the eyes of the Ashanti as symbols of former greatness and
as repositories of Ashanti custom and tradition. Those, like Opoku,
who were trained in traditional lore and etiquette, were especially sensitive to cultural and aesthetic inheritances expressed in terms of linguistic symbolism, religious or communal ceremonies, and particularly,
the dance, which occupied such a central position in African social and
cultural life.

Opoku had also received a Westernized schooling, graduating from
Achimota College before he departed for Britain, where, like Amu and
Nketia, he spent part of the war years in advanced study. Opoku's specialty was art and design, which he taught at Achimota upon his return
home after the war, eventually continuing his teaching career at the
technical college in Kumasi, concentrating on sculpture and more particularly on wood engraving. During his tenure at the Kumasi college,
Opoku also became associated with the Asante Cultural Centre, a civic
enterprise founded by his cousin, Alex Kerematen, during the 1950s as
a concrete expression of Ashanti culture, a place where Ghanaians might
regain contact with their traditions, relearning the classical culture in
direct and tangible ways.

A practicing artist, Opoku nevertheless turned his energies at the
center away from paint, wood, or ceramics and focused on the dance.
"To us," he has said, ". . . dance is life expressed in dramatic terms."

> For a deeper insight into our way of life—our labours, material
> culture, aspirations, history, social and economic conditions, reli-
> gious beliefs and disbeliefs, moments of festivity and sadness—in
> short, our life and soul, and the realities, perceived, conceived, or
> felt, that make us the people that we have been and are at present,
> are revealed to the serious seeker in our dance. It has been said
> that drama puts a strong spotlight on a significant aspect or face
> of human life and experience, drawing special attention to the in-
> ternal and external conflicts which shape our lives. The African
> dance serves a similar purpose in our community.

With the help of others Opoku organized a dance group at the center, naming it after a song by Amu that expressed the poetic notion,
"those who play and dance together are children of a drum and there-

fore of love." One of the members of the royal house at nearby Mampong–Asante gave formal inauguration to the group, pouring a libation and announcing that "God has brought this thing in its proper time." Opoku quickly discovered, however, that many of his fellow Ashantis had lost touch with their dances, that he was obliged to conduct classes in fundamentals before moving on to various forms of popular and court dancing. The public response was enthusiastic, and in its first four years Opoku's school trained over five hundred individuals who came to the Centre twice a week for instruction by experienced dancers and who developed skills that soon transformed training into recreation. In time, the Ashanti dance school gained a reputation that led to command performances to entertain visiting dignitaries. Programs of Ashanti dances were mounted, and, at festival time, special presentations included dances from other regions in Ghana.

It was not long before Opoku found himself traveling to Legon on weekends where, at Nketia's behest, he conducted informal dance classes along the same lines as those at the Kumasi Cultural Centre. In collaboration the two men began to lay plans for organizing a troupe of dancers and musicians, professionals capable of presenting for national and international audiences the dances and music of Ghana, converting the results of field research in traditional forms to performances that would be a tangible expression of the Ghanaian people as a whole. In 1960 Opoku came to New York where he spent a year studying under Martha Graham, taking time out during the interval to advise Agnes De Mille in her choreography for the musical drama, *Kwamina*.

The work at Martha Graham's school was not designed to expose Opoku to the idiom of modern dance; rather he sought a greater understanding of body movement and staging, for what he and Nketia had in mind was a dance company for Ghana that would preserve the character of traditional dance and music while reshaping them for theatrical presentation before nonparticipating audiences. Here was a plan both exciting and hazardous. The old would be retrieved, but with a new function far removed from the original purpose of African dance. Novel in conception, it was an idea long in gestation. When Opoku was still in London, he and other Ghanaians had looked forward to the day when they could form a traveling team that would visit the country's regions, not to play soccer matches but to exhibit the nation's many dances.

At this period in Ghana's early independence, there was great public interest in the indigenous arts. An arts council had been formed at Nkrumah's request and was attempting to formulate artistic programs of national dimension. There were ambitious if vague plans for a national theater, and numerous individual music and dance companies had come into existence, vying for popular attention and government support. The collaboration between Opoku and Nketia, however, brought together understanding of traditional modes with an awareness of the exigencies of modern theater; these qualities, wedded to a practical management, made possible the perilous leap of African dance from an ancient religious and social rite to an aesthetic form for popular enjoyment.[8]

"There were practical problems," Opoku later observed. "In the old dances, everybody faced the king, but in the theater we could not turn our back on the audience. Exits and entrances had to be worked out. Moving dancers across the stage without collisions, creating patterns pleasing to the eye, devising movements that were physically possible, shortening lengthy ceremonies and giving them dramatic impact, all without losing essential authenticity—these were real problems." When criticized for daring to choreograph traditional dances, Opoku insisted that some form of choreography had always been present. In earlier times the dances were arranged and changes constantly introduced to meet new circumstances; his was only a modern version of an old process, he pointed out. Just as the sculptor, Oku Ampofo, experimented with new woods and techniques, just as Ephraim Amu redesigned the traditional flutes, so Opoku tried new patterns, new tempi, to gain new insights and to revive and heighten the aesthetic experience.[9]

So often the innovation that emerged came from necessity. For example, while a traditional solo dance performed ritually was appropriate in a small village compound, on a stage in a large hall such gestures might become lost in their subtlety, the single dancer remote in a too vast space. Opoku thus amplified the dance by staging it for a quartet of performers, thereby enlarging the movement for all to see. Again, a particular Ewe dance contained very beautiful passages, but with such rapid movements that they could not be followed by an unfamiliar observer, and the dance was over before the audience could grasp its character. In this case Opoku began presto, then introduced a reprise in slow time before returning to the original quick pattern. Authenticity was compromised but comprehension enhanced. In still another instance, Opoku eliminated the supporting drums of a particular sequence so that the talking drum could be clearly understood by an audience that did not speak the language of the drummers. Interpretations of this sort, done poorly, could destroy form and intent, but in the hands of a knowledgeable and perceptive artist, they could enhance the old and create something new.

In pursuing his plans for a creative renascence of traditional dance, Opoku had the support of his experience. At Kumasi, for example, he had constantly experimented with dances from different areas of the country; more often than not he found that his innovations were incorporated by the practitioners and brought back for use in their own villages. In Africa, experiment and change, not static sameness, was as much a part of artistic life as anywhere. Opoku recalled the comments of an experienced African weaver who had pointed out that, contrary to common understanding, the design patterns of *kente* cloth were constantly changing in response to new demands, the insights of individual craftsmen, or the exigencies of new events in need of commemoration.

At the same time innovation had to be keyed to tradition. In whatever form, the old modes reached deep into the individual psyche, fulfilling and satisfying needs that had long lain dormant. When *Kwamina* went on the road before its New York opening, it played briefly in Toronto. There Opoku was approached during the performance by a Ghanaian, apparently quite moved by what he was seeing. "Thank you," he said to Opoku, not in English but in his native tongue. "Thanks for lifting our faces up. I feel so very proud."

The powers of the dance seemed without bounds. In Kumasi there were chronic skirmishes and occasional public violence between adherents of the Convention People's Party of Kwame Nkrumah and the Ashanti-based National Liberation Movement, but these disturbances invariably vanished in the dance arena. It was the one place where all could literally bring about the cooperation of the people of Ghana. Dance was also a phenomenon that touched all, high or low. The traditional chief, Opoku explained, must dance, and dance well, or he may be shamed out of his office. "At his enthronement the dance speaks of the achievements of his predecessors. So he must be able to dance. . . .

If he can't, he takes lessons. If you're not dancing well, the drummers can be insulting . . . passing some very rude commentary on their drums."

The dance had the same power for modern politicians. On one occasion Nkrumah planned a visit to Kumasi despite its political opposition. There was much apprehension until the occasion was defused by concentrating public appearances on cultural and social functions. Nkrumah was met by groups of Ashanti women dancing with handkerchiefs in traditional fashion. "We met him in an Ashanti way," Opoku recalled,

> . . . with the women dancing. Nkrumah waited until he got to a place where the NLM and the CPP people were seated opposite . . . and he got hold of a handkerchief. He could not really do the dance but he went through the motions with the women. And all these people were swept off their feet. They rushed up to him and started dancing with him. He conquered them straight from the Cultural Centre. . . . And he went to each group and did something like what they were doing. Then they said, 'He is a man of the people.'

This was no exclusively Ghanaian phenomenon. Later, when the Dance Company of Ghana visited Nigeria, the Nigerian head of state, General Yakuba Gowon, danced at one of the performances to the delight and approbation of his own Nigerian compatriots.[10]

One thing in particular that Opoku and Nketia noticed from their study of traditional forms was the similarity between the dance and music of different peoples and regions within Ghana. Often the variations were minor and easily recognizable. As a politician, Nkrumah was also sensitive to these similarities and recognized their potential for national cohesion; at the same time, he viewed the dance as a visible manifestation of his concept, the African Personality. For independence day celebrations he encouraged performances in Accra of regional dance troupes, a popular entertainment that, however, became difficult to manage and to appreciate because of the large numbers involved. Opoku, therefore, was encouraged to form a nuclear dance company of individuals from the various regions, performers who possessed pride in their own culture but were also able to see virtues in the culture of others and to share in the differences. In this way the Ghana Dance Ensemble was formed in 1962, with Nketia as director and Opoku as artistic director.

An experiment in intramural cooperation, the ensemble was also a carefully conceived device for the revival of traditional culture through study and performance. This was no casual pickup company but the product of a disciplined program operating from the School of Music and Drama at the University of Ghana, its object the development of professional performers in dance, music, and drama, and the renascence of traditional forms, chiefly from Ghana but also from other parts of West Africa. It was an experiment, Nketia acknowledged, but withal a creative experiment.

> We have tried . . . to work out a form of presentation which highlights and clarifies the essential forms of the dances without destroying their basic movements and styles, their emotional, symbolic and cultural values or their vitality and vigour. . . . We have tried to use . . . the comments and criticism of experts in our villages. . . . We have tried to see our dances with Ghanaian eyes and not with the eyes of Hollywood or the squinted eyes of the amateur dance-anthropologist. . . . We have insisted not only on correctness of movement but also on the quality of movement. . . . We have followed the warning . . . that a dance form which does not re-create . . . stagnates and dies.[11]

Such aspirations were exportable. Kwame Nkrumah had seen the Dance Ensemble and its traveling arm, the African Dance Company of Ghana, as a political tool with pan-African and international ramifications. When the Ghanaians visited New York in 1968 on their first American tour, however, the audiences were touched spiritually and aesthetically. One critic was impressed by what he saw as the "classic" character of the performances. Speaking of purity of movement, elegance of stance, the combination of physical dexterity with ceremony, he concluded, "The accent was upon decorum, graciousness, regal behaviour. . . . Earthiness, physical force, the recurrent use of pelvic actions were present, and these were exciting, indeed, but even in the swiftest, most emotional moments, the contours of classicism were retained."

Perhaps another critic came closer to the ulterior purpose of the ensemble. "Folk music," he observed, "is a mass response to common problems." Through dance all rejoice in marriages and mourn the dead. "The African Dance Company of Ghana last night created this intangible community bond."[12]

## Les Ballets Africains

The Ghana company was not the first to display its talents before a New York audience. Almost a decade earlier, in 1959, another group had captivated urban sophisticates and impressed the metropolitan critics. "The Ballets Africains of Keita Fodeba has . . . taken the town," announced the dance reviewer of the *New York Times*. He added that this was no little achievement, for ethnic dance was constantly menaced by the twin quandaries of too much authenticity turned to dullness or entertainment that degenerated into just another musical review. "Mr. Fodeba . . . seems to have grasped the basic problem and solved it with the instinct of an artist," the *Times* critic concluded. "In the theater the dancer is first of all required to communicate with his audience. In [this] performance . . . there is a tremendous amount of communication, yet there is no denying that social ritual, religion, the realities of village life all exert an irresistible power over the dancers. Indeed this power is one of the things they succeed in communicating.[13]

This had been no spontaneous achievement. Toward the end of the Second World War Keita Fodeba had turned up in Paris, a young man seeking to complete the schooling he had begun in his native Guinea and later in Bamako and the Senegalese town of Saint-Louis. Fodeba had trained to become a schoolteacher, and indeed, for a time, he taught school in Paris after concluding his studies there. Nevertheless, it was the theater that was to become his consuming interest as well as his chief source of income.

The change was to some extent accidental. Schooling was expensive and the young Guinean began to augment his financial resources through musical performances in local Paris nightclubs, using song and dance materials from his native land and more generally from West Africa. There had always been a community of Africans living in Paris, many of them students like Fodeba, and after the conclusion of the war, the numbers increased dramatically as France sought new political and cultural relations with her colonies. Thus there was a considerable African audience to appreciate the talents of the young performer, supplemented by those Frenchmen with a taste for the exotic.

Fodeba was early aware of the need to preserve authenticity while at the same time touching his audience. In Africa, he later observed, "Nobody dances for his neighbor, everyone dances for himself." It was his constant care, therefore, "to avoid leading the audience into error in presenting to them a picture of a fictitious Africa," yet "stage presentation being different from life, we have . . . recourse to a slight scenic adaptation."

Though basically a drummer, Fodeba could perform creditably on a number of other instruments to accompany his dance and his songs. Versatile and talented though he was, there were initial difficulties, and for a time Fodeba's father was obliged to send food from Africa. Soon, however, the performances developed their following, and the performer his reputation. By 1946 he had acquired an agent and was touring France and other parts of Europe, journeying as far as Italy, Switzerland, England, and Scandinavia.

Individual success prompted expansion. Fodeba began to recruit a company drawn first from Africans living in Europe, then he reached out to Africa and the Antilles. In 1953 he returned to West Africa, where he traveled systematically in further search of performers and material. Stopping in each of the territories of what was then French West Africa, Fodeba conducted exhaustive auditions, inviting selected individuals to join him in Dakar and incorporating local dance and music into his growing repertory. For a year he remained in Dakar, rehearsing and polishing. By 1954 he was ready, and the *Ballets Africains de Keita Fodeba,* some thirty-seven performers, made its European debut, visiting a number of countries both east and west.[14]

At some point during the 1950s, Fodeba's objectives began to transcend the purposes of entertainment, converting more and more pointedly to a projection of black art and culture. In Paris he had used Europeans, mixing them indiscriminately with African artists, training them to the level where they could function as expertly in an African idiom as could their black counterparts. Further, the repertory was drawn from experience; no particular effort was made to present African dance in any systematic fashion. The revues, moreover, took on a chic polish, resembling in form if not in content the stylishness of French music hall presentations, staged with the expert but characteristic elegance of French designers. The very name *Ballets Africains de Keita Fodeba* reflected the personal rather than the institutional character of the group.

By 1957, however, Fodeba seems to have changed his objectives. Perhaps it was the growing imminence of African independence, perhaps the increasing intensity of the debate over Negritude. Writing in that year Fodeba spoke of the African dance in more purposeful terms. He proclaimed the survival of black culture in various parts of the world despite the wrongs done to men of color by the so-called civilized peoples of the earth. And it was the dance, he insisted, that gave cohesion to African societies. "We know that only the voice of the *tam-tam* possesses enough strength and magic to speak to the African in his essential tongue. So different in form and origin, our dances seem nonetheless to come from the same spirit. It is a spirit at which we never cease to marvel. For us it is a law, a law of perpetual ascendant movement. To the dynamism of thought responds the dynamism of the dance, transposing that thought to the world of the body."[15]

The intensity of this vision broke through the necessities of entertainment and the stylishness of the Western staging, costume and set design provided by Fodeba's French collaborators. It was assimilation at its best. When the *Ballets Africains* reached New York, the European overlay was immediately identified, but, somewhat surprisingly, far from detracting, it served to heighten the authenticity of an essentially African expression. It was a personal triumph for Fodeba and realization of his concept, "a wonderfully successful concept that sees the free and broad dimensions of African culture in terms of a living and international theatre."[16]

Fodeba's concept, it was also his valedictory. The group that visited New York in 1959 was already in transition, its founder no longer associated with his own company. Fodeba had become a minister in the government of his native Guinea, and the company was soon to become the *Ballets Africains de Guinée*, a national dance company limited to Guinean performers and a repertory that presented only the music and dance of Guinea. Others also left the company for government posts, but a number of the original players remained—for example, Kante Facelli, a celebrated griot and performer on the twenty-one stringed cora, and the master drummer, Ladji Camera. When the group returned to New York in 1960 it presented an almost totally new program, but one that was still pleasing, and still capable of projecting the quality of African dance with verisimilitude.

There were other changes. Like his counterpart, Kwame Nkrumah, President Sékou Touré of Guinea saw the national dance company as a medium for projecting an African presence in the world; hence the *Ballets Africains* toured extensively and its performances took on a political purpose. Further, the company survived its founder. Caught in the complexities of national politics, Keita Fodeba eventually fell from power. In 1969 he was arrested, convicted of plotting the overthrow of the government, and presumably executed. The *Ballets Africains* still survives. Expanded to two companies, it tours in Guinea, in Africa, and in Europe.[17]

# 6

## Literary Perspectives of
## Cultural Independence

### Three Novels

In Africa, as elsewhere, literature has commented on society as it is
and as it might be. In traditional times this was done essentially
through the oral media of drama and poetry. As literacy arrived,
commentary began to turn to written forms such as histories, essays,
news reporting, and eventually to that most Western of Western literary forms, the novel. Produced of necessity by Westernized Africans, written tracts in the nineteenth century were couched primarily
in European languages learned, partly for want of indigenous orthog-
raphies and readers, partly for the convenience of communication
among the literate few. Whatever the form, it was a lively exchange,
expressing through literary treatise, scientific study, political argument, journal essay, or published correspondence, a wide-ranging commentary that included, among many interests, ongoing concern with
the impact of the West on traditional African civilizations. This particular preoccupation may be seen in such disparate writing as Boilat's
1853 anthropological study, *Esquisses Sénégalaises*, and the constitutional commentaries published in the 1920s by the Gold Coast barrister, J. B. Danquah, in the variegated output of generations of newspapers, reaching back into the early nineteenth century in West Africa
and eventually spreading throughout the entire continent.

As a literary form and social expression, the novel was a late arrival, its appearance not noteworthy until after the Second World

War. A possible early exception was Casely Hayford's *Ethiopia Unbound*, possible because it reads more like an intellectual autobiography than a work of fiction. Published in 1911, *Ethiopia Unbound* chose as its theme the disintegration of African society forced to submit to political and cultural colonization and argued for survival through adhesion to time-tested traditional verities. Almost a half century later, a rising flood of writing in Africa was addressing this perennial theme—for example, the essential message of Negritude contained in Camara Laye's *L'Enfant Noir* of 1954, and the concurrent early novels of Chinua Achebe that depict the disastrous effect of intrusive Western culture on the previously sheltered world of African society.

In time, African writers abandoned the subject of colonialism for newer themes as Africa faced the complexities of the post-independence era. The dilemma of Africa and Europe remained, however, part of the perplexing question of what should be the shape and purpose of sovereign, self-directed societies. The question held fast, but as time passed the mood seemed to change: first, the euphoria of independence, then the doubts of the sixties and seventies with their political and economic uncertainties, and then the eighties when a cautious optimism appeared, almost a wishful thinking that Africa could win through at last if her peoples combined hard work with faith in the cultural institutions that had sustained them through the ages. The progression from optimism to renewed hopefulness by way of the uncertainties of self-doubt may be illustrated in various literary and artistic manifestations, in this case through the medium of three novels that appeared at intervals between 1960 and 1980.

*Independence*

Nineteen-sixty, the year that symbolized African independence, was also a year of ambivalence in some quarters. Sékou Touré had already led his country to freedom, shouting defiance at the threat of Gaullist reprisal, and Ghana had long since begun to chart its own course under Nkrumah's dynamic leadership. Others were not so sure. Léopold Senghor and Aimé Césaire had sidestepped politics to stress the cultural autonony of their Negritude, while Houphouët-Boigny vainly sought alternatives to a political independence he viewed with misgivings. In Nigeria, independence was delayed until reluctant emirs

from the northern region could be persuaded that freedom was prefer-
able to their comfortable relations with colonial administrators. Other
subject territories achieved national autonomy only to discover fatal
divisions within their own societies. Ugandan independence was unable
to digest the hard stone of Baganda nationalism. By 1960 the Sudan
was already four years a sovereign state, but it would soon be forced
to face civil revolt by southerners who had viewed independence only
as the substitution of a domestic for a foreign tyranny.

By and large, however, these were minority views; the prevailing
mood was euphoric. Nineteen hundred sixty was indeed the symbolic
moment of African independence. Coincidentally it also marked the
appearance of an uncommonly fine novel that spoke eloquently of
another African liberation, recounting an earlier struggle for equality
in the face of economic and racial discrimination.

Sembene Ousmane's *God's Bits of Wood* tells the story of a strike
that took place against the Dakar-Niger railroad between October 1947
and March 1948. The basic facts were simple—workers demanding
higher wages and improved conditions to overcome the poverty, mean-
ness, and dangers of their lives. After months of privation, punctuated
by violence, the workers gained all their objectives. In the process they
discovered they had gained something more—the strength of unity,
pride in achievement, affirmation of racial dignity.

Unity came hard. The railway stretched eight hundred miles from
Dakar to the Niger River beyond Bamako, tapping a million square
miles inhabited by scores of peoples between the Wolof of Senegal
and the Bambara of Soudan. The Bambara combined warrior traditions with a sense of superiority and tended to regard the coastal Senegalese as effete, corrupted by European contamination. The aged
mother of Bakayoko, one of the strike leaders, refers to Senegal as
the country of the *toubabous dyions,* the slaves of the white men.
"Slaves and sons of slaves," she pronounces. "They are all liars and
cheats," speaking the white men's language instead of an honest African tongue, following the white men who are also liars and cheats.[1]

Perhaps she is right. In Dakar, N'Deye Touti, a young schoolgirl,
escapes the squalor of her surroundings by living a fantasy formed by
cheap romances and the cinema, "a universe in which her own people
had no place, and by the same token she had no place in theirs." On
one occasion she misreads the theater program and finds herself

watching a documentary on Pygmies. "She had felt as if she were being hurled backward and down to the level of these dwarfs"—they were not her idea of real Africans. She dreams of a Prince Charming who will bring her love, far different from the polygamous arrangements of her family and neighbors, their "lack of civilization" standing out bleakly against the "parties and costume balls, weekends in the country and trips in automobiles, yachting trips and vacations abroad, elegant anniversary presents and the fall showings of the great coutouriers. Real life was there; not here, in this wretched corner, where she was confronted with beggars and cripples at every turning." Each time N'Deye Touti left the theater, returning to her own world, "she would be seized with a kind of nausea, a mixture of rage and shame."[2]

There are other divisive factors; for example the conventions that govern the behavior of men and women—conventions, however, that are showing signs of wear in a modern world. N'Deye Touti wears a brassiere under her Western clothes despite the taunts of her relatives, and the young stepdaughter of Bakayoko wants to learn what it means to be a man for she hopes some day that men and women will be equal and she will drive a fast locomotive just as her father does. Her mother, however, belongs to the old ways. "A perfect wife: docile, submissive, and hard-working," she is not even consulted before her marriage, which was arranged by her parents; then she is turned over to a man she has never seen after a ceremony appropriate to a family of ancient lineage. When her husband dies, she is married, according to custom, to his younger brother, Bakayoko, who takes her child as his own. "Assitan continued to obey. . . . She was as submissive to Ibrahim as she had been to his brother. . . . He faced dangers she knew nothing of, but that was his lot as a man, as the master. Her own lot as a woman was to accept things as they were and to remain silent as she had been taught to do."[3]

To achieve ultimate success the strikers will need and will gain the assistance of the women, but still other divisions remain to be surmounted. At the outset the railway workers remain alone, unsupported by other unions; there are, moreover, those Africans who have sided with the *toubabs*, African collaborators hated and despised even more than the Europeans whom they serve. Such a one is El Hadji Mabigué of Dakar, overdressed in his yellow slippers, pink parasol, and rich tunics, his red fez wrapped with a scarf in the fashion of Mecca, ever ready to point out that he has made the holy pilgrimage and is thereby due the special respect of his position. The strike has meant hungry days for many, including Mabigué's sister, who approaches him for help, but in vain. "The designs of Providence are unfathomable," he intones with a gesture of his soft, pink, womanly hand.

The whole strike is foolishness, Mabigué goes on. It is the cause of all the misery. Why do not the women urge the men back to work? "Do you think the *toubabs* will give in?" he continues:

> I know better. . . . Everything belongs to them—the shops, and the merchandise in the shops, even the water we drink. . . . It is not our part in life to resist the will of heaven. I know that life is often hard, but that should not cause us to turn our backs on God. He has assigned a rank, a place, and a certain role to every man, and it is blasphemous to think of changing His design. The *toubabs* are here because that is the will of God. Strength is a gift of God, and Allah has given it to them. We cannot fight against it—why, look, they have even turned off the water.[4]

Such sanctimonious remarks are savagely rejected by the frustrated woman, but lack of water and food are far more serious than fraternal defection. Starvation hovers over many households, and the children especially suffer, listless and sickly. Even under normal conditions they dwell in squalid compounds surrounded by refuse heaps that breed maggots, decay, and disease. Her own compound shelters some twenty "God's bits of wood" in an earth-colored shed perched on bricks and complemented by mud huts and wood and tar-paper shacks. One of the main rooms contains an iron bed shared by all the children and covered with a worn spread patched together from many old cloths.

The brood of children plays in the courtyard and, since there has been no water that day, they go unwashed, "their scaly, dried-out skin . . . streaked with dirty cracks, and their eyelashes . . . caked back against their brows." Their mother studies them anxiously, "but her primary concern was for . . . her next-to-last. The child wobbled unsteadily forward, on a pair of rickety legs. His shining belly was so distended that it appeared to precede him." She admonishes him. "You've been eating dirt again." He picks at his nose, then sucks his finger. "Stop that!" she cries. "Stop eating that!"

"I'm hungry," the child screams. She tries to calm him, then rocks the baby in her arms, thinking—the ceaseless hunger, swelling the bellies of the children, defleshing their limbs and bending their shoulders.[5]

Sooner or later all suffer, old as well as young, from famine, sometimes from worse. In the railroad center of Thiès an old man is driven away by well-fed Syrians, then, hungry and ill, he faints, then dies, and is eaten by rats. In Bamako a worker is tried by his fellows for having given up the strike and returned to his job. He is found guilty, his punishment worse than a beating—only the knowledge of his defection, a treachery that he must bear for the rest of his days. During a street riot in Thiès a blind woman loses hold of one of her twins, hears its cry cut short as the infant is crushed under a vehicle. Her other baby survives, sickly, with puss-filled eyes.

> She cradles the child against her bosom. Later she asks a friend.
> "Is she pretty?"
> "She is a beautiful girl. . . ."

Thiès is the nerve center of the strike, appropriately so since it is the junction for the line running north to Saint-Louis as well as the location for maintenance and repair shops. It is also the soot-blackened coal-dust begrimed wasteland that is every railroad town in the world:

> Hovels. A few rickety shacks, some upturned tombs, walls of bamboo or millet stalks, iron barbs, and rotting fences . . . a vast uncertain plain where all the rot of the city has gathered—stakes and crossties, locomotive wheels, rusty shafts, knocked in jerrycans, old mattress springs, bruised and lacerated sheets of steel. And then . . . piles of old tin cans, heaps of excrement, little mountains of broken pottery and cooking tools, dismantled railway cars, skeletons of motors buried in the dust, and the tiny remains of cats, of rats, of chickens, disputed by the birds. . . . In the midst of this corruption, a few meager bushes—wild tomato, dwarf peppers, and okra—those pitiful fruits were harvested by

the women. Bald-sided goats and sheep, clotted with filth . . . a place where everyone . . . had a face the color of the earth.[6]

Thiès is also the headquarters for the railway workers' union and it is there that the strike order is given. There is a momentary exultation, a sense of achievement; the men have defied the *toubabs* and shut down the railroad. All up and down the line there is an air of festivity. There are parties, excursions into the markets, shopping sprees with what little resources each family can muster. The old ways are revived, ceremonies and pageants long forgotten: "Men armed with staffs or cudgels performed the saber duels whose ritual dated from the reign of El Mami Samori Touré. Women dyed their hands and their feet with henna . . . and colored their lips with antimony. The young girls wore incredibly complicated hairdos of elaborately combed and braided tresses and strolled gracefully through the streets, abandoning themselves to the rhythms of the Bambara dances that were played on every corner."[7]

Gradually more sobering thoughts intrude. There is anxiety over the consequences of the strike, but there is something more; paradoxically, there is a sense of loss—loss of the machine. The people accept the dirt and ugliness. It is part of their lives, part of the railroad—the "smoke of the savanna" drifting across the fields, rising above the houses, the flicker of colored lights in the marshaling yards, the distant wail of the locomotive. Africa is no longer just a vast garden for food. The machine, this is their life as much as the dancing and the drumming. The railroad has changed everything. Now that the strike has closed the line, the smoke has disappeared, the engines are silent. There is only the sighing of the wind. The stillness is disquieting.

> Like rejected lovers returning to a trysting place, [the men] kept coming back to the areas surrounding the stations. Then they would just stand there, motionless, their eyes fixed on the horizon. . . . Sometimes a little block of five or six men would detach itself from the larger mass and drift off in the direction of the tracks. . . . They would wander along the rails and then . . . hasten back to the safety of the group. . . . Again they would . . . squat down in the shade of a sand hill, their eyes fixed on the two endless parallels, following them out until they had joined and lost them-

selves in the brush. Something was being born inside them, as if the past and the future were coupling to breed a new kind of man. . . . They said nothing . . . only their eyes betrayed an inner torment brought on by the mounting terror of famine and an inconsolable loneliness for the machine.[8]

Hunger comes from dwindling resources; it is also the result of official policy. The management of the railway has the full cooperation of the colonial administration. Supplies of rice, millet, and maize are cut off, the shopkeepers are warned to cooperate with the authorities. Water is suddenly in short supply; if trouble starts, there are the police and the soldiers.

In Thiès the regional director of the railroad rages over the strike, his fury fed by his contempt for the strikers. He knows his natives. One must never give in. There can be no sign of weakness; certainly no pay increases and family allowances. "Give family allowances to these people?" His voice rises in scorn. "The minute they have some money they go out and buy themselves another wife, and the children multiply like flies!" He will not talk to the workers. They must simply go back to work. He begins to formulate plans for a rival union, bribes in the right places, better still, some sort of empty title. "They are all alike . . . more interested in titles than in money. I know my Africans; they're rotten with pride."[9]

The strike drags on. Among the Africans hunger inches closer to famine. For the Europeans small doubts begin to intrude. Those in Thiès live in a district on the edge of town, a collection of comfortable houses set in garden plots that feature roses, daisies, snapdragons, and cascades of bougainvillea. It is an easy life but monotonous, and monotony gives rise to irritability. Now fear has banished boredom. One of them has shot and killed some boys. There are reassurances but these sound forced. "After all, one or two children more or less. . . . The number of children . . . is incredible. . . . The women don't wait to have one before they're pregnant with another. . . ." There is incessant talk about the strike, about Africans, stressing their dependency on the whites, citing endless examples of barbarous behavior. The houses are secured and secretly vigilante committees are formed.[10]

The killings force a meeting between management and strikers, a great encouragement for the workers, who have seen the other side give first ground. The regional director is angry and frustrated. The mere fact of a meeting is demeaning, he tells himself. How can one discuss anything with inferiors whose function is total obedience to absolute authority? He sees himself being maneuvered by circumstances into concessions, but, by God, he will not budge on the issue of family allowances: "To give in on the question of family allowances was much more than a matter of agreeing to a compromise with striking workers; it would amount to recognition of a racial aberrance, a ratification of the customs of inferior beings. It would be giving in, not to workers but to Negroes, and that Dejean could not do." At the meeting the regional director is belligerent in manner, the strikers calm but unyielding. "Monsieur," he is told, "we are here for a discussion among equals, and not to listen to your threats."[11]

It is too soon for a settlement. That must come later, after more suffering, more company losses. The clerics, imams and priests, are enlisted by the government to undermine striker unity, especially through the women, but this only intensifies their determination. The women organize a march on Dakar that finally swings the other unions into support. A general strike follows and at last it is the authorities who collapse. All union demands are met. The strike has been won.

Sembene Ousmane offers many reasons for the success of the strike. Workers solidarity, the support of the women, the faltering of the *toubabs* are all factors. Through all these, however, there is the faith these people have in themselves. Ousmane's characters proclaim it on every page. "We're the ones who do the work," says one. "In what way is a white worker better than a black worker? . . . Only the engines we run tell the truth . . . they don't know the difference between a white man and a black." The unionist Bakayoko presses home the point. "It isn't those who are taken by force, put in chains and sold as slaves who are the real slaves; it is those who will accept it, morally and physically." Later he stresses moral strength. "There are a great many ways of prostituting yourself. . . . There are those who do it because they are forced. . . . And then there are others who sell themselves morally."

Perhaps it is moral stamina that Ousmane places above all else. Bakayoko's young daughter puzzles over a riddle told by her grandmother. Water washes, says the old woman, but what washes water? At last the girl finds the answer. "It is the spirit," she announces in triumph. "The water is clean and pure, but the spirit is purer still."[12]

## Uncertainty

For Sembene Ousmane there is no question about the success of an independent Africa. The *toubabs* can be defeated. The only danger lies in self-doubt. With Yambo Ouologuem, however, the prospect is far less promising, a dim future that is the natural consequence of a barbarous, exploited past. *Bound to Violence*, Ouologuem's brutal novel of a corrupt African world, appeared in the late 1960s at a time when the initial bloom had faded from African independence and new nations were beset with faltering economies, political division, and the beginning of an era of military coups and dictatorship. The gloomy perspective of *Bound to Violence* seems in tune with those years that saw the fall of Nkrumah, the outbreak of civil strife in a number of states, and widespread social complications that led to such displays of misgovernment as Idi Amin's obscene regime in Uganda and the Napoleonic caricature of Colonel Bokassa's Central African Empire.

*Bound to Violence* appeared at a moment of contemporary uncertainty, but Ouologuem's text deals primarily with the past, a history of excess and inhumanity that stuns the reader and spares no civilization—if such a word can be applied to regimes of unbridled lust, murder, rape, torture, and psychic abnormality. Ouologuem begins at top speed, his savage irony in full cry. "Our eyes drink the brightness of the sun and, overcome, marvel at their tears," he states. "To recount the bloody adventure of the niggertrash—shame to the worthless paupers . . . the true history of the Blacks begins . . . with the Saifs, in the year 1202 . . . in the African Empire of Nakem."[13]

From the Fezzan south to the equatorial forest and as far west as the ocean, assorted tribes are conquered and absorbed into Nakem, the survivors enslaved, others butchered or buried alive, expectant mothers disemboweled, children slaughtered, husbands forced to rape their wives before killing themselves. "The village chief," Ouologuem tells us, ". . . drew the conclusion that human life was vain"; nevertheless he is obliged to keep order by displaying the earlobes of unsuccessful rebels. "The Crown forced men to swallow life as a boa swallows a stinking antelope."[14]

We have only reached the third page devoted to these depravities, but Ouologuem is just warming to his task. One Saif deposes his brother, marries his father's wives, including his own mother, then throws his brother into a dungeon to be eaten alive by worms. The Saifs claim Jewish descent, but the implication is that they are "plain ordinary niggers." Black Jews or not, they produce, with one exception, an unbroken line of rogues and tyrants. When Europeans begin to sail the African coasts, the reigning Saif extends the slave trade with the connivance of southern chiefs: "Niggers, who unlike God have arms but no soul, were clubbed, sold, stockpiled, haggled over, adjudicated, flogged, bound and delivered—with attentive, studied, sorrowful contempt." Consigned to the middle passage with its "orgy of fever, starvation, vermin, beriberi, scurvy, suffocation, and misery," the cargoes lose 30 percent en route, "and, since charity is a fine thing and hardly human, those amiable slavers were obliged . . . to pay a fine for every dead slave."[15]

Ouologuem showers scorn on his targets with a fine impartiality. "The Arab conquest," he relates, ". . . settled over the land like a she dog baring her white fangs." Slaves are gathered to be shipped off east and west, "at prices as ridiculous as the fleabitten dignity of the niggertrash. A strong man in good health cost a little more than a she-goat and a little less than a he-goat." But there is justification, Ouologuem points out, his irony unrelieved. Arab universities are founded and spiritual values sustained. When in time European slaving is replaced by colonial occupation, the intruders are deceived by the ruling Saif. "With the help of the local notables a colonial overlord had established himself long since, and that colonial overlord was none other than Saif. All unsuspecting the European conquerors played into his hands. Call it technical assistance. At that early date! So be it! Thy work is sanctified, O Lord. And exalted."[16]

Saif remains on his throne, ruling much as before the Europeans. Assisted by the notables, he provides the French administration with labor gangs and the French clergy with souls for conversion and salvation. Informers and poisons are used to eliminate undesirables, including when necessary the foreign administrators themselves. Despite the carnage Ouologuem makes his "niggertrash" rejoice over their resourceful prince; in the popular eye he has become a great and just leader, his tyranny an eternal glory. "Twilight of the gods? Yes and no. More than one dream seemed to be fading; a turning point of civilization, or should one say a convulsion presaging its ultimate end? Presaging a new birth? Or merely a sempiternal agony, presaging nothing? A tear for the niggertrash, O Lord, in Thy compassion."[17]

The Europeans may be guilt-ridden over their conquest; some appear to find special merit in the arts and culture of Africa, concocting, says Ouologuem, pretentious nonsense about the spiriutal power and religious symbolism of African art, all the while encouraged by the wily Saif who buries quantities of carvings later to be exhumed and sold at great profit in the markets of Europe. In particular there is the anthropologist, Shrobenius—a scarcely disguised caricature of the German ethnographer, Leo Frobenius—part fool, part artful entrepreneur, who finds metaphysical meaning in everything, including the shape of the palaver tree, but who ships off carloads of carvings for profit and establishes himself in a prestigious university chair where he presides over the acolytes of "Shrobeniusology."

Saif is fully equal to the demands of this charade, producing improvised discourses on Nakem culture and history. "Ever so often," he announces, "the tools used to carve a mask were blessed seventy-seven times by a priest, who, all the while flagellating himself, gave blessings until the third day of the seventh year after the tree to be felled was chosen amid incantations revealing the genesis of the world." Shrobenius responds in kind: "The plant germinates, bears fruit, dies, and is reborn when the seed germinates. The moon rises to fullness, pales, wanes, and vanishes, only to reappear. Such is the destiny of man, such is the destiny of Negro art: like the seed and the moon, its symbolic seed is devoured by the earth and is reborn sanctified . . . in the sublime heights of the tragic drama of the cosmic play of the stars." "Negro art," Ouologeum remarks, "found its patent of nobility in the folklore of mercantile intellectualism. . . . [Shrobenius] exploited the sentimentality of the coons, only too pleased to hear from the mouth of a white man that Africa was 'the womb of the world and the cradle of civilization.' In consequence the niggertrash donated masks and art treasures by the ton." Here is an indictment of European hypocrisy and African acquiescence that is echoed in scholarly terms by the philosophers Marcien Towa and Paulin Hountondji, who make the same point in arguing for a realistic view of African civilization uncluttered by romantic appeals to an idealized past.[18]

Against his backdrop of bloody, antic lunacy, Ouologuem gradually narrows focus, concentrating on the fortunes of a single family. Kassoumi, a serf in the Saif household, marries Tambira, another serf, who bears him several children, including Raymond Sparticus. Raymond is clever and does well at school. His mother, intent upon her son's advancement, gives herself to Saif's sorcerer in order to insure a successful examination. Subsequently she is raped by some of the emperor's henchmen and ends up either a suicide or murder victim, her corpse buried in the filth of the serfs' latrine.

Perhaps her sacrifice will prove worthy of the intent. Raymond Sparticus passes and is sent to France for further study. He becomes infatuated with European civilization and sets himself a regimen of cultural assimilation, turning resolutely from what he regards as the barbarisms of Africa. But no; there seems to be no escape from an African destiny. It is Europe that now makes free with Ouologuem's "niggertrash." Inadvertently Raymond seduces his sister who, unbeknownst to him, has come to Paris to take work in a brothel; later he becomes the doting male mistress of a Frenchman. It is inevitable that Raymond's lover leaves him, and eventually Raymond settles down to marry the unattractive daughter of a laundress, "living the life of a middle-class white nigger," for "the society in which his mother-in-law moved was no better than an 'advanced' nigger, living among Whites, was entitled to aspire to."[19]

Fashions in colonial rule change, however, and the time has come for Nakem to elect a deputy to the French assembly in Paris. To his delight, Raymond is nominated. He returns home, alighting at the newly inaugurated airport to be welcomed by the assembled dignitaries and acclaimed by the people, delirious with enthusiasm. Here is vindication indeed. He is certain of election to an office that will place Raymond Sparticus, this son of serfdom and violence, in a position of national leadership, that will at last put an end to the tyrannies of the Saifs. Poor Raymond, he cannot rise above his fate: "Kassoumi the shrewd calculator had miscalculated: armed with his degrees and the support of France, he had expected to become his old master's master, when in reality the slave owed his election exclusively to the torch of Saif, more radiant than ever. . . . Kassoumi thought sadly of the legend of the Saifs, a legend in which the future seems to seek itself in the night of time—prehistory in a tail coat: there stands the African. . . ."[20]

## Affirmation

Yambo Ouologuem is uncompromising in his pessimism. There appears to be no hope for an Africa destined to be victimized by its own leaders or by others, always despised, ever self-despising. For a time such a view seemed to be shared by the Ghanaian writer, Ayi Kwei Armah. Like Ouologuem, Armah portrayed the European and the Arab as slave mongers, white men who preyed on the African for profit. Like Ouologuem he expressed contempt for the African, in this case for the new leaders of a modern independent Africa who aped the materialism of Europe and destroyed their people in the process. Still, with Armah, there seemed to be some element of hope—his first novel, *The Beautyful Ones Are Not Yet Born*, raged at the corruption of modern African society but ended with the image of a flower growing from a dung heap.

That was in 1968. Ten years later Kwei Armah gave a more explicit affirmation of hope. There is a future for Africa was the message of his 1978 novel, *The Healers*. Africa's destiny, said Armah, lies not in foreign ways and modern technology, however. It rests with the traditions of the past that once held the black people of the world together as one.

*The Healers* is an historical novel, dealing with characters and events surrounding the occupation of Kumasi in 1874 by a British army under the command of General Sir Garnet Wolesley. This advent of colonial rule on the Gold Coast scarcely seems the stuff of optimism, and indeed, much of Armah's tale is occupied with stupidity and duplicity displayed by various representatives of the Akan people from the coastal Fante to the Ashanti of the interior. The corruption and shortsightedness is contributed primarily by royalty, coastal princes besotted by gin and beguiled by European trappings, Ashanti kings blinded by jealousy and fearful of treachery that might cost them their thrones. The main action, however, concerns a young villager, Densu, caught up in the great events of the day, which he shares with a community of practitioners in traditional African medicine whose activities give the book its title.

The basic action is simple. Densu is forced to flee his coastal village of Esuano, accused of murdering the heir apparent to the Esuano throne. He makes his way inland to the forest, taking refuge with the healers and gradually learning the wisdom of their craft, a way of life that greatly attracts him. Eventually he becomes involved in an abortive effort to turn back the columns of Wolesley as they march on Kumasi. Returning finally to the coast, Densu is tried and acquitted as the true culprit is caught. The novel ends with the British in control, but with a new unity among the Akan, born from the effort to oppose the European invaders.

Kwei Armah's characters are more archetypical than real. Densu is cast in heroic proportion, excelling mentally and physically, serene in spirit with a lofty idealism that contrasts sharply with the power-hungry villainy of Ababio, the village elder who is Densu's protector and ultimate betrayer. Ababio wants the throne of Esuano and tries to involve Densu in his plotting. Rebuffed, Ababio commits the murder in such a way as to throw suspicion on his young protégé.

Densu accepts his exile with fortitude; indeed, he had already been searching for the healers, attracted by their philosophy and repelled by the materialism and divisiveness he had encountered at home. He asks puzzled questions about the ritual games celebrated annually by his people. For Densu the games have no purpose beyond a test of individual strength and skill, a test that ends in pride for the victor riding over a multitude of envious losers. His questions go unanswered. A few of the older inhabitants recall vaguely that the games were a ritual marking community cooperation at a time before the Akan became divided.

The way the people who still remembered talked of them, these had been festivals made for keeping a people together. They were not so much celebrations as invocations of wholeness. . . . The truth was plain: among the wandering people some had chosen homes deeper in the heart of the land. . . . This was division. Some had pushed their way eastward. . . . This was division. Some . . . had gone westward. . . . This was division. . . . Some had moved south. . . . This, too, was division. . . .

When Densu asked . . . what the games were for, some said
they did not understand the question. . . . Others asked . . .
why had such a question become so important to him? They
asked, because at Esuano the remembrance of a larger community
had become a faint remnant from a forgotten past. There were
people who knew stories of a time when the black people were
one. But they were not easy to find. Even when found, they were
rather silent, as if the question raised in their minds a regret that
overwhelmed their tongues.[21]

All this is disturbing to the young man. Despite his superior skills
he purposefully loses at the games, withdrawing from some contests
and conceding others.

In his imagination he could see different rituals. . . . There would
be no competitors, only participants. There would be a community whose members would be free to work together in the cool of
the morning; they would be free to run, swim, jump, play, to cele-
brate health in the late afternoon; they would dance to their own
songs in the quiet of the evenings. These things were good. . . .
What sense was there in excluding the whole community from the
centre of the field, leaving only a few grim battlers? . . . The
idea of a society separated into a small, active group of competitive fighters flying high above a massive mass of mere spectators
with uplifted faces, brought ugly pictures to his mind; a very few
lean, sinewy, strong champions dominating a soft shapeless crowd
beneath their feet.[22]

In the quiet forest, among the healers, Densu begins to find what had
escaped him at home. Damfo, a leader among the healers, explains the
principles of his craft. The healer, says Damfo, tries to see the world
through understanding, not merely as a series of discrete, unconnected
phenomena but as a unity in comprehension. Hence, where the average
person might see a child bitten by a poisonous snake lying near death
in the forest, the healer sees in the leafy bed of the forest the antidote
that will bring the child back to health. "Those who learn to read
the signs around them," Damfo goes on, "reach a kind of knowledge . . . that . . . follows you everywhere. . . . It says there are

two forces, unity and division. The first creates. The second destroys; it's a disease, disintegration."

Disintegration, Damfo informs the young acolyte, comes from spiritual blindness. Those who cannot see the spirit try to force and trick the body into selfish action, a manipulation that divorces the body from the inspiration of the spirit. "A people can be diseased the same way. Those who need naturally to be together but are not, are they not a people sicker than the individual body disintegrated from its soul? Sometimes a whole people needs healing work. Not a tribe, not a nation. Tribes and nations are just signs that the whole is diseased. The healing work that cures a whole people is the highest work, far higher than the cure of a single individual."

Such has been the fate of the African people, Damfo assures Densu. Scattered, the people forgot; forgetting, they began to pretend they had always been organized into "these silly little fragments each calling itself a nation." And it is not just the Akan; they were part of a greater whole—"a people that knew only this one name we hear so seldom these days: Ebibirman. That was the community of all black people." Here is literary affirmation of the pan-African unity of Nkrumah and Cheikh Anta Diep.[23]

The center of Kwei Armah's action shifts to the impending invasion of Ashanti. The British are powerful and ruthless. Wolesley bribes the coastal kings and plies them with alcohol to obtain the necessary labor for a road that will take him to the interior. When these methods prove insufficient, they are replaced with force. Villages are burned, hostages seized, populations terrified. Missionaries compel their converts to join the labor brigades. "The purposes of the Christian god were not so mysterious after all," says Kwei Armah. "They were whatever white men decided they should be."[24]

Some Africans are persuaded, among them Ababio. The whites are going to control the land, he has already assured Densu, but they will need the help of blacks they can trust. They will need soldiers, porters, provisions, labor. "If we do not help the whites," Ababio continues, "we shall be left by the roadside. And if we are such fools as to stand against the whites, they will grind us till we become less than impotent, less than grains of bad snuff tossing in a storm. . . . We shall be on the side of the whites. That is where power lies.[25]

Densu sees things differently. On the coast he observes the British colonial official, Captain John Glover, assembling an army to invade Ashanti, attacking from the east as Wolesley advanced from the south. Glover is everywhere, a dervish of energy, ordering, explaining, instructing, demonstrating. "Here indeed was the white man in action. Glover the god-like, Glover the white man descended among the black people to do magical wonders. . . . Here he was a god, a god among mere men, a beloved father-god among infant-men. . . . Here he was, the one white man who could boast he could tell black men to do anything, no matter how difficult, and they would do it immediately out of love for him, Glover. Here he was, Glover the father of the Hausa fighters, protector of loving slaves."[26] Glover's manic energy and lofty self-image in fact hide a morose, solitary being, racked with self-doubt, duped by the local rulers who accept his gifts while deluging him with praise and promises of men and matériel they have no intention of providing.

Armah's contempt for Glover is contempt for a fool. When the time comes to march on Kumasi, Glover is a commander without troops and he remains powerless on the coast. There is contempt for Wolesley as well, but it is tempered with a grudging concession. Wolesley is a little man impressed with self-importance. When he stands erect, he strains to appear a giant, but he has no doubts about his mission and he gets things done. In Kwei Armah's eyes Wolesley is more malign than foolish. Against opposition and in the face of steady sabotage, Wolesley builds a wide road from Cape Coast toward Kumasi. Labor is conscripted to clear the ground, smooth the surface, build bridges, and erect storehouses. Mysterious craters appear in the road while bridges are wrecked, but new conscripts are set to work repairing the damage. When ablebodied men are unavailable, women and children are pressed into service. The road goes forward. A bridge is built to span the Pra River. Wolesley crosses the Pra into Ashanti country. He does not even get his feet wet.

Still there is no need for despair, Armah reports. The Ashanti have a general, Asamoa Nkwanta, who is equal to the occasion. Asamoa has a plan that will exploit the weakness of the whites and lead them to destruction. "I knew their greatest weakness," Asamoa explains. "It wasn't military at all. It was a weakness of the spirit, the soul. The whites are not on friendly terms with the surrounding universe. Between them and the universe there is real hostility. Take the forest here: if they stay long in the forest they die. Either they cut down the forest and kill it, or it kills them. They can't live with it."[27]

Asamoa's plan is simple. He knows Glover cannot put an army in the field. Glover is ignored while Asamoa concentrates on Wolesley. He will let Wolesley advance deep into the forest, then he will attack the cumbersome supply train and isolate the British far from their base. "We shall . . . oblige them to stay in these forests and fight till death. The whites fear the forest. They will not survive—if we keep to our plan."[28]

Asamoa's strategy is well conceived but it is a plan that is doomed. The general serves royalty and, as the healer, Damfo, has observed, it is royalty that is a major cause of the divisions among the Akan. In discussions with Asamoa, Damfo has already suggested the superfluity of rulers, a world without kings, without slaves, without the ritual killing that has claimed Asamoa's nephew, a world the way it used to be before the division of the Akan people. Asamoa struggles, torn between his sense of duty to the Ashanti monarchs and his desire to save his people. The hold of the monarchy is too strong. Asamoa returns to Kumasi to organize his campaign. "Asamoa Nkwanta is a good man," Damfo observes.

> But all his goodness has been spent in the service of Asante royalty. Among our people, royalty is part of the disease. Whoever serves royalty serves the disease, not the cure. He works to divide our people, not to unite us. . . . We know that to the royals the healing of the black people would be a disaster, since kings and chiefs suck their power from the divisions between our people. How can Asamoa Nkwanta do healing work while remaining trapped in a group serving the disease?[29]

The answer comes in the treachery of the Ashanti rulers. Unbeknownst to Asamoa they cancel the encircling attack on Wolesley's supply train, and Wolesley is able to fight his way into Kumasi. The queen mother explains. "If Asante followed Asamoa Nkwanta's plan and resisted the whites, there would be nothing to stop Asamoa Nkwanta from becoming king of the inviolate nation. . . . The wisdom of a king lay in knowing at all times what to do in order to remain king. If what should be done now was to yield a bit to the whites, better that than to lose all power to an upstart general." Putting aside such an insupportable prospect, the kings carry out their treachery and gain another twenty years of failing authority. For the coastal peoples it is all over. Their independence is converted into the British Gold Coast Colony.[30]

Still, by a strange alchemy, circumstances begin to bring the divided people of Akan together in adversity. At Cape Coast there is a ceremony as General Wolesley departs. A contingent of West Indian soldiers plays Western marches, Wolesley then says a few words and steps into the surf boat that will take him to his waiting ship. As he leaves, the mood suddenly changes. "The stiff, straight, graceless beats of white music vanished. Instead, there was a new, skilful, strangely happy interweaving of rhythms, and instead of marching back through the streets the soldiers danced. Others joined them. They . . . took their procession meandering through the streets of Cape Coast. All the groups gathered by the whites to come and fight for them were there and they all danced." Here were Opobo warriors from the east and their neighbors from Bonny. Here were Hausa and Kru, men from Dahomey, Anecho, Atakpame, Ada, Ga, and Ekuapem. There were Fante policemen, Temne from Sierra Leone, and Susu swordsmen. "All heard the music of these West Indians who had turned the white men's instruments of the music of death to playing such joyous music. All knew ways to dance to it, and a grotesque, variegated crowd they made, snaking its way through the town." "It's a new dance," said one. "It's a new dance all right," said another, "and it's grotesque. But look at all the black people the whites have brought here. Here we healers have been wondering about ways to bring our people together again. And the whites want ways to drive us farther apart. Does it not amuse you, that in their wish to drive us apart the whites are actually bringing us work for the future?"[31]

Damfo has already stated the objective: The work of healing is work for inspirers working long and steadily in a group over the generations, until there are inspirers, healers wherever our people are scattered, able to bring us together again.

"This is seed time," says Damfo. In the future there will be the harvest.[32]

# 3

*Educational Independence*

# 7

## *The Search for a Usable Past*

### *The Uses of History*

In Africa, or anywhere else, history is relevant. The emphasis may change. The philosophies will alter. The purpose remains the same—to secure the present.

As African nationalism intensified after the Second World War, there was marked ambivalence concerning the role of history in the realization of an independent Africa. On the one hand, a need for past achievement in support of future freedom created an intense interest in earlier times, and ultimately produced a whole new generation of historians practicing innovative systems of historiography. On the other, there were those who felt that history served little purpose, was indeed potentially harmful, for it could divide and alienate peoples who would have to come together in willing union if new nations were to survive and prosper.

There were compelling arguments on both sides. Those who favored a fresh appeal to the African past pointed to the evident necessity for cultural as well as political divorce from Europe, with its patronizing disregard of Africa's civilization and its denial of the very existence of a history of what were regarded as barbarous peoples before the advent of European colonialism. It was essential, therefore, to banish the sense of inferiority that a century of colonial rule had engendered, to substitute an impressive past, equal to Europe's own in accomplishment, in powerful empires, in great and influential rulers.

Such use of history was subscribed to by most African nationalist leaders intent upon uniting their peoples, for they realized that self-respect was companion to self-determination, while economic growth and technological advance might falter among a people who lacked confidence in their destiny. In this respect the remarks of Kwame Nkrumah were typical, as he participated in the ceremonies inaugurating an African studies institute at the University of Ghana. "One essential function of the Institute must surely be to study the history, culture and institutions, languages and arts of Ghana and of Africa in new African centered ways—in entire freedom from the propositions and pre-suppositions of the colonial epoch. . . . By the work of this Institute, we must re-assess and assert the glories and achievements of our African past and inspire our generation, and succeeding generations, with a vision of a better future."[1]

Nevertheless, for one of Nkrumah's turn of mind, these were dangerous waters. By all odds the most genuinely revolutionary of Africa's modern nationalist leaders, Nkrumah sought to create a new Ghana and a new Africa, in the process destroying the old ways that the new were designed to replace. An appeal to the past, however, was also an appeal to tradition and an ancient culture, much of which was healthy and virile, and highly resistant to political fashions that now decreed its demise. The chiefs were far too conservative for the dynamic Doctor Nkrumah; for them the world changed but slowly and the past had an immediacy that made it sometimes indistinguishable from the present. Worse still, from the point of view of a modernizing innovator, historical research might produce ethnic histories that reinforced local pride, introducing a fatal tribalism that would confound efforts to create a modern nation-state. Nkrumah thought he had the answer in pan-Africanism, an appeal to a wider continental unity that transcended national, let alone local, loyalties.

Nkrumah, of course, was far from alone. Most nationalist leaders of the independence years felt much the same as he and for the same reasons. Economic expansion and a rising standard of living had to be achieved and quickly. Popular support was essential, but an appeal to cultural heritage could not be allowed to compromise national development. It has been observed that where there was considerable cultural diversity, as in East and Central Africa, little was said about heritage or history, while in South Africa it was the white-controlled government that appealed most strongly to the abiding importance of the past.

In balance, however, the usefulness of the past far outweighed its potential disadvantages; indeed heritage came to be an ideological imperative for national independence. Colonialists had argued that it was Europe that created modern African states, reshaping the elementary societies and economies of African peoples. Why should not this process continue in partnership, they demanded, a process that owed so little to traditional Africa and its culture? If there were no African past of consequence and no modern Africa except that which followed Europe, there was no point in an independence that was bound to fail in its pointlessness.[2]

Here was special pleading unlikely to persuade Africans who well understood the sophistry behind a definition of partnership originating in colonial Europe, and who also knew that self-respect came from a sense of identity in achievement, both past and present. Such an awareness was in fact of long standing, dating back to the early years of colonialism and before, when Africans first welcomed the technological prodigies of European culture. Deeply impressed, they also experienced their first need to maintain psychic security as external ideas and institutions threatened to engulf them. Reaching out for new techniques, new machines, and new ideas, they also moved closer to African culture and tradition. Bishop Crowther did it, preaching Anglican orthodoxy but in the Yoruba tongue. Africanus Horton did it as he called for a European-styled university dealing with African subject matter. Edward Blyden granted Europe only a portion of God's perfectibility, reserving for Africa its share and reaffirming the continent's ancient and distinguished past. Others went further and wrote extensive histories of their people. These were no antiquarian exercises, but histories with a purpose, and it is interesting to listen to the reasons given by authors who devoted years of research and writing to these labors.

Three examples suggest themselves—three West African societies forced to endure basic changes of circumstance, their sense of security shattered, their identity brought into question. In Sierra Leone, the receptives of Freetown, refugees from slavery, were a conglomerate population drawn broadly from many parts of West Africa, quite literally a population without a past. No people should lack a history for in it rests their immortality, said A. B. C. Sibthorpe, a recaptive descendant who produced his *History of Sierra Leone* in 1868 and watched it gain

popularity through three editions issued over half a century. Sibthorpe
was a schoolteacher, and he tells us he wrote his history in part to provide himself with materials for his classes. But there were also deeper
purposes: "Considering the pleasure and interest with which the public
in general read histories of foreign nations, and finding that everyone
in the colony has not the privilege of hearing or reading the history of
his father's or mother's nation; and as we have been compelled by fortune and nature to become one people or nation, of mixed generation,
on this soil—I have endeavoured to give in a condensed form the history of the place we now inhabit." Without its history, Sibthorpe observed, a nation is like Jonah's gourd, grown in the dawn but perished
with the twilight.[3]

Sibthorpe's sense of history, though clear, was lightly born, and in
this respect he differed from his contemporary, the Gold Coast cleric,
C. C. Reindorf, who produced his sober, almost ponderous, *History of
the Gold Coast and Asante* in 1889. Reindorf was of Danish descent
but numbered ancestors from the Ga people of Accra on both sides of
his family. His long life was spent in the service of the Basel Mission
located near Accra, but missionary labors were forced to share his attention, for he felt greatly attracted by the customs of the country. But
for his European background, he remarks, he might well have become
a pagan priest instead of a practicing Christian. Over thirty years
Reindorf collected traditional materials from more than two hundred
individuals, and these accounts, along with some written sources, formed
the basis for his history, the only study of the Gold Coast written by an
African during the nineteenth century.

Reindorf says he was intent on bringing the past into view because
it was the measure of the present and a means of discerning either
progress or retrogression as a basis for future guidance. He does not
reveal his conclusions in this respect, but his long account of chronic
warfare, disease, famine, and slavery is the story of coastal peoples
caught between two forces—the violently aggressive Ashanti nation of
the interior and the dangerous European intruders, Danes, Dutch, and
British whose ambiguous diplomacy was confusing and provocative. It
is an unhappy tale of peace-loving villagers trying vainly to contend
with phenomena often beyond their understanding. Of the two, it is the
Ashanti who seemed more comprehensible, despite their cruelty. In the

end, however, the Europeans prevailed and British authority was established throughout the Gold Coast. The people of Accra were forced to submit. Reindorf, Christian missionary and part European, ruefully acknowledged that the Africa of his forebears would have to accept its lot and adjust to the new reality. In the event, however, his history would insure self-awareness and an understanding of their fate.[4]

Warfare, slavery, disease, famine, and European intrusion also characterized nineteenth-century Yorubaland, and the events of the civil wars among his people became a major theme in Samuel Johnson's monumental *History of the Yorubas*. Like Reindorf, Johnson was an African working on behalf of a European missionary society. Like the Gold Coast historian, he spent years in the painstaking accumulation of traditional accounts, "that the history of our fatherland might not be lost in oblivion." Echoing Sibthorpe, Johnson pointed out that many of his countrymen were acquainted with British, Greek, or Roman history but knew nothing of their own. "This reproach," he said, "it is one of the author's objects to remove."

Once again the African historian is found hard at work recording a period of great unrest, his effort not only to preserve the past but to save the present, to emphasize a people's common sources, to expose the futility of faction and violence, "the spirit of tribal feelings now rife among us." For Johnson Yoruba survival lay in unity and peace. During the last phases of the civil wars he was directly concerned with diplomatic efforts to bring an end to hostilities. He helped in advising the war leaders in Ibadan, preparing letters for the military command and eventually acting as liaison between the Ibadan chiefs, the authorities at Oyo, and the British who were established in Lagos.

British intervention in 1893 finally brought an end to the wars along with the beginning of colonial rule throughout Yorubaland. For Johnson, however, the intervention was a divinely inspired act, and his warm, if somewhat uncritical, regard for British activities must be seen in light of their role in terminating hostilities. Other of Johnson's interpretations may be open to question; for example, his belief that the Yoruba had once comprised a unified kingdom centered at Oyo and Ife. In the main, Johnson produced an authoritative, detailed account created to insure that the history and culture of an African people might yet endure.[5]

*Negro Nations and Their Culture*

Whatever individual nationalist leaders may have felt about reviving the past, there were those historically minded individuals, professional or amateur, who were in no doubt as to the importance of history in the struggle to be free of colonialism. The new historians were in the tradition of predecessors like Samuel Johnson, but there was a difference. For all their size and scholarship, the histories of Sibthorpe, Reindorf, and Johnson were small in scale. They wrote for a parochial audience; those caught up with the postwar African independence movements were concerned with a larger canvas—a new nation at the very least, more appropriately the whole African continent and beyond. Their purpose was also more ambitious. To be sure, they wanted to insure a knowledge of the past and a sense of psychic security. For them, however, the past was essential to the present, an assertion of national, continental, or international black strength, an affirmation of cultural self-assurance that justified and supported the freedom movements then underway.

Such support came in many guises. The people of the Gold Coast, for example, on their way to becoming the independent nation of Ghana, produced two histories, *The Gold Coast Revolution* by George Padmore—friend, confidant, and political advisor of Kwame Nkrumah—and *African Glory*, a panegyric survey of black history suggested by its title.

Padmore's book was a punchy, unsentimental political tract designed to legitimize Ghanaian independence and particularly to emphasize the pivotal role of the Convention People's party and its great leader, Kwame Nkrumah. Padmore, the communist revolutionary turned pan-Africanist, knew how to utilize historical analysis for political advantage. He wasted no time on orthodox Marxian dialectical formulas and jargon; rather the book moved swiftly in chronology, selecting material in a cumulative assessment that projected Nkrumah as the essential social revolutionary for his own country and a splendid model that other African nationalist leaders might emulate with profit. Beginning with early European connections in West Africa, Padmore firmly linked the newcomers with the slave trade, then proceeded to the first reactions of Gold Coast nationalism, citing the Fanti Confederation formed in 1868, the Aborigines' Rights Protection Society that came together in the

1890s, and J. E. Casely Hayford's later National Congress of British West Africa. It was a major function of these groups to keep the pressure on colonial administrations, Padmore asserted, for British colonial policy always spoke grandly of ultimate self-rule but never revealed a timetable. "The rate of progress," said Padmore, "is set by degree of pressure put upon the imperial authority by the natives themselves."

Moving to the postwar period, Padmore described the rising aspirations of the Gold Coast people for economic betterment and political freedom, but he was careful to qualify the independence roles both of the traditional rulers and of the conservative business and professional classes located in the coastal towns. "Africa can only be economically developed with the active cooperation and willing support of the Africans themselves," said Padmore, "and their goodwill will not be secured until they are given the opportunity of shouldering the political responsibilities of self-government." In this we must beware, Padmore continued, of self-serving groups like the United Gold Coast Convention of J. B. Danquah and his colleagues, made up of "typical bourgeois gentlemen . . . desiring political power for themselves . . . [having] nothing in common with the workers, farmers, market women, petty traders and other under-privileged sections of the common people."

Founded in 1947 the UGCC had tried to make common cause with the chiefs but was rebuffed by native rulers uncertain whether to play their hand for or against imperialism. It would have been an unsavory alliance in any case, said Padmore, for there was a growing body of opinion in the Gold Coast and other parts of the continent that the days of the chiefs were numbered. Many feel, he concluded, "that chieftaincy is a social anachronism that must adapt itself to the rapidly changing social order or disappear, if Africa is to take her place in the modern world."

In Padmore's perspective this left the road clear for Kwame Nkrumah, who had served briefly as secretary of the UGCC, then split with his conservative patrons to form the Convention People's party in 1949, for Padmore the true arm of the Gold Coast revolution. Nkrumah, along with Padmore, had been an active participant at the pan-African Congress held in Manchester, England, in 1945, and had been instrumental in drafting Congress resolutions that called for African independence—by peaceful means if possible, by force if necessary. In the Gold Coast Nkrumah confronted a concrete colonialism ready to be tested. As Padmore put it, "Nkrumah's genius lies in the fact that he has been able to translate these injunctions [the Manchester resolutions] into practice within such a short time." *The Gold Coast Revolution* was published in 1953, by which time Nkrumah had established his CPP, called a general strike in defiance of the administration, swept to power in the elections of 1951, and, as newly chosen parliamentary "leader of government business," set the nation on the road to independence, which came for Ghana in March 1957.[6]

*African Glory* was more extensive in range but less ambitious in reach. Appearing a year after Padmore's volume, it was the work of J. C. deGraft-Johnson, a university economist and member of an old Gold Coast family. Despite its elevating title, it made little attempt to connect the African past with the brushfires of nationalism then crackling about the continent. Despite its effort to establish black history as an integral part of man's past, it offered nothing new in method or material, nothing that would have been unfamiliar to Africans writing a century earlier.

Drawn from secondary sources, *African Glory* presented a number of familiar themes—that ancient Egyptians were part negroid; that black genes are widely distributed among the world's races; that Akan speakers from the Gold Coast came originally from the savanna regions of ancient Ghana; that the conquest of Spain was accomplished by Africans. Stressing the long-lived integrity of African civilization, including a sometime familiarity with writing and the plow, deGraft-Johnson credited the Atlantic slave trade with the disintegration of African societies that ultimately led to European colonial occupation. The account closed with an examination of early nationalist movements on the Gold Coast, led principally by a Western-educated elite from the time of the Fanti Confederation to the days of J. E. Casely Hayford, barrister, newspaper editor, and legislator, whose National Congress of British West Africa flourished between the two world wars.

In 1966 *African Glory* was reissued, thereby enabling deGraft-Johnson to add a note of personal disenchantment, for, only two years earlier, he had been imprisoned by Nkrumah without formal charges, one of the many individuals detained by the Ghana government as politically hostile. "It is ironical," observed deGraft-Johnson, more in sadness than in anger, "that leaders who fought for freedom and justice for their people, should elect to deny these very people freedom of speech and freedom of movement, and should demand unqualified sycophantic loyalty. Situations have developed on the African continent where the image of a leader abroad has been the exact opposite of his image at home."[7]

During these same years there appeared another study of African history, one that reflected both the purposefulness of Padmore and the scale of deGraft-Johnson. It was called *Nations Nègres et Culture,* appearing first in 1954, and quickly reissued by *Présence Africaine.* The author was Cheikh Anta Diop, a young Senegalese studying in Paris whose wide-ranging interests in the arts and sciences were focused on a fixed idea—the total reconstruction of the history of Africa. Indeed, it was more than reconstruction, for Diop was prepared to demonstrate a new design for African history, a new philosophy of history that challenged accepted truths concerning the long-lived relationship between Europe and Africa.

Diop, the thoroughgoing iconoclast, placed conventional wisdom on its head—it was Europe that depended on Africa, he said, not the reverse. Far from having no history at all, as European scholars had been assuring themselves, Africa was now recognized as no less than the source of mankind. Furthermore, Diop added, much of its best thought and culture had been transmitted to Europe via the Mediterranean in ancient times, where it helped civilize and elevate barbaric nomads like the early Greeks wandering through the bleak chill of northern latitudes.

Diop had arrived in Paris in 1946 and the ensuing years were crowded with both curricular and extracurricular events. These were the days of the *Rassemblement Démocratique Africain,* an interterritorial political grouping that sought to coordinate the energies and aspirations of Africans in France's possessions of West and Equatorial Africa. Diop was an active pan-Africanist among his fellow students, working for territorial unity and political freedom, just as his studies were concerned with the integrity and vitality of African culture. Diop was trained as an Egyptologist with enough emphasis on Greco-Latin culture to produce a doctoral thesis comparing the social and political systems of Europe and black Africa in ancient times. Beyond this he gained a grounding in philosophy, archaeology, and the natural sciences, working for a time in the laboratory of Frédéric Joliot-Curie.

These varied interests combined with the knowledge of oral traditions in his native Senegal to produce a second thesis, this one dealing with patrilineal and matrilineal systems in antiquity.[8]

Several more volumes and numerous articles followed over the years, supplementing the basic thesis of *Nations Nègres,* all replete with massive documentation drawn from history, linguistics, archaeology, along with selected arts and sciences. Yet the essential thesis was simplicity itself. African civilization, and a good deal of the culture of Europe, Diop insisted, came originally from Pharaonic Egypt, which was incontestably a Negro civilization. Thus, the views of Thales on matter, Platonic idealism, Epicureanism, Judaism, Islam, and much of modern Western science originated in Egyptian cosmogony and science. Any African historian, Diop continued, "who evades the problem of Egypt is neither modest nor objective . . . he is ignorant, cowardly, and neurotic." To ignore Egypt is comparable to a Westerner writing a history of Europe without reference to Greco-Latin origins.

Diop's emphasis on a black Egypt as the source of much of the ancient world's knowledge was not original with him. Many others have made like assertions, for example, W. E. B. Du Bois, but Diop's concentration on this theme and his overwhelming scholarly support went well beyond previous efforts. With ancient Egypt as a base, Diop could envision the unity of African history and culture stretching backward to Louis Leakey's monogenetic thesis that places man's origins squarely in East Africa, and forward through the ages to the present era of independent African nations. For Diop monographic exercises and parochial histories had small place in this grand design. The history of Benin or Zimbabwe, of the Yoruba or Nubians, of the ancient empire of Ghana or the Mossi kingdoms were but facets of the larger, single black culture, its unity preserved by its history, its present diversity more illusion than reality.

The historical studies of Cheikh Anta Diop were at once theoretical and practical. When speaking of his work, Diop displayed a serenity that knew no uncertainties, no qualifications, yet the majestic vastness of this historical scheme did not end in some flawless but unreal paradigm. The unity of African culture exists today, Diop recently asserted. It is for Africans to bring it back into living, working focus. At present, he continued, Africa is backward in terms of technology, partly because of the impediments of colonialism that were thrust into the long flow of Africa's history. Africans must learn technology from the West, but first they need to reaffirm their own culture as a solid base on which to borrow and build.

Culture, said Diop, is the cement that unifies a people; otherwise they are but a collection of individuals. The West has modernized but it has maintained its closeness to its classical sources. It is inconceivable to imagine modern Europe cut off from this long-lived past. Look at Western history, legal systems, sociology, or philosophy, Diop insisted, all rooted firmly in Greco-Latin culture. This is what has given modern Western civilization its strength. Must it not also be thus with Africa?

> It was necessary to find the roots of the African people, in their own territories, not ideologically but through scientific research in the different areas of human sciences. It was necessary through historical studies to discover our past, whatever it was. . . . We are the result of all that. That is what interested us. . . . We knew that we were here, on this ground, our ancestors had existed, and these were the experiences of our ancestors. . . . That is all. The rest is only accidental and secondary. And we knew also that this gave us our strength. . . . That is what gave us our feeling of unity. . . . That is what we wanted to recover and reinforce.

From such strength in self-awareness, Diop continued, great things flow. For one, Western technology could be absorbed without fear of cultural annihilation, as with a people drifting unsecured by the knowledge of their own institutions. More than that, the cultural past would serve the future, said Diop, for it foreshadows the arrival of a federal state for all of Africa.

But, the objection was raised, this has not happened. Africa is very far from unified.

Diop's self-assurance was unshatterable. "That does not matter," he insisted. "It is a necessity. Every new day's experience shows that it is a necessity."

But, is it not only an ideal?

"No matter. For the moment it is an ideal, but more objective than reality. Reality is today's mediocrity. Reality is permanent defeat. Reality is fragmentation. The ideal? That is the one road that will permit the resolution of all these difficulties, and the recovery of political and economic health. So, on the one hand, there are the risks of distintegration and even of existence. On the other, there is survival."[9]

## History at Ibadan

If there was some divine or natural law revealed in the work of Cheikh Anta Diop it was not the historical inevitability of Marx but Diop's own certainty that past culture shaped future politics. Federation will come, he said, because African culture is one, and in federation lies Africa's future greatness. History of such heroic conception was necessarily rare, in Africa as elsewhere; more common was the belief that historical study was essential to the firm grounding of newly independent nations. After the Second World War in Nigeria there emerged a school of historical studies of great vitality and importance, paralleling the work of Diop, but with different emphasis, different concepts, different results. More eclectic and more parochial than Diop's splendid panorama, the work of the Ibadan school nevertheless struck out in a number of directions—exploring new methods and new materials, attempting broad educational objectives in the schools and among the public at large, encouraging official support for the collection and preservation of historical materials, training a generation of professionals to deal with historical problems. Cheikh Anta Diop offered a daring new personal concept of African history. At Ibadan the emphasis was institutional and corporate.

The initial steps were tentative, painful. Nigeria's first university, at Ibadan, had been founded in 1948, a response both to growing nationalist pressures and postwar changes in the theory and practice of colonial stewardship. A year later the department of history recruited a young Nigerian lecturer, K. O. Dike, whose recently completed doctoral dissertation at London University explored nineteenth-century commercial activities in the Niger River Delta. Dike's natural impatience for a quick start in his teaching was intensified when he discovered that his department was staffed by Englishmen engaged by the British administration and offering a syllabus that gave scant recognition to the existence of African history apart from its connections with Europe. Such limitations were hardened by the status of the new institution as an associate university college of the University of London; hence, any changes in syllabus and degree structure for higher education in Nigeria were subject to approval by various boards and councils of the University of London.

It was frustrating and vexatious. As a graduate student Dike had been warned by his thesis advisor about the use of oral materials in his doctoral research, a practice then heavily frowned upon among British historians. Later he was to learn that the administration at Ibadan would attempt to recruit a British Africanist to head the department because "the ideas I held of African history were dangerous . . . they didn't want to entrust the teaching of African history to me. . . . They tried to replace me with somebody more orthodox, more to the imperial idea."

In those days "dangerous" did not necessarily mean revolutionary or politically inflammatory. It was widely felt among British academics that there was no substantial, credible history to be had from the preliterate societies of Africa, which, in any case, were far from the mainstream of important developments in the world. Fifteen years later a leading historian in England would still pronounce African history unrewarding, its locale irrelevant, its subjects barbarous. At this earlier point in time, the young African felt hard pressed, his new department headed by a man whose own specialty was not history but theology and who used literature like Harry Johnston's *Colonization of Africa,* a book, Dike observed, that few would recommend, even then. "I was naturally horrified," he added, "to have . . . Africans subjected to theories which were then acceptable . . . to the European colonizer, not necessarily to the African groups or . . . communities." Disillusioned, at one point Dike resigned.[10]

Times were changing, however. In Britain a small but respected group of specialists was making a successful effort to secure African history as a legitimate field of study. In Africa colonies were rushing toward political independence. At Ibadan Dike found his ideas slowly prevailing. The department of history gradually changed character and personnel. In 1956 Dike became chairman and subsequently was named vice-principal of the University College. His authority and influence waxing, Dike was now able to move ahead on a number of fronts.

The argument that Africa had no history rested partly on the fact that much of the past survived in the form of traditions orally transmitted from generation to generation, partly on a paucity of documentary source materials from which secondary works could be written. Already Dike had been able to arouse the authorities in Lagos to the need for preserving historical documents. He was appointed supervisor of public records in 1951, a position that enabled him to travel throughout the country during the long vacation periods between terms. Official papers and private collections he found in varying stages of neglect and decay, preyed upon by insects and brown rot, stored in haphazard fashion or total disarray, many documents lost through inadvertence and lack of uniform policies governing preservation. Where possible, Dike collected and stored materials in Ibadan; more than that, he began to formulate a systematic plan for preserving and organizing the Nigerian archives. To this end he submitted a report, published in 1954, recommending the establishment of a public record office for the conservation and administration of state papers and other historical records.

Dike's recommendations were accepted in substance and a national archives was established under the education ministry. With Dike as director, the process of collection and preservation was stepped up, storage centers were established in the regional capitals of Ibadan, Enugu, and Kaduna, and the main collection was located in a new archives building located on the Ibadan university campus. A number of students were sent abroad to study the principles of archival administration, while plans were laid for a system of classification, an appropriate distribution of papers among the different centers, an orderly method for destruction and weeding of records, and an extension of archival control over available private collections and the important records of Christian missions that had long labored in Nigeria.[11]

Archival materials offered a major historical source, a source, however, rich but limited. By its nature, historical research in Africa required more than the written record, more even than verbal tradition. Archaeological study, analysis of languages, genetic explorations of man, his animals and his crops, examination of climatic changes over time—such investigations could reveal much in regions where the written word was scarce and oral recollections uncertain. For Dike these complexities opened up intriguing possibilities for new methods of historical research. Could not the different disciplines be coordinated, concentrated on a particular historical problem with results far beyond those of more conventional inquiries?

By the mid-1950s a sea change was apparent in attitudes toward African history. Growing interest among scholars as well as governments encouraged Dike to suggest a multidisciplinary study of the kingdom of Benin, occupied by the British expedition of 1897 but once a paramount power, its hegemony extending from Lagos to the Niger Delta. Rich in history, art, and tradition, Benin also had a long-lived association with the Yoruba people and was in early contact with Europe through its connection with fifteenth-century explorers and traders. Funds were soon forthcoming from the colonial administration in Lagos as well as from research and philanthropic organizations in Britain and the United States. In 1956 the Scheme for the Study of Benin History and Culture was launched, its base at Ibadan with Dike as its coordinator.

The Benin project set a pattern to be followed by others, in Yorubaland and in Nigeria's northern region. It showed the way for interdisciplinary studies, utilizing the talents of historians, ethnographers, and archaeologists, attempting to show how the past in Africa might be reconstructed with verisimilitude despite the lack of conventional sources and methods. Much information and experience was gained, particularly with the complexities of a multidimensional project. Written records of European origin, local oral traditions, the sociology of contemporary Benin, and the material remains of the past were all studied in detail and with profit. Difficulties arose, however, in relating information from different sources to form a coherent integrated picture of the past. No single person appeared capable of absorbing such diverse materials to produce one synthetic whole. It was often like adding apples and pears. As one scholar observed, "It must be seen as the stray components of a multidimensional structure seemingly held together by a few threads, although instinct tells us it has a unity."[12]

The search for historical materials continued. At a later time Dike would once again attempt coordinated research, this time through a university-based institute of African studies. At the moment, however, he was more concerned with training a generation of Nigerian historians, and seeing them launched on monographic studies related to aspects of the Nigerian past. Promising undergraduates were sent abroad for doctoral study; on return they were invited to join the department, their theses published under the Ibadan University Series, an arrangement worked out between Dike and the Longman publishing house in London.

By 1959 the first Nigerians were coming home to lecture on African history. Two, J. C. Anene and J. F. A. Ajayi, would eventually head the department and publish their theses in the Longman series. Ajayi recalls how he was encouraged in his postgraduate studies at London University, first by his thesis director, Professor G. S. Graham, who had earlier helped Dike withstand the African history skeptics, and then by a series of interdisciplinary conferences that Professor Roland Oliver organized during the 1950s at the School of Oriental and African Studies. Oliver's conferences brought linguists, social anthropologists, and archaeologists together with historians in discussions of methodology in the field of African history; thus young students like Ajayi were early exposed to the more advanced thinking on the subject and these new approaches became part of their intellectual baggage as they returned to take up their teaching responsibilities.[13]

The Longman series produced a substantial number of works, chiefly in Nigerian history but also touching other parts of the continent. By the 1970s some dozen volumes had been published, the historians at the University of Ghana and University College, Nairobi, Kenya, had paid Ibadan the compliment of imitation with a similar project, and new manuscripts continued to arrive. Dike, however, had been concerned with a variety of outlets for African historical scholarship. The first volume in the Ibadan Historical Series was Professor Ajayi's *Christian Missions in Nigeria,* which first appeared in 1965. Nine years earlier, Dike had formed the Historical Society of Nigeria with its own journal. Nationalist fervor in Nigeria had produced a lively interest in local history both in academic circles and among the general public. Scholarly output now had a vehicle, partly through the meetings of the Society— which were stimulating and widely attended—and partly through the journal, which published important research that might not otherwise have appeared because of its local character.[14]

Dike was particularly effective in the encouragement he gave others, providing them with essential organizational and financial support for their activities, placing his growing prestige behind their work, and thereby creating a series of institutions and procedures that broke new ground in standards and directions for historical studies in Africa. This left little time for his own research, which suffered accordingly, but his administrative responsibilities increasingly engrossed his attentions and drew him away from the field of history that had been his early preoccupation. By 1960 Dike had moved on to become principal of the university college, and his energies were also absorbed by other extracurricular responsibilities—for example, preservation of the country's traditional art, a responsibility that fell to him as chairman of the Nigerian Antiquities Commission. The development of historical studies at Ibadan was thus assumed by others who, fortunately, were fully equal to the start Dike had made.

There was still much work to be done. Paradoxically, Dike had made least headway in his reforms within the history syllabus itself, where only a single paper was offered on Africa and the degree structure was dominated by European and English history. The status of Ibadan as a university college associated with London University virtually ruled out any significant change in curriculum; it remained for the independence of Nigeria in 1960 to break the impasse, bringing in its wake the establishment in 1962 of the independent University of Ibadan, with its own governance and consequently its own power to develop its own system of degrees.

Between 1959 and 1961 the historians worked hard at a new syllabus, striking both at content and form. The London-associated program had offered both a general and an honors degree heavy with irrelevancies like Greek, Beowulf, or the economic and social history of Tudor England. Under the new arrangement, students could take an honors degree in history that began with generalized study covering a number of different fields in the humanities and social sciences, culminating during the final year with a concencentration on one or two subjects, for example, history, or history and politics. Within the history department itself, the offerings on Europe were somewhat compressed, thus permitting the introduction of several African history papers. The first year featured a two-part survey of Africa followed in the second year by more specialized subjects such as Islam in Africa, Nigerian history, South Africa, East Africa, and so on. During the final year a series of special subjects were available, seminar-type courses in which the students were encouraged to work directly with original sources.

The tradition of written documentation died hard. "The European scholar . . . tended to equate written documents with history," Dike remarked in 1965, "and to take the absence of documents to mean the absence of events worthy of historical study." Some fields had previously been disallowed in London because it was felt that not enough was known about the subject, meaning not enough documentary material was available. Even under an independent university structure there was a strong tendency by British-trained Africans to maintain a heavy reliance on documentary evidence. The special subjects were based primarily on written sources, and efforts were made to prepare books and articles that would assist students in the more generalized offerings.

Gradually the department took shape as an independent growth rather than a foreign transplant. There were still many Europeans on the history faculty—individuals sympathetic to the development of a department with strong and varied curricular offerings. The Islamic specialist, H. F. C. Smith, for example, supervised much of the day-to-day work of the department and laid the basis for study of Islam in Nigeria through the collection of important Arabic materials. J. D. Omer Cooper from South Africa edited the *Journal of the Nigerian Historical Society,* and A. F. C. Ryder of Great Britain carried the historical burden of the Benin research scheme along with his teaching responsibilities. At the same time Anene and Ajayi headed a growing number of Africans who had completed their doctoral studies and were busily teaching the new courses they had created for the syllabus.

It was hard, grinding work, unspectacular but satisfying, trench warfare to Cheikh Anta Diop's aerial flights. The new courses were developed, tested, revised. Documents were assembled and reproduced. The library acquisitions grew steadily, including a valuable microfilm collection that featured early West African newspapers and voluminous representations from missionary reports and correspondence. A valuable bibliography of journal articles dealing with African history was published and in 1963 the history department organized workshops for schoolteachers from the four West African Commonwealth countries of Nigeria, Ghana, Sierra Leone, and Gambia, introducing them to the newly developed materials now available for use in revised West African school syllabi.

The workshops produced two volumes, *A Thousand Years of West African History,* which Ajayi helped to edit, and *Africa in the Nineteenth and Twentieth Centuries,* of which Anene was coeditor. In 1965 the department launched *Tarikh,* a periodical devoted to short essays on various aspects of African history. The syllabus was broadened beyond Europe and Africa. A course in United States history was introduced and plans were laid for offerings on Latin America, Eastern Europe, and China. Graduate training began with a group of Ibadan graduates. At the same time the historical society remained active, with a full complement of meetings, their papers appearing subsequently in the pages of the society's journal.

Much was achieved that might not even have been ventured in more static times. "In *One Thousand Years of West African History,*" Ajayi recently observed, "I had to give an introductory paper, a survey of West Africa in 1000 A.D. I knew next to nothing about that but I had to face the exercise. . . . In the end, people thought it was publishable. It was published," he concluded. Such efforts brought results. By 1966 the Ibadan history department had become exceptional by any standard. Then in January of that year came the military coup that led to the Biafran secession and war, an event that changed many things in Nigeria, among them the University of Ibadan and its department of history.[15]

## *The Question of Oral Tradition*

In the West, historians have tended to take historical sources for granted—they are simply the available documentary material. Indeed, with Europeans, the association of historical sources and the written word became for a time so strong that it led to an eventual perversion of cause and effect. From the position that documents served history, the scholar proceeded to the reverse—no documents, no history. Forgotten for the moment was the fact that early Western history relied on oral traditions where written evidence was lacking—the Homeric epics or certain sections of the Bible, for example. Forgotten too was the obvious fact that the quality of the source is based not on form but reliability. "Sources are sources," says Jan Vansina, who pioneered the development of oral history in Africa. "They can be good or bad but there is nothing intrinsically less valuable in an oral source than in a written one."[16]

Largely preliterate until the late-coming period of European colonialism, African societies were limited in their historical sources to extradocumentary materials. It is no prodigy, therefore, that the modern African historian has turned to archaeological, linguistic, anthropological, even astronomical data as well as evidence orally transmitted. These different disciplines are utilized to reinforce each other, providing chronology for events that often lack sequence, or illuminating an obscure oral testimony through reference to some aspect of a society's present-day culture.

Much of the early work dealing with the use of African oral tradition was done by the European scholar, Jan Vansina, working before the era of independence in the Belgian Congo and the United Nations trust territory of Ruanda-Urundi. He identified various types of oral literature—such as legal precedents, commentaries, tales, and genealogies—and clarified the understanding of these traditions by a study of current language and culture. Other methodological techniques followed. It was necessary to make distinctions between tribal, village, family, or royal history, to recognize the varying character and function of official linguists and the more informal tellers of stories, and to learn how to check authenticity by matching accounts and weighting their veracity through other types of evidence. All this was enormously painstaking and time-consuming, but it produced history where none was otherwise available, and it provided methods of procedure that others might follow with profit.[17]

Others did follow. Indeed, in the case of B. A. Ogot, a young Kenyan student at Makerere University College, it was a question of beginning even before he became aware of Vansina's work. In 1950 Ogot was an undergraduate studying mathematics, but he says he was already deeply interested in African history and culture, a preoccupation that increasingly came into conflict with his formal studies. Subsequently, as a postgraduate student in Scotland, Ogot switched from mathematics to history, but when faced with Scottish clan history offered as a university subject, Ogot could not help but wonder: if this is a subject worthy of university study, why then not African history as well? By the time he left Saint Andrew's with a master's degree in European history, Ogot had determined to work on precolonial Africa and to concentrate particularly on the problem of oral history. Consequently he declined an offer to study aspects of colonial history at Oxford and turned instead to London University, where he found sympathetic encouragement from Roland Oliver of the School of Oriental and African Studies.

Oliver's reassurances did not necessarily extend to the rest of the London faculty, at least among the historians. Kenneth Dike had previously encountered opposition at London despite the fact that most of his thesis was based on documentary evidence. Now, only a few years later, here was another young African proposing a research topic on the history of his own people, the southern Luo of Kenya, that would rely almost totally on oral evidence. Many were certain it could not be done, and none was sure that it could. "I wanted to . . . get people at London University to take me seriously," Ogot later recalled. Oliver and some of the linguists were encouraging, but for the rest, "This was the biggest hurdle . . . to be accepted and to be taken seriously, that this was a thing that could be done. They [could] not see how anything could be done without documents. . . . If you want to study folklore, they said, join the Department of Anthropology."

If Ogot was determined, Oliver was cautiously optimistic. "As to the subject," he wrote a colleague, as the young Kenyan began his studies in the autumn of 1959, ". . . I have no doubt that a Ph.D. could be obtained . . . especially if he did a good deal of field-work of a more or less anthropological kind. As for the History Board . . . I shouldn't expect a trouble-free passage . . . because . . . like most worthwhile things, it is an innovation. . . . The greatest danger is not the History Board, but the undoubted difficulty for Ogot of breaking into a new field where he cannot hope to draw very much on the experience of others. This will require great qualities of perseverance." Apparently the perseverance soon made itself known. Six months later, as Ogot penetrated more deeply into his research, Oliver was increasingly confident. "He is shaping *extremely* well," Oliver wrote. "I have no doubt that the ultimate result will be a milestone in African history."[18]

As anticipated by the skeptics, by Oliver, and by Ogot himself, problems of methodology soon emerged. At London Ogot had busied himself with background reading, but his main concern was to formulate techniques, including linguistics study, that would serve to translate the raw material of oral evidence into historical texts susceptible to orthodox historical criticism. At this time Ogot had only sketchy knowledge of Vansina's work, a fortunate omission as it turned out, because Vansina's techniques proved to be ill-suited to the types of societies under Ogot's investigation. Vansina had worked with peoples whose social and political organization was articulated in a pyramid-shaped hierarchy that rose from local village heads through regional chiefs to a central kingship, presided over by a sovereign much as with the monarchies of Europe. The Luo and analogous Nilotic peoples, by contrast, were held together by clan ties, and even more, by the closeness of individuals who had endured the passage of puberty rites together, irrespective of differing clan or even tribal affiliation. Quite another approach was needed in dealing with the traditions of such peoples with their decentralized, horizontally ordered social and political institutions.

It was procedure by trial and error. As Oliver had surmised, Ogot's inquiry involved new methods in a new field. There was little to fall back on. At London Ogot read widely, mainly in early medieval European historical and archaeological materials, only to discover techniques that would not apply in his case. There was a considerable body of material already published dealing with Nilotic traditions, and this Ogot consumed, but it was raw data, the traditions themselves as recorded, without any attempt at analysis. As Ogot later remarked, the lack of analysis was an unforeseen blessing because the collecting had been done by missionaries mainly interested in linguistics, and their analysis, had it been attempted, would have proved an impediment.

Thus, arriving in East Africa for his fieldwork, Ogot came without a sure methodology. Vansina had keyed his units of analysis to such factors as clans, families, or village elders and these worked for people with centralized political systems. Among Ogot's Luo, however, traditions were comprehensible in various ways depending upon the people under study. In many cases the unit of analysis was defined by the time when people were born and when they were circumcised. Territorial systems, group and personal relationships, ideas of state and polity were all related to these age grades that transcended other types of social or political organization. Ogot found that in other cases the basic unit was the clan, some of them spread all over East Africa from the Sudan to Tanzania, others involving different people like Luo, Teso, or Acholi. All were aware of their mutual membership but never saw each other, all linked by a bond that cut across such fundamental differences as marriage taboos, inheritance or language, indeed across different societies. In some cases old clans joined to form new clans, all in all a tissue of complexity that threatened to overwhelm the young scholar.

When it came to gathering the raw materials for analysis, there were greater similarities to Vansina's experience. "The main idea," said Ogot, "was to get from the people themselves what they regarded as historically significant and why." Initially he went to the clan elders and asked that they convene all those recognized as experts in the history of the region. Ogot met with these in a four-day marathon conference from which much information was forthcoming, including the names of many more individuals known to be knowledgeable about their history.

Eventually all informants were interviewed and their historical texts recorded in the vernacular. Next, the traditions were collated, the origins of various versions traced, and the role of oral traditions examined for each society. Were they meant, for example, to justify a particular institution, or to prove prior occupation of a piece of land? Finally, the texts would be subjected to critical analysis similar in technique to that employed by historians anywhere concerned with old manuscripts.

Here again complications arose. As the material accumulated, the number of clans grew. Twenty, thirty, then forty, going forward and backward in time, stretching geographically across thousands of miles from the foothills of the Ethiopian highlands westward to present-day Zaire and south to Tanzania. Were there not larger units for the southern Luo? Ogot wanted to know. No one seemed to be aware of any. Then, finally, one or two elders spoke up. "Yes," they said, "you can reduce all of us to three groups." The first came directly from an original Luo settlement along the frontier that had been located between the southern Sudan and Ethiopia, sped on their way by Galla invaders during the fifteenth century. A second group came later, but was less pure, pausing north of Lake Victoria, intermarrying with Banyoro, Soga, and others before finally arriving in Kenya. The third group also came to Kenya via Uganda and showed much mixing with other peoples such as the Teso and Karamoja.

The discovery of three main groups was a major breakthrough that greatly simplified Ogot's work and formed the basis for later research in Uganda that both utilized and sustained this classification. It also served to bring forth a wide range of economic and political information, for subgroups and clans varied greatly. Some lived as farmers, others as cattle herders, still others as traders; some formed highly centralized states, others were decentralized, but all came from the same original stock.[19]

For Ogot there still remained the problem of chronology, always a difficulty for those working with oral traditions. Partly this is due to the fact that in traditional African society there is such a sense of closeness between the living and the ancestors that there is often no clear differentiation between past and present. Occurrences are frequently related in the present tense and with a fervor that suggests the informant was present during an incident that may in fact be hundreds of years old. "When these chaps start talking," said Ogot, "they talk as if things happened yesterday. . . . They really talk as if they were there. . . . The whole thing is so vivid and so fresh. . . . They are not talking about something dead. Some even get up and demonstrate to you how they were fighting."

A second problem arises from the lack of absolute chronology; that is, signposts that place a particular event on a particular date, not merely in relation to another event, equally unfixed in time or perhaps associated with a reign that itself escapes any absolute chronology. Ogot's solution, which he regarded as only partially satisfactory, was to construct a time sequence in terms of generations and, where possible, to link this system to an absolute chronology through the use of events known to the outside world. He obtained a genealogy from each of his expert informants, coordinated these, established a generation time interval, and began to attach names and events to the chronological ladder thus conceived. In this fashion the body of information grew and held fast to a sequence that developed its own internal consistency, and was related to outside events through occasional fixed knowns like a solar eclipse, a volcanic eruption, or an incident described in Arab or Portuguese sources. Basically, however, Ogot's chronology was restricted to its own relative dates, as with research in archaeology or historical linguistics; consequently there was a lack of the sharp temporal precision that marks history based upon documentary evidence.

How effective, then, is oral history? Lack of precision, says Ogot, does not necessarily invalidate the idea of history, or even of chronology. His own work brought forth a time depth of about four hundred years, and he was able to show an articulated recollection of the past for a people whose way of life was politically both centralized and decentralized. If details were sometimes imprecise, there was clarity of sequence and historical causation. If sources were occasionally questionable and contradictory, this was not peculiar to oral tradition— such conditions obtain equally with history based on documentation.

In gathering his material, Ogot first sought personal information from his informants. Who were they? What about their families? How did they earn their livelihood? Next, he investigated the movements of peoples. Where did this or that group originate? What places did they pass through? Who led them at such and such a time? A third line of inquiry moved toward greater generalization and included such questions as what was the religion of the Luo, or how was iron obtained and utilized? Expert testimony was needed for much of this, but gradually what took shape was a multidimensional picture that dealt with all phases of life—cultural, religious, philosophical, as well as economic and political. Unlike other oral historians, Ogot found no important difference in the availability of information between societies politically centralized or decentralized. What is important, he has insisted, is to identify the right historical unit for the people in question, that is, "what is historically meaningful in any particular society." Properly defined, that will lead the historian to the information he seeks.[20]

There have been, of course, limitations on what oral history can achieve, as Ogot has readily admitted. Some researchers have been confounded when studying peoples with little or no apparent interest in their past. Others have felt that their methodology has failed them, yielding too little material to be useful—too vague or fanciful in matter, too restricted in its geographic extent. For Ogot, the chief shortcoming has been chronological—that is, the inability of oral evidence to provide absolute dates and a refined temporal precision. On the whole, however, Ogot insists that oral studies have greatly enriched African history, oral methodology is now being used with profit in European historical research, and oral historians have stimulated the study of historical linguistics and iron age archaeology, which have joined with oral history to make new and important contributions to history and historiography in Africa.[21]

## A Usable Past

Alan Ogot published his book on the southern Luo in 1967, a year that probably represented a high-water mark for historical studies in Africa. The department at the University of Ibadan had already achieved a peak of activity. Teaching and research in both Nigeria and Ghana had been encouraged by the creation of institutes of African studies at their respective national universities. A stimulating program in history had just been established at the new Tanzanian University of Dar es Salaam. Thriving departments were hard at work in Nairobi and Kampala, and everywhere Africans were returning from postgraduate studies to occupy university teaching positions that had been held previously by outsiders. Even in the more rigidly controlled curricula of the French-speaking universities at Dakar and Abidjan, there appeared to be growing attention to national and continental history.

The flourishing condition of African historical studies was more apparent than real. At Dar es Salaam the program had been conceived and staffed by expatriates and they were already beginning to leave by the late 1960s. The Nairobi department continued to prosper under Ogot's direction, but political uncertainties in Uganda and Ghana soon complicated developments in those countries. French-speaking Africa failed to produce significant historical studies, with the exception of the works of Cheikh Anta Diop and Joseph Ki Zerbo of Upper Volta. At Ibadan almost two decades of constructive development was compromised by the secession of Biafra in 1967 and the civil war that followed.

The history department at Ibadan also suffered from its own strength. In a new country with severe shortages of trained leadership, many talented scholars were drawn off to fill positions in government or to staff administrative posts in the new universities that began to take shape across the nation. Similar manpower strains occurred in other countries; moreover, as the decade of the seventies opened, the problems of independence seemed to grow in complexity, their solution more elusive. A faltering economic development and chronic political instability complicated the routine of day-to-day living. There was less time, if not enthusiasm, for such esoterica as eighteenth century Yoruba history or Bantu movements in eastern Africa. In university budgets, moreover, there was less support for the humanities as governments turned their interest increasingly toward the sciences and technology.

Disinterest in historical studies occupied a more profound level, however. The uncomplicated enthusiasm of the early independence years had ended, and with its demise had expired the spontaneous joy in rediscovering an African past. In 1980 Michael Crowder, the widely respected British historian of Africa, commented on the stagnation that had overtaken African history during the 1970s. "Where African history used to be so adventurous, where it was constant excitement in the sixties . . . it has become almost old-fashioned, repeating itself. . . . The doctoral students . . . tend to be pursuing the interests . . . of their supervisors. Where is the psychohistory? Where is . . . landscape history, a new and exciting discipline . . . of immense significance . . . in the African context? . . . What attention is being paid to the history of popular culture . . . changing fashion, changing dress design?" Crowder went on to point out other gaps— the need for textbooks, for wider ranging syntheses, for histories of independent nation-states that explain to their citizens what it means to be caught up in new cultural and political loyalties. "It does seem," Crowder concluded, "that African history had its first great fling because it had an outside opponent which it was able to attack. . . . Now they do not have that opponent. . . . What they need is to turn inward and look at history without constant reference to what the outside world thinks."[22]

Alan Ogot has pointed to other factors. Many Africans, he suggests, are preoccupied with faltering economic development. Those who are historians tend to see African history only in terms of Third World dependency on the industrialized West. All else they regard as extraneous antiquarianism. Others go even further and question the ultimate utility of any history. African history, they say, has been a celebration of the past that has degenerated into sentimentality and nostalgia, an obsolete Negritude. Those dealing with present problems look to the past for a vision of the future. They are looking for a usable past, says Ogot, but what they find instead is a pointless story of wanderings and warfare by aimless peoples. They turn in despair from such bootless activities.

Such pessimism is unwarranted, says Ogot. History will always fulfill an essential role, for it must tell a people who they are by telling them whence they came. To this, the Nigerian historian, J. F. A. Ajayi adds specifics, pointing to the dynamic character of historical research, ever changing direction and emphasis to meet the new needs of a changing present. "For the historian," Ajayi says, "the search for relevance is a constant preoccupation . . . what is significant or relevant keeps changing with the present." During the struggle for political independence, Ajayi continues, African historians were concerned to establish a long-lived past antedating a colonialism that itself needed to be studied from the African, not the European, perspective. As independence came, African historians were able to shift to the study of powerful and stable states in Africa's past, to the creation and direction of large empires comparable to those complex territories coming into existence as the new nations of independent Africa.

As African governments encounter the complexities of technological development and political cohesion, says Ajayi, new historical insights can help promote better social coherence and ethnic understanding. Thus, the general history of Africa sponsored by UNESCO stresses a continental, pan-African perspective of African history and attempts to place the contributions of blacks in Africa and elsewhere within the totality of human endeavor. If there is a momentary popular disinterest in the shifting aims of historical research, Ajayi adds, it may only reflect the need to bring new objectives more clearly into popular view.

Ogot's conclusion is forward-looking, optimistic. The search for historical relevance, he says, is the search for a philosophy of African history in terms of African needs and aspirations, quite independent of foreign systems of thought. Cultural and intellectual independence must follow accompanying and supporting political freedom. Then will the present clarify and Africans will recapture a usable past.[23]

# 8

## The Idea of an African University

### Early Educational Theories

The first universities in black Africa were imports, their purpose the indoctrination of a foreign culture. At the height of the Mali and Songhai kingdoms, the scholars of Timbuktu's Sankore mosque were concerned with propagation of the Islamic way. Fourah Bay College, offering a number of university courses after 1876, began life as an Anglican seminary for the training of African clergy and missionaries.

During the nineteenth century West Africans who came under the influence of European missionaries were persuaded that a Western-style education was the key to success for themselves and their compatriots. The few who could afford it journeyed to Europe for their education. Many filled the mission schools, some for the spiritual solace they found in Christianity, others to master vocational skills or the mathematical and linguistic literacy they associated with achievement in the world of affairs.

There were those, however, who envisioned education in an African context, not an uncritical introduction of foreign learning but a shaping to African circumstances of skills and perceptions from abroad, a marriage of indigenous and foreign wisdom that would help the African to find his way in the modern world. Africanus Horton was such a one, proposing Western medical and technical training for Africans in a tropical setting and urging the establishment of a university in West

Africa that would apply the latest European curricula to African conditions. As a medical doctor, Horton displayed greater innovation in the sciences. He was inclined to accept Western literature, history, philosophy, or languages uncritically and without substantial change, but in such areas as biology, chemistry, geology, and physics he insisted that these disciplines be focused for the first time on the tropics, thus to unlock the mysteries and riches of Africa.

Horton's recommendations were tempered with a practicality that linked education to economic development; basically, he was content to apply Western learning to African problems. Quite a different point of view was put forward by a number of Horton's contemporaries, however, most notably the Freetown businessman and civic leader, William Grant, and the West African clergymen, James Johnson and Edward Blyden. It is fair to say that Grant and Johnson were influenced to a considerable extent by Blyden's educational philosophy, including his ideas for university development, and these concepts rested in turn on racial theories that Blyden had evolved to challenge white supremacy and to secure black culture and self-respect in a competitive world. Blyden saw the races of the world as complementary, each possessing unique characteristics, some good, some bad, but all combining in the total perfectibility of God's divine purpose. For Blyden it followed that racial mixing, cultural or biological, dulled the fine edge of racial genius, weakening character, and corrupting those very traits that were the special contribution of each race to world civilization. This being so, said Blyden, a European education, whatever its merits, would be fatal to the black man who required a training that cultivated his special talents and fostered the development of African racial instincts.

In 1872 Blyden offered a blueprint for a university in West Africa. He did not reject Western learning out of hand. There was much to be gained from Europe, he said, especially from a study of classical languages and civilization as well as from Western science and mathematics; these enlivened the spirit and disciplined the mind. It was the modern period of European studies that had to be avoided, Blyden continued. History that featured the barbarisms of the slave trade and literature or sociology that was, at best, patronizing toward the black race was counterfeit, pernicious, and unfit for the instruction of those who knew these messages to be false. Much better the African be tutored in his own history, languages, and customs, to hear his own songs and learn his own traditions, taught by Africans who knew and respected an indigenous culture so misunderstood and discounted by foreigners, studying at an inland university center far removed from the deadly effects of alien influences. In this way, concluded Blyden, the African would develop the racial strength needed to fulfill his destiny. In this way the value of the black man would be demonstrated for all the world to see, not only to his own advantage but for "the advantage of humanity—for the purpose of civilization, of science, of good government, and of progress generally."[1]

Blyden's recommendations for a university in West Africa were never acted upon as Africans were drawn ever more deeply into the toils of colonialism and European proconsuls brushed aside consideration of advanced education for subject peoples. While Africans remained divided on the merits of a Westernized schooling, colonial administrators saw no need for a university establishment to instruct those whose ultimate independence lay far in the future. Much better, it was felt, to concentrate on elementary education and industrial training, practical schooling that would provide a supply of productive labor.

Such an attitude changed in time. During the interval between the two world wars the question of higher education in the British colonies was examined on several occasions, but with the conclusion of the Second World War the prospect of independence for colonial peoples in the foreseeable future lent immediate urgency to a debate that had previously been conducted at a leisurely pace. An independent leadership would have to be a trained leadership, university-trained.

In France and Belgium the realization of colonial independence came late, as did the consequent move toward establishment of universities in former dependencies. The Belgian Congo inaugurated the bare beginnings of a university in 1954, while the University of Dakar in Senegal emerged as a fully accredited member of the French university system only in 1957. The British colonies fared better, benefiting from the considerable study that had already taken place. By 1945 concrete plans had been drafted for higher education in the colonies, and between 1946 and 1949 university colleges in the Sudan, Uganda, Nigeria, and the Gold Coast were established in special relationship with the University of London.

As conceived, each colonial university system reflected the predilections of its parent. Lovanium University in Léopoldville was rigorous and paternalistic, Dakar largely indistinguishable from other provincial French universities. In the British territories the aim had been for institutions with curricula of highest quality that were at the same time relevant to the needs of a people moving toward independence. Indeed, at Achimota College in the Gold Coast there already had been admirable precedent for such a development. Achimota had combined a Western curriculum with study of African civilizations, and it was a condition of employment for expatriates who joined the teaching faculty that they engage in research bearing on Africa.

Academic quality in the university colleges was insured by the arrangement with London University, which supervised syllabi, courses, and examinations, and provided each successful graduate with the certification of a London University degree. Physical facilities were designed with a liberal regard for requirements in teaching and research, and great care was taken to insure recruitment of a teaching staff of high caliber.

Assimilationist educators in France saw no paradox in a French university at Dakar, but those who planned the new universities for British Africa seemed well aware of the need for an education fitted to local conditions. While necessity forced initial reliance on British models and expatriate staff, these were regarded as temporary expedients until local cadres were trained and research yielded the materials for syllabi that reflected and supported the societies they were meant to serve. One purpose of a university, it was observed, is to refine and maintain the best of indigenous culture, and it was understood that research would begin at once in the social sciences, in history, in local languages and comparative linguistics, as well as in areas in the physical sciences, medicine, and engineering. The vice-chancellor of London University, while noting some of the difficulties of adapting current syllabi in Britain to new needs, appeared prepared to go beyond minimal adjustment. "Something more will be needed than the adaptation of existing syllabuses," he pointed out. "It is . . . likely that a new form of subject or grouping of subjects will be necessary."

Unfortunately, a genuine flexibility toward innovation seems to have eluded the special commissions created by the British government to develop the new universities in the colonies. There was much lip service, even enthusiasm, for the proposition that high quality would have to be matched with high relevance, but no concrete stipulations were introduced that would have extended the Achimota research commitment, either in the Gold Coast or elsewhere. Basically the impulse lacked determination to institute change that went beyond "minor modifications in the British pattern of higher education." Such was the conclusion of Eric Ashby, distinguished British educator and a close student of the history of Britain's overseas universities. The commissions might have been expected, said Ashby, to concentrate a major share of their attention on the creation of a new university form to meet the new demands of a non-Western society.

> But this was not done; an opportunity was lost to give emphasis and prominence to the fact that although the first colonial universities established by Britain would inevitably be facsimiles of British universities, they must not remain so if they are to be viable in their new environments. . . . The Asquith and Elliot commissions did not ignore this problem. Indeed, quietly diffused through the reports of both commissions is much sensible and pertinent advice on the first steps to be taken in adapting curricula to local conditions. What is missing is a sense of the critical importance of the issue. No-one reading the reports is likely to come away with the impression that the long-term prospects of these universities depend upon their becoming indigenous, and that research, design of curriculum, pattern of government, should all contribute to this end.²

## African Education at University College of the Gold Coast

The University College of the Gold Coast that opened its doors to some ninety students in 1949 combined in purest form the merits and demerits of the British university effort in Africa. On the quality of its offerings there was no compromise. The special relationship with London University insured this excellence as did the appointment of the first principal of the university college, David Balme, a classics don from Cambridge with an unbending devotion to highest academic standards. Balme held an equally firm conviction that the only consequential civilization in the modern world was the culture of the West as inherited from Mediterranean antiquity, a culture which therefore should dominate the curriculum of any university, quite apart from

whatever culture obtained locally. As inaugurated, the degree structure in the Gold Coast held closely to the pattern of postwar British
universities. Eager to introduce the heritage of Greek and Latin civilization, moreover, Balme took special pains to establish departments
of classics and philosophy.

Unbending in his academic judgments, Balme was a democrat in
his determination that all, Africa as well as Europe, should share in
the best, while a university should be administered not by a hierarchy
of its senior officers but by the rank and file of university teachers.
While the nominal governance of the university college rested with
a lay council established by law, the actual control was defined by a
set of bylaws drafted by Balme that placed authority squarely in the
hands of an academic council elected by all members of the teaching
staff. In time the lay board lost much of its authority through inaction.
Within the framework established by London University, the university college became in effect self-governing, master of its own affairs
from entrance and degree qualifications to staffing and curriculum design.[3]

There was a justifiable pride among those in Britain who had worked
to create the university colleges in the colonies. Higher education the
equal of anything at home was established in some five territories that
were soon to be independent nations, and there were plans for several
more. In the Gold Coast a splendid campus arose on Legon Hill outside Accra—a series of dazzling white stucco buildings set off with
bright orange roofing and natural timber trim, featuring quadrangles
that enclosed trellised bougainvillea and lily pools, and crowned by
its bell tower at hilltop to mark an exciting educational adventure.
It was an expensive establishment, expected to cost some £10 million
for a student population of one thousand, but even the expense was
symbolic of the effort; was not the best only just good enough for
the training of future leaders in a new and important nation to be?

So it seemed, and yet, in time, there were second thoughts and
troublesome doubts. To begin with, building costs were extravagant,
perhaps excessive, for a small nation of modest resources that also had
to meet a substantial annual budget involving, among other expenses,
full scholarships for all students and vacation travel at first-class air
rates for expatriate staff returning home at each summer recess. What

was more, entrance requirements were difficult to meet. Ten years after its inauguration, the university college had an enrollment of only 450 to fill its thousand places; worse still, a high failure quotient limited annual graduates to some fifty baccalaureates, a tiny trickle for a young nation with such desperate needs in trained manpower.

The degree structure came to be another sore point. Under the London formula two possibilities were offered—a general degree in which the candidate pursued three subjects, and an honors degree concentrating on a single field of study. For university students in a newly developing country, a broadly conceived general degree might have been the more appropriate; but in practice many chose the honors track, which was known to be a less-rigorous, yet prestigious, a condition that reflected academic preconceptions in Britain rather than the imperatives of African national development. Although considerable effort was made to introduce courses dealing with African materials, the curriculum by and large was a version of what was available in any metropolitan British university. For example, a student pursuing the general degree might study Latin or Greek, one modern language, and history. If English were the chosen modern language, it would involve a full measure of Old English, Beowulf, and Chaucer, all in all a questionable education for those who were expected to one day direct the affairs of an independent nation in Africa.

The murmurs of discontent persisted and grew. On the eve of independence a Uganda educational commission criticized the application in Africa of entrance requirements designed expressly to fit postwar conditions in Britain. Nigerian undergraduates chafed over the inapplicability of the London degree structure, which often left them unqualified for postgraduate study in fields deemed important to national development. Graduates from the university college at Legon sometimes saw their sociological or anthropological training set aside as they were assigned to teach English civics in secondary school. In 1958 a Ghanaian professor of agriculture openly questioned the relevance in his field of standards that were, if not wholly theoretical, then designed primarily to meet farming criteria in the United Kingdom.

The response was uncompromising; standards were standards. Anywhere. Everywhere. They were absolute and immutable, insisted David Balme, as applicable in Ghana as they were at any other compass point across the world community of intellect. Such pronouncements were hardly more palatable when enunciated by expatriates and former colonial masters, speaking on behalf of curricula that largely ignored local culture and kept an expensive university half full in a country begging for sorely needed graduates.[4]

At issue were differing images of the twin concepts of quality and standards. The two often seemed to be used synonymously, but there were in fact important distinctions. Quality in higher education was an intangible yet identifiable property; it was simply the best that was available in student and teacher, in research and instruction. Quality was absolute, the same the world over, but the standards utilized for its achievement varied enormously, keyed to differing parochial requirements for admission and graduation, for syllabus and degree structure. Confusion and dispute erupted when, through curriculum, standards from one society were applied to another without due regard for local needs and aspirations.

It was one thing to insist that universities in Africa concern themselves with a Western culture to which Africa already had a deep commitment. It was something else, however, to compel an almost exclusive concentration on the heritage of the West, neglecting other bodies of knowledge, particularly those involving Africa. It was imperative that African universities address themselves to the study of the societies from which they had sprung. University graduates could scarcely serve their own people unless they understood and sympathized with indigenous social structure and political organization. Future teachers would never be able to reach their students without a firm grasp of aesthetic and philosophical principles that had guided Africa's peoples through the ages. The future could only grow from the seeds of the past. Many Africans understood this, including Ghana's head of state. In 1960, on the creation of the Republic of Ghana, Nkrumah promised a university that would "reflect African traditions and culture . . . [to] play a constructive part in . . . national awakening and reconstruction."[5]

Unfortunately, those charged with creating the universities of Africa lost sight of the primary objective. Determined to provide the best, they allowed their enthusiasm to be diverted from the best needed to the best they knew.

*Nkrumah at Legon*

Kwame Nkrumah has been charged by many critics with creating a program for the development of Ghana that lacked coherence or consistency, basing action on a flimsy tissue of ideas, vague and unformed, and thereby bringing Ghana to an eventual impasse of economic confusion and political chaos. There is little dispute that the politics and economy of Ghana floundered under Nkrumah's stewardship. Much that was undertaken by the Convention People's party and its leader proved ineffective. What is far less clear is that there was no intelligence at work, that Nkrumah was hopelessly muddled as to objective and the means to achieve it, that the shortfall was not more in the execution than the conception. Ghana may have collapsed under the weight of inexperience and incompetence. It did not falter for lack of policy.

It has been said that Nkrumah was not the most Cartesian of thinkers. He created no philosophical systems. He envisioned no Platonic society. Master politician, he was an indifferent administrator, and his thinking was intuitive rather than logical. He did, however, perceive certain imperatives consequent on political independence— a better life for his people, the realization of the black man's potential in the modern world.

Nkrumah's ideas came mainly from theory and practice in developmental economics with some gesture toward Marxism. He saw political independence as the essential first step, providing the opportunity to organize national and continental resources, not for the benefit of others but for those to whom they belonged. He hoped to create an efficient agriculture for food production and profitable export, to build public works that provided necessary power, transport, health and educational services, to form an industrial establishment that would help raise the standard of living and give his people at once closer association and greater freedom in dealing with the world of nations. Sooner than most he detected the phenomenon of neocolonialism and warned of its dangers. He urged that Africa and other nations of the Third World unite in order to make their presence felt in the face of European economic cohesiveness or the vigorous policies of superpowers. He saw Africa's strength in its unique cultural characteristics and idiomatic traditions—qualities essential to preserve, but in new and effective forms that dealt with the exigencies of modern living.[6]

These were objectives shared by most developing nations, unexceptionable in orthodoxy, even to the extent of assuming a large and active role for state and government. As an independent Gold Coast evolved from hope to expectation to reality, Nkrumah reached out to shape the policies and mark the direction of a new nation. There were a great many things to be done, some problems demanding immediate attention, others less pressing, still others inaccessible because of circumstances. Higher education was one of these last. The university was launched, but initially it remained firmly in the hands of outsiders, individuals much needed to secure a promising start but not necessarily sharing Nkrumah's educational objectives. At the outset Nkrumah and his party leaders were preoccupied with securing independence and gave little attention to Ghana's new university. There was lip service to academic quality, and press reports on the university affairs were generally favorable. As late as 1961 Nkrumah himself remarked on the importance of the high standards that had been set at Legon.[7]

Defense of standards was not acquiescence in educational philosophy, however. Educated at Achimota, Nkrumah might well have regarded the Legon curriculum as unbalanced if not retrograde. If Balme was committed to the necessity for a grounding in Western culture, Nkrumah was equally determined that the university in Ghana would produce graduates who could function in an Africa that was in process of liberating itself from colonial rule by representatives of the very Western culture extolled at Legon. Nkrumah sought to create a brand of socialism to accommodate Africa's needs. Would the university be permitted to proceed in its established pattern, producing a small ruling elite who thought like Europeans, or was it meant to break new ground in providing the many trained individuals needed to assist in creating a new Ghana and a new Africa? The latter meant a radical shift away from the courses and degree structure already established at Legon. It also meant a political change—replacing those who directed the affairs of the university with an administration and faculty sympathetic to the objectives of a government that was footing the bill.

Changes came hard. Balme's system of governance was firmly in place and jealously guarded by the Legon faculty, including a small but growing number of Africans. Even after national independence there was genuine reluctance in Ghana to cast off the special relationship with London University. There were important groups within the population—principally those educated in Europe—that equated excellence with a British degree and a Western curriculum; Legon students, moreover, were fearful of the possible effect on their careers if they were graduated from an institution that did not bear the established label of the English university system. Even within the government there were differences of opinion. Whatever Nkrumah's personal convictions concerning the role of a university in Africa, he was subject to pressures from diverse quarters within his own party, some ideological and some political.

Thus hindered, Nkrumah moved at first with circumspection. Balme's departure in 1957 presented the opportunity for a fundamental shift in policy, but the government was content to accept the recommendation of British university educators and appointed another expatriate from England, leaving unchanged the essentials of curriculum, enrollment, and administration. On Legon Hill there was a collective sigh of relief. The university college survived, still untouched by political pressures that could have become severe since it was at this time that the Ghanaian professor of sociology, Kofi Busia, left his university post for a career as leader of the government opposition.[8]

The early years of independence in Ghana were politically trying. Opposition to the government tended to be regional, ethnic, and potentially secessionist, a serious concern for those committed to national unity; centrifugal forces were by no means theoretical, as the melancholy history of independence in the Belgian Congo was to prove. Under the circumstances the university college remained suspect within the councils of government, embarrassed by Busia's former affiliation, and regarded as a potential if not actual source of opposition to the authorities. There began to be hostile speeches from ministers, Nkrumah included, fed by a growing feeling within the government that the expensive institution on Legon Hill trained not only irrelevant classicists but a politically irreverent elite, urged on by a hard core of Ghanaian lecturers. There was also the resentment of many party supporters against those whose better education had secured much-prized university entrance, a sense of irritation if not insecurity that may have been shared even by Nkrumah himself.

Later, as chancellor of the independent University of Ghana, Nkrumah presided over many official functions. Among friends and supporters he seemed relaxed and showed little concern for the formalities and dignities of office. Facing a critical audience, however, he became defensive, betraying annoyance over tactless though inconsequential breaches of etiquette. He was visibly vexed, for example, at the time of his investiture when an audience of supercilious students tittered when the president was introduced as "Doctor" Nkrumah. This uncharitable, unambiguous, comment on Nkrumah's honorary American doctorate was then followed by a pointed coolness and token applause in response to the chancellor's address.[9]

Small wonder that Nkrumah, along with others in the government, developed antipathies that were directed at students as well as faculty. The zeal of expatriate professors was interpreted as neocolonialism, while Ghanaians joining the faculty were suspected of being more interested in social prestige and a steady income than the health and prosperity of their country. Students, supported at great expense, seemed almost perverse in their attitudes, which ranged from indifference to contempt toward a regime they saw as increasingly dictatorial and intolerant.

Mutual antagonism erupted first, in 1959, when the government raised questions over the deluxe travel policy for staff members on summer leave, an expense that consumed over 10 percent of the college budget. At Legon this action was regarded as an attack on university self-government; if not resisted, it could lead to interference in more serious matters. To the ministers in Accra the Legon faculty was protecting unnecessary perquisites, invoking the principle of academic freedom on behalf of nothing more elevated than special privilege and material comfort. For Nkrumah, however, the shortcomings of the university college involved far more serious and fundamental matters than these administrative inadequacies.[10]

Nkrumah saw Ghana and Africa moving out of the era of colonial control into an age where socialism fashioned the shape of societies and Africans came together in a union of states that spanned the continent. To achieve this objective he sought a university that produced citizens whose way of thinking about the world was in tune with his own, who were aware of the kind of historical imperatives he felt were then unfolding in Africa. Just as Oxford University trained individuals sympathetic to the great traditions of Western thought and culture, so for Nkrumah the universities in Africa should draw their inspiration from an African past, fusing ancient traditions with modern, chiefly Marxist, ideas, and training peoples capable of working and living in the context of a new liberated Africa.

Clearly the university of David Balme was totally irrelevant to Nkrumah's objectives, a vestige of the despised colonialism Africa was in process of casting off. With the end of political controls, it was possible to terminate economic and cultural domination as well, said Nkrumah, while bringing to flower the qualities of Africa's own civilization that lay fertile in her traditions and her past. At the very least this meant a thoroughgoing change in curriculum; perhaps even more, it meant a new form of university establishment that would serve new national and pan-African ends.

In Nkrumah's view, then, an African university in Ghana should engage in intellectual decolonization, a process at bottom as political as national decolonization following national independence. It was political to train individuals in a new way of looking at the world. It was political to pursue research in African history, culture, the arts in order to create a new kind of African man. It was political to turn deliberately from the values of the West, to resist the mixing of cultures that brought confusion and indecision. Like Mensah Sarbah and Casely Hayford before him, Nkrumah was affirming the old faith in the strength of Africa's civilizations. With such ideas he hoped to build a new Africa. But he needed a university to help do it.[11]

Such sweeping objectives in mind, Nkrumah still moved with moderation, though the public atmosphere was charged with growing hostility between government supporters and the university. Party members saw Legon as remote and insensitive—a center of privilege at government expense, a refuge for expatriates long since departed from other national services, an institution that perversely raised entrance requirements despite its many empty places, a nest of disloyal student agitation. At the university college the self-image took shape of a beleaguered few defending the sacred institutions of academic freedom and quality of education in a land that lacked university traditions to lend support to these ideals.[12]

Nkrumah seemed to be searching for compromise and consensus. As a step toward the creation of an independent university, he announced that a special commission had been invited to make proposals for a University of Ghana at Legon while converting the technical institute at Kumasi into a new University of Science and Technology. The commission membership was drawn broadly from Africa, Europe, and the United States, including a scientist from the Soviet Union, a leading black American educator, and Davidson Nicol, then principal of Fourah Bay College in Sierra Leone. The commission convened late in 1960 and issued its report the following May. What it recommended was scarcely a startling departure from what had preceded. A university was proposed that would remain largely autonomous, yet would seek to respond with sensitivity to the needs of the community it served. As created in an act of the Ghanaian parliament in July 1961, the new university was to develop a curriculum that emphasized "the needs and aspirations of Ghanaians, including the furtherance of African unity," an objective hardly exceptionable but one that Eric Ashby was later to describe as "frankly political."

The principal officer of the university was to be the chancellor, a post reserved by statute for the president of the republic, Kwame Nkrumah. The vice-chancellor, appointed by the chancellor, was Nana Kobina Nketsia, who had served as a member of the commission secretariat and who held a post in the Ghana ministry of foreign affairs. It was understood, however, that this was an interim appointment. Nketsia would remain only until a permanent vice-chancellor was found.

The chief governing body of the university was its council, named partly by the government, and partly by the faculty, with representation from outside universities and allowance for participation of lower-ranking staff. On paper the new institution seemed a modest alteration of its forebear. Research and teaching on Africa, already underway, was intensified and an Institute of African Studies was proposed, its director to be Thomas Hodgkin, another who had served as secretary to the international commission and a widely respected student of African affairs in his own right. Things should have gone well. In fact the new university was launched in an atmosphere of increasing bitterness and mutual recrimination.[13]

Suspicion between government and university had gone too far, and rumor operated in place of communication. Morale sagged at Legon, where the findings of the commission were greeted with skepti-

cism; its conclusions were just what the regime wanted, it was said—
a smokescreen of generalities to mask dark purpose and provocative
action. There was frustration in government, as well. An interim council was appointed to smooth the transition from a single university
college to two universities and an additional university college to be
established at Cape Coast, yet the council failed to make much headway as Nkrumah repeatedly postponed its deliberations. Ghana's at-
torney general, the Englishman Geoffrey Bing, had recommended a
university patterned on the model of an American land-grant college,
and later made an attempt to introduce a social science course that
he regarded as more appropriate to the training of African civil servants, but these efforts came to nothing. Another of Bing's suggestions,
however, was put into effect, the result a sharp reaction at Legon and
an outcry of protest that was no less than international in extent.

For some time the government had wanted to rid the university
of a small number of faculty felt to be provocative or incompetent,
but the policy of life appointments as a basis for academic freedom
had prevented any action. Bing argued that with the divorce from
London and the establishment of an independent university, there
was no longer any legal impediment to dismissal. He counseled that
a letter terminating contract be sent to all of Legon's teaching staff,
with the prospect of immediate reappointment except in the few cases
regarded as unacceptable. Balme's successor as principal had already
resigned in the face of a persistent rumor that he was to be replaced
by Bing. Now, as the letter went out in May 1961, it reached a faculty
already supercharged with anxiety, yet with little freedom of action
since it was too late in the academic year to resign and seek a post
elsewhere. There were a few resignations, and six contracts terminated,
but most of the faculty remained, convinced that henceforth the university would be politically controlled both as to appointment and
curriculum.[14]

Their worst fears seemed justified. In June the progovernment
*Ghanaian Times* produced a lengthy editorial congratulating *Osagyefo*
Kwame Nkrumah on assuming office as university chancellor, then
fell to castigating the reactionary character of the defunct university
college. It was a bastion of bourgeois mentality, the *Times* asserted,
ignoring Marx and the exigencies of African economic development.
It featured the classics and falsified Africa's history in support of

British imperialism. It recruited conservative professors from Britain while discriminating against appointments of Africans. Now there would be a new era in the annals of academic freedom, the *Times* went on, taking account of African socialism and emphasizing the sciences, welcoming lecturers from all quarters, East and West, and producing at last young men and women prepared to help Ghana toward the way of socialism and to promote the redemption of Africa according to the doctrines of Nkrumah himself. "Africa is in revolutionary ferment . . . ," the *Times* exulted. "Higher education in Ghana has taken a qualitative leap. . . . Bravo to Osagyefo! Long live the New Ghana! Long live the African liberation movement!"[15]

In fact there was little immediate change and the basic structure of the institution remained largely unaltered. Professors taught the same courses in the same way. Admissions policy, degree structure, university autonomy, and freedom to pursue teaching and research survived much as before. The reasons for this were various. Balme's successor as principal had achieved little, partly because of strong faculty resistance to any alterations in the Balme program, partly due to a lack of understanding of what Nkrumah wanted for higher education in Ghana. Under Nana Kobina Nketsia the university structure remained untouched for different reasons. Nketsia had no previous experience in university administration and, in any case, saw his function essentially in closing the gap between campus and government, spending much of his time cultivating those in authority at party headquarters in Accra. The primary reason, however, was traceable to Kwame Nkrumah.[16]

### Nkrumah Chooses a Vice-Chancellor

The political system developed by Kwame Nkrumah and his associates in Ghana was a complex of forces. Power was diffused among factions within the Convention People's party, among related organizations like the civil service, judiciary, or armed forces, and among pressure groups such as business interests, teachers, or church leaders. Nkrumah possessed ultimate power; on any particular issue his word was final. He was also the locus of influences that competed for his support. As a practical matter his decision on a specific question represented a resolution of conflicting positions, not necessarily all that he wanted but all that might have been possible under the circumstances.

By disposition, moreover, Nkrumah was more compromiser than tyrant, one who was searching for consensus within the definition of his ultimate objectives. A sympathetic but acute observer, Thomas Hodgkin, had many conversations with Nkrumah, especially on the subject of higher education. "Whenever I talked to him about any issue that mattered," Hodgkin recalled, "he always gave the impression that there were various people who would have to be consulted. . . . Nkrumah can be regarded . . . as a Utopian." Hodgkin continued, "[He] wished to achieve revolutionary objectives, at both a Ghanaian and an African level, with quite inadequate resources. [He] believed that fundamental conflicts could be overcome by manipulation, that inadequacies in others could in the last resort be overcome by taking over their jobs himself, that fundamental problems could be resolved by admirable pronouncements and blueprints."

What Nkrumah attempted to do, therefore, was to place in controlling positions those individuals whose loyalty, reliability, and sympathy toward his ideas and objectives could be counted upon. "So long as the appointee was approved, enjoyed the confidence of party and president," Hodgkin observed, "he was given a remarkably free hand, permitted to go ahead and do his job in his own way. . . . Once he lost this confidence he was liable to be removed . . . or subjected to intermittent pressures and attacks from party and press."[17]

Nkrumah knew what kind of university he wanted. In 1961 he also seems to have known whom he wanted for permanent vice-chancellor at Legon. He had met Conor Cruise O'Brien on two previous occasions about the time of O'Brien's temporary association with the United Nations secretariat, and it was the latter that Nkrumah invited to assume direction of the University of Ghana. An experienced diplomat of scholarly achievement, O'Brien had just resigned from the secretariat following his controversial tenure as special United Nations representative in Katanga. Nkrumah had greatly admired O'Brien's actions over the Katangan affair and clearly regarded him as a person of unimpeachable academic credentials who would also understand Nkrumah's own objectives in higher education. Hodgkin had urged the appointment of a Ghanaian as vice-chancellor, but Nkrumah wanted international acceptance along with change and feared a Ghanaian academic who might come to share the strong distaste that most of the Legon faculty and student body held toward Nkrumah's own political beliefs and objectives. After some hesitation O'Brien accepted the post, obtaining at once the confidence of both the faculty and the government.

The honeymoon lasted for one year. O'Brien assumed his duties in the autumn of 1962 and quickly struck a new note over the old issue of academic freedom. With no previous experience in university administration, O'Brien may have had a somewhat idealized view of what a university should be, but he also recognized that universities differed over the world, that Ghanaians wanted and needed a school reflecting national independence and African objectives—something quite different from the "made in England" institution he had inherited. The university would change, therefore, O'Brien informed his faculty, adapting itself to a revolutionary mutation in the local environment—that is, to the vital shift from colonial status to national sovereignty. He urged his colleagues to support him in this position. This would have no effect on the concept of academic freedom, O'Brien went on, but academic freedom in practice would have to accommodate important qualifications. First, it could not be made to include privileges placing university faculty above the law. Second, it must not be an excuse to ignore the views of government regarding such matters as enrollment and curriculum.

For Nkrumah this was a good beginning and helped to enrich an already cordial relationship between chancellor and vice-chancellor. Legon and O'Brien were left to pursue their own affairs. At the end of the 1962–63 academic year, Nkrumah asked to visit the vice-chancellor at dinner, an unusual request that was meant as a gesture of full approval and confidence.[18]

The strength of the association between the two men was also its chief weakness. Both had similar objectives for the university, but both were determined to be active in their roles. A clash of wills would have occurred sooner or later, but in fact it was events outside the university that brought a chill to the relationship and introduced a period of deepening crisis involving public criticism and official interference that continued until O'Brien left the country two years later.

By the early sixties Ghana had entered a period of economic malaise, a vexing sequel to the high expectations that had brought Nkrumah to power and the nation to independence. Low production was fed by inefficiency, while extravagance and corruption in official places joined widespread smuggling—all weighing on the national economy, feeding popular frustration and disillusionment. In 1961 a major strike by rail and harbor workers reflected the prevailing mood and had to be forcibly suppressed. Though the problems were essentially economic, the official reaction was largely political. The opposition was harassed, its leaders imprisoned or driven into exile. Nkrumah became *Osagyefo,* the victorious warrior, redeemer and life president of the Republic of Ghana. The party reached out to control all phases of the nation's economic and social life, and became, in Nkrumah's own words, the nation itself.

All powerful, all encompassing, the party began to reveal internal divisions, as groups and individuals fought for power and its riches. Amidst ambient tension, intrigue vied with rumor and officials abruptly rose and fell from favor. Nkrumah himself was not immue. He became increasingly isolated, cut off from the popular pulse. Twice within two years attempts were made on his life.

Late in 1963 Nkrumah dismissed the chief justice of Ghana following the acquittal of two former ministers and a party official charged with conspiracy. In Ghana and elsewhere the dismissal was widely regarded as political, an unwarranted interference that effectively put an end to rule by law and judicial restraint. O'Brien disapproved of the action and he said so, a statement deeply resented by Nkrumah, who felt that public comments by his vice-chancellor should be restricted to the domain of university affairs.

There followed rapidly deteriorating relations between the government and the university, marked by interference in university business, press attacks, and at one point a mass demonstration of several thousand who were led to Legon by the organizing secretary of the Convention People's party. Nkrumah exercised the right as chancellor to make special professorial appointments and insisted on the dismissal and deportation of several faculty members regarded as inimical to national interests. The Institute of Education was transferred to the university college at Cape Coast without prior consultation, students were detained or threatened with withdrawal of their grants, and a Ghanaian professor was taken into custody. There was speculation that Nkrumah may have contemplated even more radical action—for example, the detachment of the Institute of African Studies from Legon to form the nucleus of an independent university, or the special advancement for

Legon staff members who were prepared to involve themselves with the institute that Nkrumah had formed at Winneba to create and give instruction in Nkrumahism, the ideology created to observe what Nkrumah regarded as the revolution of African independence.

Those actions taken, however, were regarded by O'Brien as a direct assault on behalf of political orthodoxy against the academic freedom he had vowed to defend. Under attack, he became defensive, his sympathies closing with those of his faculty, captive, as it were, of his own boyars. The university, insisted O'Brien, deserved a better fate as a center of learning dedicated to the interests of the nation, a place where the search for truth was pursued with intellectual and moral courage. In his valedictory remarks on leaving his post at the end of his contract in 1965, O'Brien stated more in sadness than in outrage that the autonomy of the university was under attack, its constitution ignored in important respects, its academic freedom damaged, and its future thereby jeopardized.

To an extent the hostility toward the university reflected an intense conflict among the small band of presidential advisors who were grouped in competition around Nkrumah. It was also a measure of Nkrumah's own determination to construct a socialist society with an appropriately trained leadership. In its ultimate form the image of the university was shaped in the concepts of Nkrumahism, a credo that has been criticized for its vagueness, inconsistencies, and contradictions. Though sometimes ill stated, the essential principles of Nkrumahism were not obscure—the end of neocolonial pressures, the construction of a socialist economy, and a political union of African states. If the university changed little during the Nkrumah years, it was not because there was no vision of a new society and a new learning, but because of the press of circumstances. Nkrumah's own gradualism combined with the natural inertia of established institutions, while differences within the ruling party contributed to delays that were created by opposition at the university and among some sections of the population at large.[19]

# 9

## Organizing Africana

### The Pros and Cons of African Studies

In September 1960, on the eve of national independence for Nigeria, a special commission on higher education submitted its long-anticipated report to the Nigerian Federal government. The report, *Investment in Education*, was concerned primarily with the training of high-level manpower in order that a newly independent African nation might achieve a rate of economic growth commensurate with its population, resources, and aspirations. Pragmatic in focus, the report nevertheless did not overlook the importance of humanistic studies, in this connection taking special note of the paucity at the time of university-level teaching and research on Africa. "The most obvious need for innovation in Nigerian universities is in the field of African studies. . . . The future of Nigeria is bound up with the future of Africa; and Nigeria's past lies in African history and folklore and language. It should be a first duty of Nigerian universities, therefore, to foster the study of African history and antiquities, its languages, its societies, its rocks and soils and vegetation and animal life."

Such a recommendation would seem unexceptionable, but to many at the time it smacked of iconoclasm and irresponsibility. Africa's new universities, founded by European colonial powers, had begun life largely preoccupied with the study of Western civilization. The zeal to establish impeccable academic standards had brought confusion between quality of education and curriculum content; in the British territories this resulted in mimicry of what was offered in England—honors degrees that centered on the civilization of Greece and Rome, history courses exploring the British past but ignoring the precolonial eras of Africa.

The commission was therefore turning away from the prevailing orthodoxies in Britain toward a point of view long held by many Africans since the days when Doctor Horton urged the idea of an African university with an African-based curriculum. "We recommend," the report continued, "that every university . . . have a department or institute of African studies." Such establishments would pursue research concerned with developing a body of knowledge to be used ultimately for undergraduate study. "We suggest that such an institute should as far as possible be interdisciplinary, and it should co-ordinate research being done by various departments in this vital field."[1]

The commission membership was mixed, part African, part British and American, and included K. O. Dike, the recently appointed principal of Nigeria's University College at Ibadan. British trained, Dike was wedded to the concept of superlative academic standards; at the same time he knew that Ibadan would have to take African studies seriously, that the subject of Africa would have to be pursued on a broad front of academic disciplines, and that, in any case, there was no intrinsic conflict between high standards and an African-centered curriculum. The commission chairman, Eric Ashby, and several other non-Africans, were enthusiastic advocates for an African studies institute. Ashby felt that Dike may have held back at first, inhibited momentarily by his British educational background. If so, it was a temporary hesitation. As Ashby later remarked, "[Dike] did enthusiastically back the recommendation in the end."

Retrospect sees more clearly what may not have been so evident at the moment. What possible objection could there be to university-based institutes charged with the encouragement and coordination of teaching and research dealing with aspects of the very continent in which the universities were located?

As it happened, there was a good deal of opposition to the commission's recommendation. To begin with, the majority of Europeans and many European-trained Africans who formed the first faculties of the new universities brought the limitations of their own education with them; they tended to assume the primacy and relevance—even the exclusive universality—of Western culture. It was often remarked at the time that, after all, there was nothing African about the laws of physics, or that philosophy was essentially logic, epistemology, and ethics, all of which applied equally in Timbuktu and Oxford. This parochial viewpoint was most forcefully expressed by David Balme, first principal of the University College, Gold Coast, who argued that there was but a single modern civilization, one that happened to have originated in Greece. "It is high time," he stated, "we stopped calling it European as though there were some other from which to distinguish it."[2]

There were other, less-bizarre objections, however, some voiced by Africans themselves. Here the argument was not directed against the study of Africa in its various manifestations; by 1960 that need was obvious enough to most of Ibadan's African faculty members. The difficulty arose over the prospect of special centers created for the study of Africa in universities where a major emphasis on African subjects might be expected in any case. Special institutes, embedded in the university structure, created special problems, it was claimed. They absorbed much-needed funds, established power bases that competed with academic departments, and contributed little to the classroom teaching that was the essential function of undergraduate programs.

The Nigerian historian, J. F. A. Ajayi, an innovative and longtime student of African civilizations, eventually became an outspoken critic of the special African studies institute. If Dike may have entertained some initial doubts about an institute for African studies, Ajayi was no less devoted than the Ibadan principal to fostering an African content for degree programs. What concerned Ajayi was the prospect of an establishment especially created in an African university to study African problems, as if all African studies could be encompassed in one institute. African studies, he insisted, should be the responsibility of every university department.

For Ajayi there were other complications. Permanent tenured staff with no teaching responsibilities and no limits to the timing or content of their research were less likely to produce materials needed in undergraduate instruction, he pointed out. What might such individuals achieve, Ajayi asked, if they were obliged to share their research with students and meet publication deadlines that were the customary lot of a university professor? Beyond this, said Ajayi, a special African studies institute created severe financial problems, first by drawing off funds supplied by governments or philanthropic foundations that might otherwise have been invested in departmental research and teaching, then by forcing the university to invest heavily in the overhead of a permanent institute once the sources of outside funding had been terminated.

Ajayi's doubts reflected genuine apprehension in academic circles that a formal institute of African studies would usurp university research functions, defining priorities and thereby depriving faculty members in conventional academic departments of opportunities to pursue their own study interests. If there had to be an institute, the argument ran, let it be limited severely to financial and administrative activities. With financial resources an institute could support study leaves for regular faculty while arranging for the invitation of visiting scholars. As an administrative agency it would be able to organize conferences and support publications; it could provide housing, transport, and research facilities, while coordinating studies of an interdisciplinary character.[3]

These were serious objections, but the proponents of African studies institutes marshaled a formidable defense of their own. One advocate in particular, Professor J. H. Kwabena Nketia of the University of Ghana, who has spent much of his professional life engaged in the institutional development of African studies, has had much to say on the imperatives of special centers for the study of African civilization.

Nketia's association with the then University College, Gold Coast, began in 1952 when he was appointed a research fellow in African studies, attached to the sociology department and charged with research into "African languages, music, dance and folklore." "[This] was certainly a tall order for one research fellow," Nketia was later to remark, and it made him in effect a one-man African studies institute. It also gave him the experience needed to test the necessity and practicality of such organizations, and in time to help create, and eventually to direct, the Institute of African Studies that came into being at the University of Ghana in 1962. As a research fellow Nketia not only pursued his own studies, he also engaged in dissemination of the results through radio, press, and public lectures; he prepared teaching materials for the schools; he sought out and encouraged both traditional and contemporary artists; and he served on a myriad of committees organized by government and centering on the establishment of an arts council for the propagation of African culture in Ghana.

Not surprisingly, Nketia came to see African studies in broad terms that transcended the parochial biases of any particular university campus. The creation of modern African states, he has remarked recently, requires cultural as well as material development with a focus on both the heritage of traditional societies and the creative thrust of the contemporary community. If we wait for these things to develop by themselves, Nketia continued, we run the risk of haphazard growth and aimless drift; the evident need therefore is for some form of institutional organization that will provide "national integration through artistic and other programs designed to encourage cultural interaction . . . in a national program for the arts."

Nketia's early work in African studies came during the surge of African independence movements following the Second World War. In Ghana this was the era when Nkrumah's concept, "African personality," paralleled in cultural affairs the planned economic development embodied in the slogan, "African socialism." Nkrumah saw the importance of cultural awareness in generating a desire for independence, and in creating a single coherent, cohesive new nation from the disparate peoples that made up the old Gold Coast colony. Under Nkrumah, independent Ghana soon bristled with agencies concerned with formulating a national cultural policy—an arts council, youth organizations and broadcasting facilities, ministries of education and culture, and eventually an institute of African studies based in the university at Legon. The concept of African personality, said Nketia, was meant to be at once liberating and creative, bringing into focus African alternatives to Western values and institutions that had been imposed upon subject peoples by colonialism. It was important to combat the claim to universality of Western culture, Nketia concluded, to put forward an African alternative that would assert a valid African civilization, both at home and abroad.[4]

This was very much what Dike had said, and others must have agreed for eventually special centers for the study and encouragement of indigenous African cultures appeared in many universities, from Khartoum to Kano, in Freetown and Nairobi, in Lagos or Lusaka. There were many shortcomings to support the criticism of the skeptics, but there were also solid achievements. Michael Crowder, who was associated with the direction of five such institutes in Nigeria and Sierra Leone, has mounted a spirited defense of their achievements. In the early independence years, Crowder points out, African universities were predominantly Western in the orientation of their curricula. The new institutes were able to break through the crust of this imposed limitation, to encourage a greater departmental activity by example as well as through the use of interdisciplinary seminars and public lectures. At Ibadan, Crowder continued, a renascence of interest in traditional art and dance followed recitals and exhibitions produced by the African studies institute at a time when such developments were largely scorned by students as "primitive juju," and departments, even with the best of intentions, were hampered by administrative rigidity within the university.

Such flexibility, says Crowder, allowed for unusual and impressive innovation. The institute at Ibadan introduced archaeological research that produced a number of important studies and, eventually led to the creation of an independent department of archaeology. At Ahmadu Bello University in Zaria, courses in drama, music, and archaeology followed the introduction of these fields at the Centre for Nigerian Cultural Studies, which was also responsible for founding the University museum. The University of Ife produced through its African institute annual arts festivals of international proportion and repute, while degree programs in Yoruba and African art had their beginnings in the university institute.

There were still wider, more important, implications, says Crowder. At Ife, as with most African universities, the campus lay several miles from the center of town, an isolated community with little extracurricular activity, its cultural life as undernourished as that of the city from which it took its name. Crowder and his coworkers at the Ife institute could not accept these conditions. A building was rented in town, a former bar that was renovated, and converted into a cultural center and restaurant, similar to the Mbari club that had been created in Ibadan some years earlier with the same purpose in mind. At the center something was always happening, Crowder continues—dances, lectures, exhibitions, plays. Here the Ife festivals were held, attended equally by townspeople and the academic community. Seats were at a premium and there were near riots on campus when students could not obtain tickets. It was an exciting time that extended beyond the university, for both the town and the campus came together in a mutual sharing of a nation's culture, traditional and modern, overcoming those antagonisms that have so often marred relations between townsmen and the academic population in their midst. In general, Crowder concludes, the African studies institutes brought to large numbers an awareness and sensitivity to the importance of their own culture, both to the old ways and to the new.[5]

*African Studies in Ghana*

With Kwame Nkrumah as head of state, the Institute of African Studies that emerged in Ghana was bound to have a political concept and purpose, yet the government that provided all funds for the Institute's activities never interfered in such internal affairs as program priorities or staff appointments, never insisted upon curriculum definition nor made use of the Institute as a means for extending control over the affairs of the university on Legon Hill. Certainly there was much dissatisfaction within the government and the Convention People's Party over the conduct of the University, but this disapprobation did not extend to the new institute, which from the first was directed by individuals much in sympathy with Nkrumah's own educational objectives. In any case, Nkrumah's interest in the Institute of African Studies went well beyond the tactical details of university governance, settling on the essential problem of educating a new African, breaking the shackles of a colonial mentality, reaffirming ancient African verities in a new world of free men.

At the Institute's inaugural ceremonies, Nkrumah enunciated the need for a fresh version of African studies.

> I would emphasise the need for a re-interpretation . . . of the factors which make up our past. . . . African studies . . . in the West have been largely influenced by the concepts of old style "colonial studies," and still to some extent remain under the shadow of colonial ideologies and mentality.
>
> Until recently the study of African history was regarded as a minor and marginal theme within the framework of imperial history.

The study of African social institutions and cultures was subordinated . . . to the effort to maintain the apparatus of colonial power. . . .

The study of African languages was closely related to the practical objectives of the European missionary and the administrator.

African music, dancing and sculpture were labelled "primitive art." They were studied in such a way as to reinforce the picture of African society as something grotesque, as a curious, mysterious human backwater, which helped to retard social progress in Africa and to prolong colonial domination over its peoples.

African economic problems, organisation, labour, immigration, agriculture, communications, industrial development—were generally viewed from the standpoint of the European interest in the exploitation of African resources, just as African politics were studied in the context of the European interest in the management or manipulation of African affairs. . . .

This Institute must surely . . . study the history, culture and institutions, languages and arts of Ghana and of Africa in new African centred ways—in entire freedom from the propositions and pre-suppositions of the colonial epoch. . . . We must re-assess and assert the glories and achievements of our African past and inspire our generation, and succeeding generations, with a vision of a better future.[6]

This was an old story, older perhaps than Nkrumah himself may fully have realized, for he was sounding a classic position, stated many times by former compatriots like Attoh Ahuma, Mensah Sarbah, or Casely Hayford. In his devotion to a renascent African culture Nkrumah was no different from these predecessors or in fact from such an apparent antagonist as his political rival, J. B. Danquah of the United Gold Coast Convention. What Nkrumah added were his favored elements from Marxist socialism, missing in the pronouncements of earlier pan-Africanists. He was also determined to channel all activities, cultural or otherwise, to the service of political action.

Even during the busy days in 1945 while occupied with the Fifth Pan-African Congress at Manchester, Nkrumah found time to politicize the recreational activities of a group of Ghanaians, mostly students, then living in England. It was an informal group that had come together for social reasons—to soften the pangs of homesickness during holidays like Christmas or Easter, to see a familiar face, exchange confidences over work and study, and arrange entertainment that featured the songs and dances of the old country. Nkrumah managed to have himself elected secretary of this Ghana Students Union and soon tightened up the organization, endowing it with political aims that distressed those who were concerned primarily with the diversions of social intercourse.

Later, as head of state, Nkrumah continued to utilize cultural activities to further his political aims. It was he who arranged for performances of dance groups from various parts of the country as part of the independence day celebrations in Accra. It was Nkrumah who dispatched performers abroad on repeated international tours as the "peaceful arm of his global politics and diplomacy."[7]

Similar considerations lay behind the creation of an Institute of African Studies. The idea of a special institute probably originated with Kofi Busia when Busia was a lecturer in sociology at Legon during the early days of the University College. The outcome at that time had been the appointment of Nketia as research fellow in African studies, but the idea of an institute persisted, emerging periodically in discussions prompted by faculty members concerned with the development of African materials for the teaching syllabus. When the special commission was convened in 1960 to offer suggestions for the establishment of an independent University of Ghana, one of its strongest recommendations was the formation of an institute that would be concerned with research and training in fields related to African civilization, past and present.

As a member of the commission's secretariat, Thomas Hodgkin was doubtless instrumental in recommending an African studies institute. In any case he was soon charged with drafting a specific set of proposals for program, staffing, and organization, and eventually he became the first director when the Institute of African Studies of the University of Ghana commenced activities in 1962. Nevertheless, as Hodgkin insisted, the idea was supported in many quarters. "It came into being," said Hodgkin, "because Kwame [Nkrumah] and others in the cpp. . . . in the university, and . . . in the nation thought it was important that an African university should really develop work in this field, that there should be fundamental work in . . . languages and

arts, in history, sociology, and economics." It was an institute devoted
to cultural studies, Hodgkin continued, but it was an essentially political move. "The idea that people need to be trained in research in African history, politics, and arts . . . has a political purpose. It is . . .
to create a new kind of African . . . in order to break away from . . .
being cut off from one's own culture."[8]

Following the recommendations of the special commission Hodgkin
formulated plans for an institute that he hoped would be consonant
with Nkrumah's concept of "intellectual decolonization." Basically, the
institute was concerned with graduate instruction, offering a two-year
master's degree designed to accommodate prospective university or
secondary school teachers, individuals interested in journalism, those
seeking diplomatic careers or posts with international agencies, and
advanced students who wished to proceed eventually to work for a doctorate in a particular discipline. The course of study permitted concentration but also stressed a broad exposure to insure competence in a
number of fields.

Offerings were organized into four main groupings—languages and
linguistics, history, social and political philosophy, and humanities.
Each of these was further subdivided, history, for example, beginning
with Ghana, then spreading out as in a series of concentric circles to
take in much of the African continent, while reaching back into prehistory and examining related fields such as Islam or historical methodology. Again, the division of social and political philosophy dealt
with such divergent subjects as precolonial state systems, traditional
religions and philosophies, and modern nationalist movements, urban-
ization, and economic modernization.

Through such diversity, there was, nevertheless, a constant emphasis
on unity and coherence.

It is impossible [said Hodgkin] to study seriously the history,
institutions, languages, arts . . . of the peoples of . . . modern
Ghana without exploring their interconnections with the wider
West African region—and, at a further remove, with Northern
and Eastern Africa, with the Muslim and Christian worlds. . . .
There is, further, the interdependence of present and past: the
necessity for those whose main interest is in contemporary African
phenomena and problems to attempt to understand these in his-

torical depth; to realize that the so-called "new states" or "new nations" of modern Africa are unintelligible unless they are studied in relationship to the predecessor societies of the pre-colonial period.

In terms of organization the institute was designed to be an integral part of the University of Ghana at Legon, its course offerings and staff appointments subject to the same scrutiny by appropriate faculty bodies as those of the other divisions of the university. The institute received a separate budget, however, administered by the university but expressly earmarked for institute purposes. Although the Institute of African Studies was based at Legon, it was understood that its responsibilities would ultimately extend to assisting the newly formed Kwame Nkrumah University of Science and Technology at Kumasi and the university college that came into being at Cape Coast.

The institute's academic program was based upon seminars and tutorials, the former designed primarily for the master's matriculants but open to other qualified students. In addition, there was to be a mandatory one-year survey of African civilization, attended by all undergraduates and taught by members of the teaching departments as well as those associated with the institute. This was in fact a compromise solution, for Hodgkin had urged initially a foundation year for each undergraduate, its purpose the study of African civilizations, but such an arrangement would have meant a four-year undergraduate degree; hence the survey course was substituted in the form of a supplement to the more conventional three-year program. It was a popular device, and similar programs soon appeared in a number of Africa's new universities.

All in all, plans at Legon were ambitious, involving a good deal of basic research, breaking new ground in then little-known fields. Staff appointments necessarily reflected research priorities, concentrating, for example, on the history of the states of the Western Sudan, on political, ethical, and metaphysical beliefs of selected West African peoples approached through a study of their languages, on comparative studies of political systems, both precolonial and modern, or on African literature, considered both from aesthetic and historical-sociological viewpoints.[9]

As a center of serious research on Africa, the institute quickly began to attract interested scholars and to produce important work in a number of fields. To take one example, Hodgkin brought together a fine collection of Arabic manuscripts gathered mainly in the northern territories of Ghana, a resource that was of critical assistance to Professor Ivor Wilks in his seminal examination of the influence of Islam in Ashanti. Again, Margaret Field's studies of mental illness among migrant workers was conducted under the aegis of the institute. Hodgkin collaborated with the eminent Africanist Basil Davidson to begin work on a history of Africa, while research went forward recording stool histories in Ghana, particularly studying the society and culture of the area flooded by the Volta dam project.

Efforts were made to bring scholars in residence from Africa and elsewhere. Invitations went out to authorities like Ahmadu Hampate Ba of Mali, Jamal Muhammad Ahmad of Sudan, and Bereket Hapte Selassie of Ethiopia. At various times the institute played host to Polly Hill, the specialist in African rural economics, the anthropologist Peter Morton-Williams, an authority on Yoruba society, G. S. P. Freeman-Grenville, who had written extensively on the subject of the Swahili coast of East Africa, and the historian, Joseph Ki-Zerbo of Upper Volta. Though there was initial antagonism toward the institute on the part of some members of the teaching departments, there was also much cooperation involving exchange of faculty and sharing of research and teaching responsibilities.

The international appeal of the institute program and faculty was reflected as well in its student body. In addition to large, well-attended summer sessions for foreign students, the regular enrollment of about twenty-five master's candidates was drawn from several continents. In 1963, for example, in addition to Ghanaians there were six Americans, one Nigerian, one Liberian, two Poles, and one Japanese.[10]

Such swift-paced beginnings would have been difficult to maintain in any case, but Ghana's growing political and economic troubles affected the affairs of the institute as they did the university, higher education more generally, and national development at all levels. Hodgkin had understood his appointment to be temporary, and he left in 1965 to be succeeded by J. H. Nketia, only a few months before Nkrumah's fall from power. It was an unenviable and difficult position for the new director, especially when the university administration decided, with government support, to conduct a review of the Institute's work. Fortunately,

Kofi Busia was chosen for the task; both informed and sympathetic, Busia brought in a favorable report, a vote of confidence that secured the institute's future, enabling Nketia to continue its activities, assured of its position and permanence.

For Nketia this meant not only maintaining the directions of research and teaching initiated by Hodgkin but also carrying on the important humanistic elements of the institute's program that had emerged chiefly in Nketia's own creation, the School of Music and Drama. Although an integral part of the Institute of African Studies, the school had in fact a long history of its own that quite antedated the institute and drew inspiration from a wide and diverse variety of sources.

First among these was the composer Ephraim Amu, whose patriotic songs contributed much to the independence struggle. Amu published his first volume of compositions in 1933; he was, in fact, like the sculptor, Oku Ampofo, both creator and source of encouragement to others, his influence extending to Nketia when the latter was still a schoolboy during the late 1930s. Nketia himself was another important contributor, not only as the founder and first director of the school but also through the patient accumulation of musical materials during his long apprenticeship as research fellow in the department of sociology. From the first, Nketia insisted that scholarship be more than an end in itself. He realized the importance of collection and analysis of research materials; even more, however, he saw them as the means to the development of new African music. A program for training musicians— composers and performers—was essential.

Of course, music was but a beginning. There was the dance, Africa's essential art form. There was literature with its myths, its fables, its epics, and its parables. There were the fine arts and design. Finally, there was theater, sacred and profane, formal or casual, to which all the arts ultimately contributed.

During these formative years Ghana was well favored with talented individuals to fill the demands of various fields in the arts. In addition to Amu and Nketia, to Ampofo and his Akwapim group, there was Efua Sutherland, embarked on her theater projects and encouraging new impulses of creative writing through the literary review, *Okyeame*. There were the graduates of the School of Art at Achimota College, founded by the imaginative expatriate, H. V. Meyerowitz. There was A. M. Opoku, a student and colleague of Meyerowitz, who ultimately turned his talents so productively to the medium of dance. There was Joe de Graft, Mrs. Sutherland's coworker in drama. There were numerous others; these were the ones, however, that Nketia brought together, some to form the nucleus of his school, others to advise and assist in their areas of speciality.

The emergence of the School of Music and Drama was by no means a foregone conclusion. The years directly preceding and following independence in Ghana were years of ferment in which many ideas and institutions took form, some prospering, some losing their vitality, many quickly changing shape and substance. As usual Nkrumah was a potent and persistent instigator. On his initiative an arts council was founded that, in 1962, was incorporated as the Institute of Art and Culture, charged with coordinating and encouraging traditional arts and culture, and with promoting another Nkrumah innovation, a National Theatre Movement. There was, as well, the Ashanti Cultural Centre in Kumasi and the Society of African Culture, a Ghanaian branch of the black unity movement that had originated in the Sorbonne Congress sponsored by *Présence Africaine* in 1956.

Such a multiplicity of associations brought uncertainty over the division of function and responsibility. Nkrumah, for example, wanted a systematic and completely rewritten compilation of the traditional Ananse spider folktales, but which organization might best administer such a vast undertaking? The National Theatre Movement was designed to emphasize performance and new production of traditional materials wherever these existed, responsibility for encouragement and definition falling to the arts council and its successor, the Institute of Art and Culture. Such a large and amorphous enterprise was complication enough, but there were also plans for a national orchestra, the embellishment of hotels with art objects that might have sales appeal to tourists, cultural festivals, lectures and demonstrations in connection with the national museum in Accra, public programs featuring concerts, dance recitals, puppet shows, and lectures, as well as classes in such various activities as playwriting and drumming, art or drama, traditional dancing and crafts.[11]

Conceived in the heat of national independence, rapidly proliferating ideas and projects threatened chaos, but to Nketia it seemed clear that successful performance in the arts was based ultimately upon research and training, and he was able to persuade the Institute of Art and Culture to support a unit within the Institute of African Studies devoted to these purposes. When the Institute of African Studies opened its doors in 1962, therefore, it did so with a section devoted to the humanities, which quickly emerged as the School of Music and Drama.

As part of the Institute of African Studies, the School of Music and Drama was able to maintain a flexibility of activity not possible in the more narrowly conceived university teaching departments. To begin with, there were numerous courses of study available to suit both academic and practical needs. The music program, dealing in both Western and African music—as well as theory, composition, and performance—offered training that ranged from elementary courses to advanced musicology, along with formal study for matriculated university students to be applied toward the general university degree. The dance program presented work in modern dance techniques, dance notation, stagecraft, and music that complemented a basic emphasis on African dance idioms. Similarly, drama could be studied at different levels of sophistication, involving such fields as speech, acting, play analysis, and the technical aspects of production.

All this was designed to train teachers for the national school system as well as performers in musical ensembles and orchestras, in dance and drama troupes. The emphasis was on performance and composition, stressing African materials. It was not happenstance, therefore, that the faculty consisted of practicing artists like Amu, Nketia, and A. A. Mensah in music, A. M. Opoku in dance, and Efua Sutherland and Joe deGraft for theater and literature. In like vein the school became the home of the professional company, the Ghana Dance Ensemble, and a close association was maintained with Efua Sutherland's Drama Studio and Experimental Theatre.

Not that research was neglected. Fieldwork went forward on a number of fronts. Recording of traditional music and oral sources concentrated particularly on the popular "highlife" idiom. In the field of dance, the social background of dance styles was studied along with form and dynamics, and an archive of film and dance notation provided raw material for future study. The traditional literary media of folktales and minstrel poetry were explored hand in hand with analysis of modern writing forms, while drama students examined village ceremonies and festivals, and religious rites as a basis for development of modern dramatic writing.

Flexibility in the School of Music and Drama showed itself in another way. Staff members at all levels were accomplished performers. They were available, therefore, to organize and participate in community programs for the training of amateur actors, playwrights, dancers, and musicians; to assist in the development of children's drama, to organize seminars, creative writing workshops, or classes in dancing and drumming wherever they were needed.

These activities were regarded as much more than the relaxation of academic powers. "Since it is from Ghanaian communities that members of the institute acquire their knowledge of Ghanaian traditions," Nketia has pointed out, "it became important for the institute's faculty to show their respect and gratitude to the custodians of culture who helped its research personnel." Faculty from the school, therefore, was available for performance at important civic events such as public funeral ceremonies, chiefly investiture, or regional festivals. More than that, the institute was a resource of information on cultural matters. Through its library and archives, it could advise individuals and communities on such diverse questions as how properly to tie a traditional cloth, which were correct forms in naming or baptismal ceremonies, or what meanings were conveyed by patterns woven or sculpted in the handicrafts of a region. These were more than antiquarian details. They developed community stability and pride. They evoked understanding among peoples seeking to give birth to new and viable nations.[12]

### The African Studies Institute—University of Ibadan

The successes of the Institute of African Studies at Legon came from resourceful direction that supported Nkrumah's design for a revitalized Africa; its failures were a reflection more of external forces than internal weaknesses. In Nigeria similar aspirations evoked similar efforts, but the institute that emerged at the University of Ibadan never was able to match either its own hopes or the early achievements of the Ghanaians. The aspirations of each were remarkably similar; at Ibadan the execution was faulty.

By the time K. O. Dike succeeded to the principalship of University College, Ibadan in October 1960, he had resolved as thoroughly as possible to Africanize the university, changing forever the carbon-copy British model on which it had been conceived. "Dike is determined during his tenure as principal to give an authentic African character to the University College. It must be integrated into the environment." Such was the impression Dike gave one observer at the time, an impression that Dike himself was later to confirm. During the colonial era, Dike said, the educational system was patterned closely on European models following European syllabi; more than that, the system instilled in Africans thus educated unconscious assumptions concerning the inferiority of African culture and institutions in contradistinction to the unchallenged superiority of all things European.

> We were brought up on the kind of history books like Alan Burns' *History of Nigeria.* . . . There are almost unconscious attempts, almost European assumptions, that the history of Nigeria or West Africa began with an advent [Europe]. . . . That again is born of the fact that they were bringing up a community of educated Africans who began to accept these European impressions about our society, and who became so European-centered in their thinking and in their work, in their dress. When you talk about anything good in your society, it doesn't sink in. . . . We have to begin . . . to reeducate our own people, our own children, that what they've been taught by the missionaries may not be all right . . . that their past is not something of which they should be ashamed. That was in my mind. I remember it very well.

Here was Nkrumah again—a different African man but the same African voice. "I used to be surprised," Dike continued,

> to enter the home of a lecturer in Ibadan and hear the wife and husband speaking English to their children. It made me feel really depressed. . . . Everybody must have a mother tongue. What's the point of trying to talk as if to say, Ibo, your mother tongue, is barbaric, savage. . . . One of the things that made me think of having institutes of African studies isn't just blind . . . imitation

of . . . institutes that are found in American . . . or European universities. . . . It's really this . . . need for the African to recover from the culture shock of the colonial times, to begin to look at his own inheritance in a healthier way.[13]

The idea of an institute existing as a unit within the corporate body of the University College was no novelty. Already several had been established at Ibadan, mostly concerned with research and training in specialized areas. The Nigerian Institute of Social and Economic Research, to take one example, had functioned for a number of years as a center for studies in the social sciences, and a place where independent research workers come to Nigeria might find an academic base. It was linked to the teaching faculty through the person of its director, who was the Professor of Economics. Its expenses were met through a subvention from the Nigerian Federal government.

The Institute of Social and Economic Research operated to a considerable degree in isolation from the activities of the academic departments. Dike proposed an Institute of African Studies of quite opposite purpose. What was needed, Dike argued, was not a segregated research center but one that acted as catalyst, innovator, and encourager—bringing departments together in interdisciplinary collaboration, aiding the work of scholars already engaged in research that enriched their teaching, and charting new areas for investigation. Such an institute could provide seminars that easily crossed the lines of academic disciplines, raising questions and stimulating lines of inquiry otherwise unnoticed. It could furnish free time and other forms of assistance for teaching faculty who wished to pursue their particular research interests. It could open up promising fields not covered by current academic offerings. It would be, in short, a device to aid those departments already engaged in African studies and to encourage others to turn in that direction.[14]

The Institute of African Studies at Ibadan was founded in July 1962. With initial financial support from American philanthropic foundations, it quickly began a range of activities. Research professors were appointed in linguistics and archaeology, and a number of research fellows were soon at work on a variety of projects—historical research schemes in eastern and northern Nigeria, Yoruba oral literature, industrial relations in the mining industry, and a Nigerian atlas. There was support as well for an Ibo dictionary, while an impressive number of distinguished Africanists were invited to lecture under the auspices of the institute. In addition, a series of conferences and seminars was organized for both public and specialized audiences. One, for example, involved an elaborate one-week symposium on Nigerian culture and history for members of the Nigerian foreign affairs ministry. Another, principally for linguists, dealt with the use of the mother tongue in literacy.

The institute provided a special librarian to assist with the Africana collection of the main library, and a publications program was instituted in collaboration with the Ibadan University Press and other publishing houses that produced a number of important studies. Finally, the institute took responsibility for the university's collection of African art, not only with an active acquisitions program but also through displays placed in various locations throughout the university campus.[15]

Such an impressive range of activity was supplemented by special research grants for members of the teaching faculty. Here the program came close to the heart of the original concept; as Dike had conceived the institute's functions, it would break new ground where opportunities presented themselves, but in such a way as to strengthen and unify the research and teaching of the university at large. Unfortunately, far from becoming a cohesive agent, the institute gradually became competitive, its activities separated, and with a steadily decreasing impact on the rest of the university. It took many years— involving Dike's departure from Ibadan, a civil war in Nigeria, and other tribulations—but eventually the institute sank into a lethargy, isolated, largely ignored, and of negligible influence in academic or national affairs.

What happened? To begin with, an institute devoted to African studies was resented and opposed by academic departments even before it came into existence. Such rivalry was natural, and it certainly existed at Legon as well as at Ibadan. The institute at Legon, however, enjoyed strong leadership from its two directors, Thomas Hodgkin and J. H. Nketia, and they were able largely to offset the natural competition from other components within the university. This was not the case at Ibadan. Dike had originally planned for a proven scholar and administrator to guide the institute, and he had hoped to recruit Kofi Busia of Ghana, then living in exile in Europe during the Nkrumah years. When this appointment failed to materialize, Dike assumed the directorship himself, a fatal error as it developed, since his many responsibilities as principal and vice-chancellor of the university made it impossible for him to give sufficient attention to a difficult and delicate job.

Part of the complaint of the teaching departments was that the institute competed with and duplicated their efforts; another was that they had no control over its activities. Technically, this was not so since the institute at Ibadan was assisted by an advisory council that was broadly representative; too broadly, was the complaint, for it contained members from departments only casually interested in African affairs. In the judgment of those faculties more directly concerned with African fields of study, the council became too permissive and uncritical in matters of program and personnel.

The issue of personnel at the institute came to be a particularly sore point. An institute chiefly concerned with providing released time and financial aid to support the research of teaching faculty, such a facility might well have been widely welcomed. The Institute of African Studies at Ibadan, however, quickly developed an impressive establishment of its own, including three tenured research professorships, a sizable number of research fellows, diverse junior staff such as drivers, porters, and clerical help, and finally a building of its own. This was an expensive enterprise that became particularly burdensome once the initial external assistance ended and the institute, with its staff and appurtenances turned to the university budget to compete with others for available funds. Those critical of the institute were particularly irked by the fact that two of the research professorships, those in linguistics and sociology, merely duplicated strength that already existed in departments concerned with those disciplines. There were still other issues. Much of the program of the institute seemed scattered and unfocused; in attempting too much it fell into the danger of achieving too little. In any case its extracurricular activities were often criticized as doubtful of purpose within the conventional range of university functions.

This may have been a misguided judgment, for one objective of the institute was to break the university out of the constraints of too-rigid programmatic orthodoxy. Nevertheless, opposition persisted. Few members of the teaching faculty applied for research assistance, a curious omission born, perhaps, of suspicion that recipients would be obliged to devote their time to projects defined by the institute in preference to their own research interests. No doubt this was an unwarranted fear, but it is equally clear that the institute, with its own priorities and faculty, was bound to favor its own research activities rather than those of others. In the long run this proved to be divisive.[16]

# 4

*A Modern African Civilization*

# 10

## The African Personality and Europe

*Identity Quandaries*

The anticipation of political independence that greatly stimulated African humanists brought forth a surprising consistency in their message. We must reach back, most insisted, and use the past to insure the future. Neocolonialism can be cultural as well as economic; Europe can offer political freedom and still subject the soul of a people. There must be a spiritual emancipation to accompany constitutional sovereignty and insure economic self-direction. And this freeing of the African's essential nature rests upon the reaffirmation of African culture, upon a resurrected African civilization that revives the ancient qualities in forms that deal with the exigencies of the present and the future.

But were they correct, these artists and musicians, writers, historians, or educators, in arguing that the past contained its own merits, still relevant in the modern world? Was David Balme wrong and Negritude right? Was there a viable African civilization? Did the African personality really exist?

The doctrines of Negritude came into prominence during the 1950s, accompanying the prospect of political independence, and it was during these same years that Nkrumah enunciated his concept of African Personality. Negritude stressed cultural singularity, even exclusiveness; by African Personality, Nkrumah seems to have meant no more than an African presence in the world, a continent that made firm representation of its wants and needs in the councils of international affairs.

Some, both in and out of the Negritude movement, felt that the African Personality signified more than this, that there was in fact a special character or quality to the black man. The African environment brought forth a different kind of person; such was the assertion of Léopold Senghor, and the corollary went further—buried deep within the genes might be traits that set black men apart from all others. External appearance was the mark of a fundamental internal distinction.

It required no prodigy of imagination to envision such uniqueness. All peoples seem to regard themselves as unusual and superior. Tocqueville tells us that Americans never tired of proclaiming their special virtues. The French formulated the concept of assimilation because they were confident in the transplendent character of their culture; by contrast, the British stood apart from the "natives," but for the very same reason. If the white man was so sure of his preeminence, why not the black man as well?

The question implied more than a simple matter of identity. The issue was deeply existential, an African self-image that opposed and defied the image inflicted by others—outsiders, Europeans, slavers and soldiers—who imposed colonial rule and their own sense of superiority. Would Africa become a carbon copy of Europe? Could it absorb attractive elements of Western civilization—advanced technology, for example—without abandoning its own innate character? Worse still, would Africans assume the stereotype created by ignorance and contempt, a barbarous continent of no distinction and small consequence to the rest of the world? Could political freedom go it alone? Did not sovereignty necessitate a concurrent declaration of cultural independence?

## The Assault of Scientific Racism

The struggle against European prejudice was long-lived. In mid-nineteenth-century Africanus Horton had fought a rearguard action against the racist pretensions of European anthropologists whose attack on Africa's psyche and civilization paralleled the political and economic incursions on African territory. During the era of colonial rule the pressure of European scientific racism increased both in intensity and sophistication. Firmly in control on the ground, European scientists could examine at leisure: testing mine workers in South Africa, studying the effects of malnutrition in Kenya, observing epidemics on the Gold Coast, or analyzing tribal taboos in Rhodesia. The older versions of scientific racism had been naive by comparison—studies based on phrenology and cephalic indexes, on linguistic traits or cultural variations, and always concluding with assertions of European superiority that rarely troubled with factual evidence, let alone even-handed analysis.[1]

Later studies had more pretensions and seemingly were supported by firmer scientific sanction. To begin with, there was the authority of Darwin and Hegel, the former's theory of evolutionary survival and progress made to demonstrate a racial hierarchy marked by the white man's superiority, the latter's dialectics describing the process that had led to this same end. The study of anthropology soon made use of these points of departure, a notable example the work of the early twentieth-century French ethnographer, Lucien Lévy-Bruhl. Lévy-Bruhl utilized Hegel to develop the racial opposites of Western and "primitive" societies. The Western mind, he argued, is characterized by rational thought, logical progression, and the ability to develop abstract ideas, while "primitive" man is "pre-logical," posing a negative opposite to the Western mind—lacking rationality, incapable of abstraction, and relying on myth and mysticism to describe and explain the objective phenomena of his surrounding world.

Lévy-Bruhl's ethnocentric anthropology provided ample justification for European colonial rulers and was frequently supported by the findings of anthropologists, sociologists, social psychologists, and medical doctors dispatched to Africa to assist colonial administrations in the effective governing of ward societies. The widespread incidence of disease throughout the continent suggested the need for medical facilities and personnel concerned with both treatment and research. Much of the medical research was biological, but a number of interested workers were drawn to psychological problems, often with social as well as biological overtones. There was, among others, Simon Biesheuvel testing intelligence in South Africa. There were the anthropologists S. F. Nadel, working among the Nupe of Nigeria, and the celebrated Captain Rattray, with his many studies of Ashanti. East Africa was represented by Dr. H. C. Trowell in Kampala and J. C. Carothers, who long presided over the Mathari Mental Hospital in Nairobi.

In 1953 Carothers produced a monograph, *The African Mind in Health and Disease,* that appeared under the auspices of the World Health Organization. Subtitling his work, "A Study in Ethnopsychiatry," Carothers sought to summarize the state of psychiatric knowledge in Africa, a field to which he had contributed in significant measure. With the caution and detachment that characterizes treatises of this genre, Carothers presented an impressive battery of data, conclusions, and hypotheses. What emerged, however, was a statement that differed little in essence from those earlier, less-discriminating tracts that had represented the scientific racism of the nineteenth century.

Carothers was careful to present his own background as a South African who was educated in England and who spent much of his professional career in East Africa, for, as he said, in a study of this type, one's experiences "cannot fail to colour . . . assessment of the situation." He then addressed the problem. Was there any essential difference between African and European mentality? If so, could it be identified?

Some difference is almost certain, Carothers began, given a 30,000 year divergence between black and white, and even if the eminent Swedish sociologist Gunnar Myrdal argues that no racial psychic variations may be presumed at birth, the potentiality for these surely exists in genetic form, to be developed through later experience. Carothers then presented several studies of brain size, shape, and complexity, arriving at the conclusion that such differences as were apparent had no identifiable psychic consequences. Nevertheless, one study showing variations in cortical thickness was of possible significance, for, as he pointed out, both the cerebral cortex and the epidermis derive from the same elementary embryonic material.[2]

If physiological variations were inconclusive, could psychological variations be identified? Carothers cited a wide range of studies into temperament, intelligence, and aptitudes that painted a consistently dim European view of the African personality. "The African," said Carothers, has been described as conventional; highly dependent on physical and emotional stimulation; lacking in spontaneity, foresight, tenacity, judgment and humility; inapt for sound abstraction and for logic; given to phantasy and fabrication, and, in general, as unstable, impulsive, unreliable, irresponsible, and living in the present without reflection or ambition, or regard for the rights of people outside his own circle. To counteract these ruderies, he has also been described as cheerful, stoical, self-confident, sociable, loyal, emotionally intuitive, and eloquent, and as bearing no grudges and having an excellent memory, a large vocabulary, and an aptitude for music and dance.

These were images specified by various observers, all European and admittedly bringing to bear European criteria of judgment and social behavior, all sustaining the earlier observations of Lévy-Bruhl. Perhaps, Carothers admitted, such personality characteristics were more apparent than real, the result of alien standards of judgment. But no. Carothers did not shrink from a controversial conclusion. For him, as for most observers, the African character clearly differed from the European. The causes were partly to be found in disease and malnutrition, but mainly, said Carothers, they were cultural.

Usually the European child is reared by his immediate parents, Carothers continued, rather than by members of a large extended family. While at an early age there is a certain appeal to magical concepts like Santa Claus, much of causation for the growing child comes to rest upon an understanding of natural phenomena as explained and encouraged by parents. In this fashion standards of behavior become linked to the perception of consistent general principles, learned not only at home but later through a wider world of school and diverse social contacts. The introduction of letters, of balls and building blocks, and of mechanical toys add practical experience that emphasizes spatiotemporal relations and mechanical causation, teaching the laws that govern the material world and instilling a conviction in the efficacy of self-reliance. What emerges, Carothers made note, is an individual who functions by self-direction and personal judgment, who understands his material and social relationship with the world around him, and who behaves with minimum appeal to set rules.

By contrast, said Carothers, the African child is directed by a dense network of rules and taboos, the reasons usually given in mythical or magical terms that discourage speculation as to causation and emphasize the necessity for placating particular wills, both living and dead. Such a system smothers the individual ego, stressing social integration at the expense of cerebral inquiry. African education is "verbal, musical, dramatic, and emotional," insisted Carothers, ". . . the African lives largely in the world of sound, in contrast to the European, who lives largely in the world of sight." This distinction is crucial, Carothers went on, for whereas the world of sound is personal and emotional, vision introduces irrelevance and continuity that forces the understanding of cause and effect.[3]

Reared therefore as a component in a rigid social framework, the African performs according to prescribed formulas rather than through observation and reason. When confronted by situations outside the experience of local custom, he becomes impulsive, said Carothers, reacting to the immediate stimulus rather than to a sum of stored experience, present perception, or future implication.

For Carothers the consequences were manifold. First, there was mental uniformity that paralleled cultural sameness, a cultural sameness that led straight to cultural stagnation. Next, reliance on detail rather than principle encouraged good rote memory, but preoccupation with the spoken word also resulted in a concentration on external stimuli that bordered on hypnosis. Lacking unifying principles, the African tended to mislearn or misapply technical knowledge, but a preoccupation with present phenomena had its compensations. The African, admitted Carothers, was rarely absentminded and radiated a personal charm characterized by quick sympathy and a tendency to forgive and forget real or imaginary wrongs.

Despite the Eurocentric bias of his conclusions, Carothers tried to be evenhanded. "No claim is made that the European approach to life is better," he conceded. "It is achieved at a cost. . . . It may not even be more true." Nevertheless, "African culture has developed on such lines as to reduce the exigencies of living to a minimum, and . . . the integration which the rural African . . . achieves is founded on the continuing support afforded by his culture and has but little independent existence in himself."[4]

Moving on to examine the reasons for such vast differences between the mental makeups of Europe and Africa, Carothers became frankly speculative. Preliterate societies, he suggested, required social discipline for survival, but widespread disease and malnutrition apparently tend to decrease individual self-control and increase direct egotism; hence "the stern repression of individual expression and the rigid canalization of incentives of preliterate cultures." For other observers, however, the reasons lay elsewhere, deep in the psyche of primitive man, to be exhumed and explained through psychiatric techniques and analysis.

Shortly after the conclusion of the Second World War, a severe and stubborn revolt broke out in Madagascar, startling the French colonial administration and prompting, among other reactions, a study of the Malagasy under colonialism, *La Psychologie de la Colonisation.* Published in 1950 and issued a few years later in English translation under the revealing title, *Prospero and Caliban,* the work was produced by a French anthropologist, O. Mannoni, who turned from ethnography to psychiatry to explain both colonialism and the response of a subject people.

The theories that Mannoni developed were based on the psychology of dependence. Like the child who relies upon its parents for its needs and sense of security, so the primitive society, said Mannoni, requires a strong authority both for survival and psychic stability. In its classical, precolonial form, this higher authority was embodied in the ancestors who offered health, fertility, and good harvests in return for loyalty and devotion. There was no sense of inferiority, only the stability of a complicated social system—static but functional; the fulfillment of the dependency need was sufficient to bring individual and group contentment. When the white man first arrived on the scene, far from injecting a jarring note, he reinforced the dependency need, introducing a colonial regime that provided another object on which dependence could be fixed, thereby further strengthening social and psychological stability.

There was reciprocity in this relationship, said Mannoni, for the colonialist, psychologically dominant, needed the dependent as much as the dependent required the authority of the colonial system. The French settler, trader, missionary, or administrator who came to Madagascar were products of a society wherein childhood dependency gave way to adult individualism and self-assertion, but with individualism came insecurity and a sense of inferiority that was most happily assuaged in the dependency offered by the Malagasy colonial population. It was an ideal complement, Mannoni went on, until the equilibrium was upset by postwar reforms, which injected a greater political freedom that also suggested the need for initiative and responsibility. As a result, the Malagasy subject came to feel deserted and insecure, his insecurity feeding a growing sense of inferiority. Much as he may have disliked the harsh restraints of forced labor and arbitrary justice, he resented his abandonment even more.

Thus, the bonds of dependence were broken and the individual was free, but free, like Shakespeare's Caliban, only to wander in the pathless woods without guidance, without stability. As with Caliban, love was converted to hatred and erupted in the violence of revolt. Mannoni does not mention them, but contemporary risings like the postwar disturbances in the Gold Coast and Ivory Coast, or the Mau Mau of Kenya might be ascribed to the same causes, a sense of betrayal arising from the relaxation of colonial controls.[5]

### Black Orpheus

Like Carothers, Mannoni made a sincere effort to understand the differences, as he saw them, in European and African mentality, and, like Carothers, he tried to avoid the error of those earlier observers who ordered racial dissimilarity on a comparative scale of good and bad. Nonetheless unconscious prejudices intruded. The European was insecure and infantile, in need of reassurances; hence he became the aggressive colonialist seeking dominance. The "native" was reasonably well-adjusted in his dependency but was primitive and childlike. It was a perfect justification for colonialism—the noble savage ruled by the ignoble, but civilized European.

When Africans explored their own culture and mentality, comparing it with that of the European, it is not surprising that they granted differences but not inferiority. What may at first sight be arresting, however, is that they borrowed a good deal of their argument from Europeans, in the process conceding much to European assertions of cultural and intellectual superiority.

During the nineteenth-century height of Europe's scientific racism, the most thoroughgoing presentation of the African position came from the pen of Edward W. Blyden, the educator and statesman from Liberia. Blyden began by accepting the European contention that the world's races differed both physically and culturally, and he further acknowledged European claims to an intellectual vigor that had produced the world's scientific prodigies, and to political and military capabilities opening large portions of the globe to the civilizing influence of Christianity. These were impressive achievements, said Blyden, but they were no more so than Africa's own; they were simply different. For their part, Blyden insisted, African civilizations were characterized by a harmonious sense of community, by a sympathy with the rhythms of nature, and by a religious strength and communion with God. These had served mankind in the past, and Blyden was confident they would do so again. And he quoted the prediction of the psalmist, "Ethiopia shall stretch forth her hands unto God."[6]

Blyden saw world civilization as the image of divine perfection to which each race contributed an essential segment. Such a notion was remarkably like the "Civilization of the Universal," a concept that Léopold Senghor developed as part of the doctrine of Negritude. Here, as with Blyden, the European was recognized as the master of analytic reason and of science; the African was pictured as a man of feeling—intuitive in thought, sympathetic in understanding, sensitive to artistic and religious impulses, close to the pulse of nature, and bound in social order by an ancient communism. The universe, said Senghor, has evolved through synthesis, complexity coming from the communion of simpler elements. Synthesis is nuclear and biological, Senghor continued, but it is also social, and it follows that the attainment of a higher civilization can come only through the amalgamation of the riches of all races, all cultures. The African component, Senghor remarked, is of utmost importance. Modern science has progressed from the simple precision of mechanical physics to the complex indeterminacy of the subatomic world. Hence analysis becomes less useful than intuition, and it is precisely with intuition that the strength of the African lies. "[What] strikes the Negro is less the appearance of an object than its reality, its surreality," said Senghor, "less its sign than its meaning."[7]

The European aspects of Senghor's philosophy have generally been overlooked in favor of its more particularly African qualities— spirituality, communal strength, affinity to nature. Nevertheless, much of Negritude is traceable to ideas that originated in Europe—to a surrealist and existential recoil from the inadequacies of Western scientific-industrial society toward the bucolic charm of Africa; to a Bergsonian philosophy that emphasizes intuitive thought; to a methodology that draws heavily upon the dialectic processes of Hegel and Marx, to a sociology that mirrors to a remarkable degree the racial theories of Lévy-Bruhl. It was far more than coincidence that the most searching analysis of Negritude came from Jean-Paul Sartre, a leading French existentialist whose celebrated and influential essay, *Black Orpheus,* appeared first in 1948 as an introduction to Senghor's anthology of poetry by black and Malagasy writers.

Senghor's ideas on social synthesis showed the influence of the French scientist and philosopher, Pierre Teilhard de Chardin, but the dialectics came from the determinism of Marx, as Satre explained in his *Black Orpheus* essay. Sartre began with a discussion of proletariat exploitation, but at once drew a distinction between white and black since the black worker labored under the special discrimination of white racism. The white laborer is preoccupied with class struggle, said Sartre, and has little time for self-analysis. For the black man, however, his color is a constant reminder of prejudice, especially in Europe and the New World, the lands of alienation; his solution is to make an internal, subjective identification of his external blackness, delving deep into his soul in search of his essential Negritude.

This descent of the black poet into his soul Sartre called Orphic, a process suggested by the quest of Orpheus in Hades searching for Eurydice. It is an acutely difficult process, Sartre continued, because the black poet must speak in an alien language that lacks necessary qualities of expression. He succeeds by forcing words into new forms, by distorting syntax, until he can create the concepts and images he needs.

Everywhere the process is dialectical. The black, alienated through the effects of assimilation, struggles to regain his identity, his Negritude, through a conscious existential effort. "The black [dies] of the white world," Sartre explained, "to be reborn of the black soul, as the platonic philosopher dies of the body to be reborn of the truth." The black poet expresses the externals of Negritude in the customs, the arts, the songs, the dances of Africa, but the essential Negritude is internal. The white man understands technique, said Sartre, but this is superficial, merely scratching the surface. "Negritude . . . is a comprehension through sympathy. The secret of the black is that the sources of his existence and the roots of Being are identical."

But social synthesis must proceed; the dialectic must be served. Having plunged into the depths of his soul, having found his Negritude, having come so close to the essentials of humanity, the black poet must now renounce everything he has gained in a superhuman act of self-sacrifice. Having successfully survived the serpents of white racism, the poet establishes his own antiracist black racism, then, in the supreme moment of victory, he renounces all. It is a process heavy with ironies. The black claims his place in the sun. More than any other he has been oppressed in history. More than any other he feels his sense of liberty, his need to revolt. Yet, says Sartre, in pursuing his own liberty, he labors for the deliverance of all humanity.

> The Negro . . . creates an anti-racist racism. He does not at all wish to dominate the world; he wishes the abolition of racial privileges wherever they are found; he affirms his solidarity with the oppressed of all colors. At a blow the subjective, existential, ethnic notion of Negritude passes . . . into the objective, positive exact notion of the proletariat. . . . Negritude appears as the weak stage of a dialectical progression: the theoretical and practical affirmation of white supremacy is the thesis; the position of Negritude as antithetical value is the moment of negativity. . . . It serves to prepare the way for the synthesis or the realization of the human society without racism. . . . Negritude is dedicated to its own destruction. . . . At the moment the black Orpheus most directly embraces this Eurydice, he feels her vanish from between his arms. . . .
>
> From the man of color . . . can it be asked to renounce pride in his color. It is he who lives particularism to the end, to find thereby the dawn of the universal.

"Strange road," Sartre concludes. "Offended, humiliated the blacks probe the most profound depths to find again their most secret pride, and when they have finally discovered it . . . by supreme generosity they abandon it."[8]

*The Flight from Europe—Frantz Fanon*

For many blacks the poetic and philosophic flights of Negritude were potent tonic; for others they strained credulity, idle fancy that withered in the heat of reality. One who was pulled in both directions was Frantz Fanon, the medical doctor and psychiatrist from Martinique, working out his own personal identity crisis as a prelude to a broader appraisal of the being and position of the black man in modern society.

Growing up in the West Indies during the years preceding the Second World War, Fanon gradually became aware of how greatly his self-image differed from the perception of him by others, particularly Europeans. When, after the war, he came to pursue his medical studies in France, it is probably no accident that he chose to specialize in psychiatry, a field that provided tools for the examination of individual, and by extension, racial, identity. By 1952, when he was twenty-seven, Fanon had completed his formal studies and begun his residency. It was also the year he published *Black Skin, White Masks,* a powerfully searching analysis of race prejudice that shifted the problem of identity from the personal to the racial level. From this point on, writing was to be a major weapon in Fanon's increasingly intense struggle for the liberation of those tyrannized by racism, and finally for the deliverance of all men from the oppressors who dwelt in their midst.[9]

Fanon's awareness was progressive, chronological. In the years before the war, he tells us, West Indians regarded themselves simply as Europeans. There were gradations in color but these were not important. It was culture that mattered. The Martiniquan was French, certainly not a Negro; Negroes were Africans, a despised and inferior people, given to fetishes, tom-toms, and backwardness. "The West Indian was a black man," said Fanon, "but the Negro was in Africa."

The war changed such innocent provincialism. First, an occupation of the islands by Vichy forces, then, for Fanon, two years with the Free French revealed that white men made no nice distinctions between the blacks of the Indies and those of Africa or elsewhere. All were black, all were inferior, identifiable at once by the color of their skin.

Here was the stuff of trauma. For a time the islander tried to compensate, to become whiter, to prove his identity as a European. A successful marriage was one that involved a spouse of lighter color. Those who could traveled to France to be educated in whiteness, to speak French more perfectly, to return home more thoroughly Europeanized, the envy of their less-fortunate compatriots. It was no use. For the European the islander was a black man, naturally inferior, representing a stage between civilized men and the apes. To be sure, some were further advanced by dint of their perfection of white culture, but in the final analysis they were still black, still damned. The black man of the islands, said Fanon, began to despise himself, to feel the guilt of his depressed existence, an existence defined by those outsiders who observed him.

For Fanon this was a shattering discovery. He had seen himself simply as a man among men. "And then," he says, "the occasion arose when I had to meet the white man's eyes. . . . The real world challenged my claims. . . . I was responsible at the same time for my body, for my race, for my ancestors. I subjected myself to an objective examination, I discovered my blackness, my ethnic characteristics; and I was battered down by tom-toms, cannibalism, intellectual deficiency, fetishism, racial defects, slave-ships, and above all else, above all: 'Sho good eatin'.'"[10]

Then came Negritude, urged by another Martiniquan, Aimé Césaire. Black must not be put down by white. Black is good. Black is beauty and truth, said Césaire. In the islands this view was regarded at first as heresy, madness, but the war years gradually changed attitudes, for Fanon and for his compatriots. Before 1939, as Fanon discovered, the West Indian faced Europe and sought ways to escape from his color. After 1945 he realized he was black and a Negro. He began to turn toward distant Africa.

Fanon saw Negritude as a release, a liberation, a stunning solution. Black is "those without whom the earth would not be the earth," Césaire sang. Black is rhythm, countered Senghor, "the thing that is most perceptible and least material . . . the archetype of the vital element." "Blackness . . . is no stone . . . no drop of lifeless water on the dead eye of the world," chanted Césaire, ". . . it thrusts into the red flesh of the sun . . . into the burning flesh of the sky." Black rhythm, returned Senghor, "is rhythm in its primordial purity . . . rhythm in the masterpieces of Negro art. . . . Rhythm is alive, it is free."

Fanon was jubilant. "Had I read that right? . . . From the opposite end of the white world a magical Negro culture was hailing me. . . . I began to flush with pride. . . . Was this our salvation?" Césaire was singing the praises of those who had never invented, never explored, never conquered. Senghor was explaining that emotion was as Negro as reason was Greek. "I am made of the irrational," Fanon cried. "I wade in the irrational. Up to my neck in the irrational."

It was but a momentary triumph. The white man concedes nothing, Fanon soon realized. He insists that emotion is only a stage in the evolutionary scale, that the black is still a primitive, that there is nothing original in his primitiveness. Fanon was frantic. He searched for more evidence, some salvation, and he found it. Césaire had already pointed out the long-lived and rich culture of Africa, and his testimony had been corroborated by white scholars. It was all there—the great savanna cities of Ghana and Mali, the wealthy kingdom of Kongo, the learned Muslim scholars, wise interpreters of the Quran. "The white man was wrong," exulted Fanon. "I was not a primitive. . . . I belonged to a race that had already been working in gold and silver two thousand years ago." So there it was, all there—black civilization in its history, black beauty in its culture, black uniqueness in its personality.

Then came the final blow, and, paradoxically, from the very hand that had been raised in defense of the black man. Jean-Paul Sartre, writing his celebrated *Black Orpheus* essay, insisted that Negritude was in fact black racism, a step in the dialectic process leading to a society without races, "the weak stage of a dialectical progression," Sartre termed it, as he called upon the black man to abandon his Negritude and lose himself in a common humanity. Fanon was stunned. "When I read that page, I felt that I had been robbed of my last chance."[11]

It was the beginning of disillusion. Negritude had saved, but only partially. It had rescued, but only temporarily. Fanon turned to other views of the problem of racism and gradually evolved his own solution—the necessity of violence, violence that would secure racial dignity, violence that would establish individual identity. But did this mean that, for Fanon, there no longer was a black man among men, no special African personality? Alas, yes, said Fanon, he exists. Like the Jew in the eyes of the anti-Semite, the black man exists in the mind of the white racist. Jean-Paul Sartre has already shown, said Fanon, that the Jew was one whom others considered a Jew, the idea created in the mind of the anti-Semite. It is the same with the black, Fanon continued, but it is worse. The Jew, after all, is a white man. He can hide, go unnoticed, avoid the stereotype. The black man has no such luxury. "I am given no chance," announced Fanon. "I am the slave . . . of my own appearance: I move slowly in the world. . . . I progress by crawling. And already I am being dissected under white eyes, the only real eyes. I am fixed. Having adjusted their microtomes, they objectively cut away slices of my reality. I am laid bare. . . . I see in those white faces that it is not a new man who has come in, but a new kind of man, a new genus. Why, it's a Negro!"

My humanity is denied, Fanon continued. I am told I am a savage, a brute, an illiterate, despised, not by my neighbor or my enemy but by a whole race. "Shame. Shame and self-contempt. Nausea." There is, however, a solution, said Fanon. The black must create his self-image to counter the image of the white man, define his existence from within, not permit that it be imposed from without. "Black consciousness is immanent in its own eyes. . . . I am wholly what I am. I do not have to look for the universal. . . . My Negro consciousness does not hold itself out as a lack. It *is*."[12]

It is curious that Fanon did not reject out of hand Sartre's discussion of Negritude, with its unconvincing dialectic and its racist assumption of the analytical European and the emotional African. Perhaps he was too much captive of his Western education, too impressed with Sartre and the existential ideas that were to form the basis for his own work in psychiatry. In any event, Fanon began to cool on Negritude, but for other reasons that he set forth in his celebrated essay on violence, *The Wretched of the Earth*.

*The Wretched of the Earth* appeared in 1961, the year of Fanon's premature death, and must be regarded as his final views on the issues of racism. Fanon's position on Negritude, however, had already been presented two years earlier at the Rome Congress of Black Writers and Artists sponsored by *Présence Africaine*, and in the chapter, "On National Culture," contained in *The Wretched of the Earth*, basically an expanded version of these earlier remarks. The trouble with Negritude, said Fanon, is that it does not go nearly far enough. Colonialism not only imposes its rule, it also destroys the culture of those whom it dominates. The colonized, therefore, strike back, Fanon continued, establishing their own existence, their Negritude, searching the past for evidence of a civilization of value, a past culture that can be exhibited in all its brilliance. "The concept of negritude was the emotional if not the logical antithesis of that insult which the white man flung at humanity. This rush of negritude against the white man's contempt showed itself in certain spheres to be the one idea capable of lifting interdictions and anathemas."

A good start, admitted Fanon, but not enough. Colonialism rejected black culture in toto, so Negritude came to be a blanket celebration of black culture regardless of the fact that many differences existed among peoples of different nations and continents. Culture is national and specific, said Fanon. It cannot be effective as a vague and romantic image, an idealized black mystique, divorced from the realities of the struggle against colonialism. This is Negritude's first limitation.

Worse still, Fanon continued, Negritude leans strongly in the direction of nostalgia, toward the trappings of an irrelevant past. The artist and intellectual of Negritude, intent upon illuminating the way to freedom, turns paradoxically to the past, to "the castoffs of thought, its shells and corpses, a knowledge which has been stabilized once and for all." Expression becomes locked in a rigid stereotype that no longer has meaning in a changing world. It is significant, said Fanon, that it is precisely this expression from the past that is accepted, even praised, by the colonialist oppressor, intent upon fixing his wards permanently in their inferiority—the masks and drums of primitivism patronized in the studies of European anthropologists, the hoarse jazz of America admired while confirming the depressed character of the southern Negro.

Enough of antiquarianism; there must be a more supple, positive affirmation of culture, Fanon insisted, using the past to open up the future.

We must not . . . be content with delving into the past of a people in order to find coherent elements which will counteract colonialism's attempt to falsify and harm. We must work and fight with the same rhythm as the people to construct the future. . . . A national culture is not a folklore, nor an abstract populism. . . . It is not made up of the inert dregs of gratuitous actions . . . which are less and less attached to the ever-present reality of the people. A national culture is the whole body of efforts made by a people in the sphere of thought to describe, justify, and praise the action through which that people has created itself.

We must not forget the "niggers" are disappearing, Fanon cried. The storyteller abandons his tedious epics for fresh and relevant episodes, the artist frees himself from the inexpressive mask to create new evocative compositions. In America, for example, "the new fashions in jazz are not simply born of economic competition. We must without any doubt see in them one of the consequences of the defeat, slow but sure, of the southern world of the United States. And it is not utopian to suppose that in fifty years' time the type of jazz howl hiccuped by a poor misfortunate Negro will be upheld only by the whites who believe in it as an expression of negritude, and who are faithful to this arrested image of a type of relationship."[13]

## The Flight from Europe—Medicine in Africa

For all their differences, Fanon and the proponents of Negritude seem to have agreed on the actuality of an African personality. Certainly, for Fanon, the black man was his own man, unique and identifiable, existing through self-definition. Similarly, Fanon recognized the authenticity of indigenous cultures under colonialism—black or white—apparent in their national variations, an understanding that Fanon put to concrete use as director of the psychiatric institution at Blida-Joinville in Algeria during the mid-1950s. Fanon knew that physicians, like anyone else, were conditioned by their culture, that mental disorder could not be properly defined, let alone treated, without a sure grasp of local traditions and customs. His prescribed therapy, therefore, leaned heavily on awareness of the North African society in which he worked and on the quite different views of madness as seen by the Westerner and by the Muslim.[14]

Among African physicians Fanon was not alone in basing medical practice on a sociological grounding, utilizing cultural information in dealing with psychic and somatic disorders. For example, the Ghanaian sculptor and gynecologist, Oku Ampofo, was one of several medical and social scientists working in Ghana who studied the methods of traditional healers, particularly in birth delivery, and Ampofo also collected and analyzed local herbs known to be used widely by indigenous medical practitioners. Ampofo usually discovered through chemical analysis that his herbal samples contained drugs of established value, although rarely was the connection with a particular plant known to modern medicine.

Sometimes the therapeutic effect was dramatic and mysterious. Ampofo tells of the occasion when he was in danger of losing a mother because of a difficult birth infection. Walking distraught in front of the hospital, he was approached by some local farmers to whom he explained his concern.

They laughed. "You have the medicine right there," one said, pointing to a nearby sheep pen bordered by a restraining hedge. "Mash the leaves in water. Get the woman to drink it. And fast."

Ampofo was soon back, his patient already recovering. "How did you know?" he asked. They explained that normally the sheep and goats did not touch the leaves of this plant, the males never, and the females only when pregnant and nearing delivery. It was far from germ-theory medicine and the cure was not understood, but it worked.[15]

The traditional healer's craft was even more useful in the diagnosis and treatment of mental illness. Because of his deep understanding of indigenous beliefs and customs, the indigenous practitioner could frequently link psychic and organic disorders with the possibility of social maladjustment in a patient. Particularly important in psychiatry, such knowledge was not lost on Fanon, and it was the strength of the social setting that was utilized by the Nigerian physician T. A. Lambo, in establishing his psychiatric clinic at Aro, which was operated under the auspices of the University of Ibadan teaching hospital.

The Aro mental patients were boarded in typical village homes, always living with a brother, mother, or other member of their immediate family, spending their days in treatment at the clinic, where many villagers were employed, but returning to the local community at night. Lambo and his colleagues found that close contact with a familiar social environment facilitated recovery, allowing the patient to live among people emotionally healthier but sympathetic to symptoms that were often socially unacceptable by Western standards, strengthening the ego and diluting anxiety, and preparing the patient eventually for an effective return to the similar environment of his own home.[16]

Lambo's work at Aro naturally raised many questions about the relationship between mental disorder and social background and suggested the possibility of a distinctive African personality. Though admitting the need for much further research, Lambo was persuaded that the African was indeed a distinctive individual, not through color, not through Fanon's existential image, but largely through the cultural conditioning of traditional society, an hypothesis that can be traced to the theories of Lévy-Bruhl. While physical factors such as protein and vitamin deficiency played important roles in personality development, Lambo was drawn to the importance of social training, particularly the role of the family in child-rearing.

Generalizing from research on children in Nigeria, Lambo pointed out that the newborn African infant is at once introduced into a warm, affectionate environment in which needs and desires are anticipated and the security of a close-knit extended family engenders emotional security. This encourages confidence and the ability to play complicated social roles with sophistication, said Lambo, but such early accommodation ends with a shock when the child is weaned after a long period of breast-feeding. He is momentarily disoriented, consumed with a strong Oedipus complex and a dislike for authority caused by the abrupt awareness of a dominant father. The family takes hold, however, and the immediate environment of the child becomes clearly defined, his world simple and easy to conceptualize. It is a social world, said Lambo, an extended family of many surrogate fathers and mothers, a world that deals in personal relationships and suppresses any drive for individual autonomy.

The solidarity of an extended family, Lambo continued, gains strength from the conviction that ancestors are an important part of that family. From this it is a short step to perception of supernatural forces, to belief in the powers of magic, and to acceptance of dream life as objective reality. Socially, Lambo said, the African becomes totally identified with the group and manifests only a loosely defined personal ego. It is the we-ness of life that counts, Lambo concluded, establishing, along with the rich heritage of legend and myth, the sense of security that marks the character of the African personality.[17]

*The African Identity and the New African Philosophy*

Whatever the scientific evidence, the humanist in Africa seemed compelled to assert a special quality for African civilization, a special identity for the African individual. The Nigerian novelist, Chinua Achebe, has said that he writes to teach the African to be proud of his cultural heritage. K. O. Dike was moved to generate historical studies at Ibadan because of the distortions he saw in European historical writing on Africa. Efua Sutherland sought to fill an African void on library shelves, and Wole Soyinka's theater of commitment involved ultimately a whole Yoruba cosmology with implicit ethical and moral standards to counter European pretentions. In 1962 the Ghanaian philosopher W. E. Abraham produced a book with the provocative title *The Mind of Africa* to affirm a uniquely African personality. Negritude was a whole movement devoted to the demonstration of an African identity. Against the European's sense of superiority and skepticism, there had to be self-assertion, equal and opposite.

The crisis of identity was especially acute for the African intellectual. Each had received a Western education. All were cultural hybrids, recognizing the merits of both backgrounds, eager to bring them together in consonance in a modern Africa that was itself an amalgam of indigenous and Western institutions and values. Attracted to the West, they found they could not simply walk away from their Western heritage. The more they protested an African identity, the more it testified to the hold of the West. Could the Western demon be exorcized? Could African culture free itself to develop in un-self-conscious self-absorption?

The answers were various, from Fanon's militant assertion of black identity to the romantic Negritude of Kwei Armah's *The Healers;* more recently they have come from another voice, stating new views in the old debate. During the 1970s a number of professors of philosophy in African universities began speaking out on the role of their discipline in modern Africa, in the process evaluating familiar preoccupations with Africa's past and future, her relations with the West, and the interaction between doctrine and the practicalities of everyday life. A number of individuals have been involved, among others, Kwesi Wiredu of the University of Ghana, the Nigerian scholar, Peter Bodunrin, Henry Oruka from the University of Nairobi, Marcien Towa of Cameroon, and Paulin Hountondji, dean of the Faculty of Letters at the University of Cotonou in Benin.

In their assessments, these scholars have differed in detail, but there has been substantial agreement over basic principles and objectives. Wiredu, for example, appears to speak for all when he discusses the relation between modernization and the discipline of philosophy in Africa. Clearly, says Wiredu, science is crucial in the conversion of traditional into modern societies, but the pursuit of modernization must not be limited to its obvious application of technology to social and economic problems. The methodology of science—the search for coherence and system, the habit of exactness in method, rigor of thought, appeal to evidence over authority, reliance on experiment—all these call for broad application beyond life's practicalities to areas of intellectual activity that include the abstract meditations of philosophy. The discipline of philosophy, continues Wiredu, rests largely in the study of logic, epistemology, metaphysics, ethics or political philosophy as developed in the West; hence, "the contemporary African philosopher will find that it is the philosophies of the West that will occupy him most, for it is in that part of the world that modern developments in human knowledge have gone farthest and where, consequently, philosophy is in closest touch with the conditions of the modernisation which he urgently desires for his continent."

Thus, African philosophy, as Hountondji points out, is philosophy as it was developed in the West but produced by Africans in Africa. Wiredu adds that, after all, English or French philosophy is at bottom the philosophical work of Englishmen or Frenchmen, the former recognized perhaps by its preference for empiricism against the continental preoccupation with idealism.[18]

Whatever their differences, the new philosophers all agree that modern African philosophy is not an updated version of traditional African thought. Indeed, they insist, the traditional values of African societies cannot justly be characterized as philosophy in the sense of a systematic methodology applied to defined areas of analysis such as logic or ethics. Rather, traditional thought is what Marcien Towa and Paulin Hountondji have termed ethnophilosophy, its study a branch of cultural anthropology. These worldviews of traditional Africa, says Wiredu, served their societies well, creating necessary codes of conduct, bonding people into coherent mutually supporting groups, and providing a knowledge and wisdom appropriate to the exigencies of the environment from which they grew. But all this was prescientific, Wiredu continues—certainly rooted in rational thought and knowledge but also based on myth, mysticism, and magic, appealing to authority as expressed by ancestors and elders rather than to evidence presented through observation and experiment. "The crucial difference," observes Wiredu, "is that the Western philosopher argues for his thesis, clarifying his meaning and answering objections, known or anticipated; whereas the believer in folk conceptions merely says: 'This is what our ancestors said.' "

Such appeals to authority still occur in the West, but they do not constitute a modern philosophical worldview, Wiredu points out. Westerners, however, are prone to regard the traditional thought systems of Africa as the essence of African philosophy, and to compare them, usually to their disadvantage, with the philosophical structures of the West. One consequence is an exaggerated notion of the difference in nature between the African and the European; another is that this alleged difference is accepted by many Africans as a given truth. Thus, says Wiredu, we have "the spectacle of otherwise enlightened Africans pouring libations to the spirits of their ancestors. . . . That our departed ancestors continue to hover around in some rarified form ready now and then to take a sip of the ceremonial schnapps is a proposition that I have never heard rationally defended." Yet the process continues, carried along by those who feel they must demonstrate their commitment to a uniquely African culture.[19]

There is much more involved, however, than mere speculation over the existence of an African personality, and Marcien Towa has described the consequences of the backward-looking doctrines of Negritude and its handmaid, ethnophilosophy. The nations of Africa, like all developing societies in the modern world, must build a material strength, he avers, in order to guarantee continued sovereignty in their political, economic, and cultural activities. To this end, they must follow in the footsteps of the West, where modernization began with rationalism and experimental science. An appeal to the virtues of a dead African past is a barren tactic, precisely the wrong approach. It was traditional Africa that Europe conquered, Towa continues—echoing Richard Wright's Sorbonne observations—using the scientific and technological superiority it had developed to effect and exploit that conquest. In reaching back to an obsolete and impotent past, Africans will insure a continuing Western subjugation of their continent during the postcolonial era of apparent independence.

To avoid perpetual bondage and effect a genuine independence requires a total metamorphosis of African society, says Towa—a radical break with the African past and a fundamental absorption of Western modes of thought, not merely the superficial accretion of those elements of Western culture identified with the West's ascendancy over colonial peoples. As Russia turned from its ancient mysticism to create a modern society, as the Chinese abandoned Confucianism to the same end, so, says Towa, must Africans reject their past and submerge their essential being in a process of transfiguration and rebirth reminiscent of Sartre's Orphic synthesis.

> Our task takes shape. We must assert ourselves in the world of today. . . . We must reestablish our stature as men. . . . Naturally the decision to assert ourselves . . . is at the same time a decision to assume with a sense of pride the validity of our past. Such a decision, however . . . by introducing a radical change in our present condition, demands as well a similar break with a past that is responsible for that condition. The wish to be ourselves leads at once to a reassessment of the past since the essence of self comes from that past. Coldly and clearly scrutinized, the past attests that our present subservience is explained by the essence of self which is of the past. To change the present character of self means at the same time to change the essence of self, its particularities, original and unique, to enter into a negative relationship with the self.

For Towa, then, the modern African must not be a simple projection of the traditional African; rather, he must be a new man who stifles his earlier self to be reborn as he responds to the exigencies of the modern world. This need not mean total rejection of the African past; it is a matter of emphasis. In transforming our self, says Towa, we change the character of the past. Thus, "the past is placed at our disposal, not us at the disposal of the past." Then, presumably, a new Africa emerges, utilizing Europe's secret of success along with appropriate elements of traditional African culture and thought. Peter Bodunrin makes much the same point in discussing the work of Nkrumah, Nyerere, and Senghor as they have sought to establish a new African world based upon the old. "They have studied philosophy in Western schools and the influence of this training is noticeable in their idioms," says Bodunrin, continuing, "They do not claim to be merely describing for us the African traditional philosophy, nor do they claim that their work represents the collective view of the traditional African. What they are doing is trying to *base* a philosophy of *their own* on the traditional African past."[20]

Doubtless Towa would not include Senghor, the architect of Negritude, as an African modernizer, nor would Paulin Hountondji, who has joined Towa in calling for adoption by Africa of Western rationalism and scientific method as a means to modernity in Africa. As with Towa, Hountondji begins with the European attempt to describe the mind and thought of Africa, first with the work of Lévy-Bruhl, which he dismisses as hopelessly ethnocentric, and then with Father Placide Tempels's *Bantu Philosophy*, first published in 1945 and later reissued by *Présence Africaine*. Tempels, a Belgian missionary in the Congo, in effect turned Lévy-Bruhl's theory of racial mentality on its head by ascribing an articulate metaphysical system to at least one African people, the Bantu-speaking Luba of present-day Zaire. Tempels was primarily concerned with understanding the Bantu minds as a basis for introducing Christian principles into Africa, but his thesis was picked up with enthusiasm by the proponents of Negritude, who regarded it as an important contribution to their effort to establish the validity of African thought and culture.

Not so Hountondji. Along with Towa he dismisses Tempels as he had Lévy-Bruhl, another European apologist whose theory of a Bantu ontology was at bottom only a device for spiritual imperialism and continued African subservience to Europe. Senghor had adopted Tempels's hypothesis of Bantu *muntu*, or being, as a "vital force," integrating it into his system of Negritude, which already showed the influence of Lévy-Bruhl, the French philosopher Henri Bergson, and the Surrealists, with their emphasis on the unconscious mind, intuition, and irrational motivation. For Hountondji, Negritude's claim to a uniquely African intuitive mentality distinguished from the analytic logic of the European was an ideological myth that has been perpetuated by other African intellectuals, ethnophilosophers like the Abbé Kagame of Rwanda, who followed Tempels in arguing the existence of a distinctive African mentality.

Their motivation was pathetically apparent, says Hountondji, born not of ignorance but of desire. African ethnophilosophers knew full well that so-called African philosophy and the philosophy as practiced in the West were distinct and incomparable. Yet the scholars insisted on such a comparison, "setting their conceptual understanding on one side while drowning the language of science in a welter of desire. . . . African intellectuals," continues Hountondji, "wanted at all costs to rehabilitate themselves in their own eyes and in the eyes of Europe." The general African public accepted this line of argument for much the same reasons.

Those Africans who followed the ideas of Tempels, Hountondji continues, were, like the Belgian priest, mainly concerned in addressing a European audience, eager to explain the existence of an African civilization, to gain the respect of the West for a truly African culture, and thereby falling into the trap of their own making. "It was inevitable," Hountondji points out, "that they should have ended up by inventing, as a foil to European philosophy, an African 'philosophy' concocted from extra-philosophical material consisting of tales, legends, dynastic poems, etc. . . . to derive from them what they could not, cannot and will never yield: a genuine philosophy."

Hountondji states his arguments with an intensity that makes his conclusions appear categorical, but, in fact, his essential position is much like that of Towa, Wiredu, and others of the new African philosophers. He begins with modern science and scientific research as basic to the development of Africa's independent societies. Science is a method, he insists, not a body of knowledge, and philosophy, which Hountondji sees flowing from science, is also method rather than content. This extreme view appears to rule out metaphysical speculation, but it also eliminates inherited systems of thought or mythologies such as Tempels and the ethnophilosophers have identified as the philosophy of traditional Africa. For Hountondji, then, philosophy is a discourse among philosophers, in Africa among African philosophers, constantly examining and reexamining past theses for present confirmation, rejection, or alteration. Philosophical method ultimately becomes an historical process, ever-changing, always subjecting past arguments to the test of reason. Static authority gives way to the dynamism of philosophical scrutiny.[21]

In turning away from traditional African culture in favor of Western science and philosophy, Hountondji and the other new philosophers seem to have rejected the idea of a unique African personality; the African was simply Homo sapiens in Africa. They seem also to have been captured by the West in their very effort at self-liberation. Their exertions look like a new version of assimilation, Abbé Boilat in the twentieth century. It is a danger, this latest effort in dealing with Europe, but the purpose is in fact freedom, not imitation. If modern science and philosophy have developed in the West and account for the advances of Western civilization, then, as a practical matter, Africans must follow the same course to bring about an elevation of the quality of life in Africa. As method, science and philosophy lose any ethnic character and belong to all mankind.

Contemporary Africa, the argument concludes, must get on in the modern world, not by indulging in a comfortable but unprogressive romanticism like Negritude but by dealing with contemporary problems with all the resources of the modern world. Herein lies true liberation from the shackles of colonialism and neocolonialism in both their material and spiritual aspects. This new argument of the new philosophers is also an old argument, heard in earlier times when Africans like John Mensah Sarbah and J. E. Casely Hayford, Bishop Crowther or Herbert Macaulay, even the Abbé Boilat, sought to use the strengths of the West to gain African freedom from Western constraints and exploitation. In the process they often took on some of the very qualities they were at pains to avoid.

# 11

## *An African Voice*

In embracing the tenets of Western science and thought, the new African philosophers did not concede an admittedly higher Western civilization; rather, their movement was marked by recognition that Africa's independent nations needed the world's best intellectual "technology" for fullest realization of an indispensable cultural independence. At the same time, their attack on Negritude, already foreshadowed by Frantz Fanon and others, seemed to repudiate the argument put forth by numerous African humanists that reaffirmation of indigenous civilizations was an essential prerequisite to cultural emancipation from Europe, and therefore, to political and economic freedom as well.

What appeared to be developing was a basic split in African thinking, one branch arguing the verities of traditional culture and institutions, the other calling for modernization through thoroughgoing Westernization. The political strife, disunion, and faltering economic growth that marked the early independence decades pointed up for growing numbers of Africans the irrelevance of nostalgic appeals to what they regarded as a dead and useless past. Consequently, they searched for solutions to development, cultural as well as material, that had been successfully introduced elsewhere—that is, in the West. Was this a fresh approach, or only a new tack in the old cycle that opposed the ideas of Africa and the West? Was Negritude finished, an historical incident, no more? Would the new philosophy atrophy in its time, to be replaced by still another return to ancestral taproots? Was some fruit-ful synthesis possible, leading perhaps to genuinely new solutions to the old problems of independence and growth, cultural and material?

Questions such as these were given a thorough airing in the late sum-mer of 1980 at a conference held in Bellagio on Italy's Lake Como, bringing together a number of individuals concerned with the condi-tion and direction of the humanities in Africa. There were some eigh-teen in attendance—writers, artists, educators, historians. Most were African by birth; others were longtime and sympathetic students of African affairs. At the conference their major preoccupation was cul-tural and political rather than aesthetic, their concern to explore the effect of humanistic expression on independence movements and the creation of the new nations of Africa.

Other than this general definition of interest, there had been no ini-tial effort to predetermine the nature of the discussion; but, as the meeting unfolded, two dominant themes emerged. First there was the conviction that the humanities in Africa had to find expression in an indigenous idiom, that genuine political or economic independence could not thrive without concurrent cultural autonomy. The second theme of the Bellagio conference offered a sharply different perspec-tive, expressed in the judgment that modern technology was essential in providing the better life that had been a primary objective of Afri-can independence movements. Those at Bellagio were therefore not suggesting a simple retreat into an idealized past. On the contrary, the conference members repeatedly made note of the pervasiveness of Western ideas and institutions, and their unanimous support of high technology as developed in the West was a firm endorsement of these outside influences.

It might seem that these two themes were antithetical and contradic-tory, as many of the formal and informal discussions appeared at first to suggest. The modernizers insisted on the introduction of technology at its most advanced level; the traditionalists argued with equal inten-sity the importance of Africa's traditional cultures to the realization of a genuine African independence. Often both views were expressed by the same individuals, embracing the essential split that had so long characterized African thought. It was almost as if the two antithetical worlds of Europe and Africa were being forced together in a single embodiment, indicating that whatever solution to African development

might be forthcoming, it would have to be in the form of a reconciliation and synthesis. At Bellagio, those in attendance felt they had begun
to show the way to that synthesis.

## In Defense of African Culture

The discussions at Bellagio ranged widely over the humanities. There
were papers dealing with African history, the press, university education, creative writing and politics, philosophy, and the arts in their
various forms. Commentaries and dialogue dealt with the specifics of
these and related matters, but the essential argument from the first
seemed focused on justifying the effectiveness of the humanities in the
development of national independence. Assuming the difficult but important role of critic, the British political scientist, Dennis Austin,
pointed out a number of shortcomings, beginning with the new African
universities. Many were becoming structures without life, he argued,
training an elite irrelevant to national needs, ignored or harrassed
by governments that questioned their utility. As centers of learning,
Austin continued, the universities lacked the resources in teaching
and research to pursue a basic body of knowledge that was international, if not Western. When they turned inward to concentrate on Africa, he said, they risked a descent into parochialism.

The African defense was sometimes vigorous, sometimes apologetic.
The Ghanaian writer, Kofi Awooner, agreed with Austin that universities in Africa had not contributed greatly to the mainstream of contemporary affairs, but their isolation, he insisted, was rooted in their
European origin and continued domination by Western educational
philosophy. The conflict between Kwame Nkrumah and the university at
Legon should be understood, Awooner said, as one effort by an African
political leader to break this Western intellectual monopoly. Others
challenged some of Austin's assumptions. J. H. Nketia, for example,
argued the effectiveness of African studies institutes as an especially
flexible component of the university that was able to reach out to the
community at large, reviving knowledge of traditional culture and
thereby developing pride in cultural achievement, which was an important element in the assertion of a true spirit of independence.

Nketia's comments regarding institutes of African studies were part
of the generally expressed view at Bellagio that an independent Africa

would thrive to the extent that it supported and drew strength from traditional African values and institutions. This position was defended repeatedly, perhaps most interestingly during the discussion that followed the paper by Abiola Irele on recent trends in French-African thought. Irele, a perceptive student of Franco-African literature, reviewed intellectual developments in French-speaking Africa from the days of Negritude to the era of the new African philosophy, a discourse providing Paulin Hountondji with ample opportunity to expound his thesis that African societies required a large dose of Western science and philosophy if they were to succeed in their development as modern nations. Hountondji's position was challenged by Irele and the Senegalese writer, Pathé Diagne. Irele, for instance, pointed out that Hountondji's adherence to Western standards and ideas of modernity ignored evident shortcomings in Western civilization, both material and spiritual, and left Africa with no alternative to a Western perspective, including new ideologies that might be built upon Africa's own past. Irele also noted that Hountondji's argument for Western philosophic tools revealed a confidence in the independent African that, ironically, may have derived from the efforts of those who had earlier dared suggest a break with the West in favor of the values of traditional Africa.

Whether favoring Westernization or revitalized African traditions, the Africans at Bellagio were nevertheless unanimous in their judgment that the artist and writer were obliged, by the very nature of their special talent, to assume an active role in the political and social life of their developing nations. Within this blanket commitment there were numerous variations. The Sudanese poet, Taban lo Liyong, suggested that the writer possessed special qualities of insight that obliged him to act as social critic, a view in which Efua Sutherland concurred, although she, along with Demas Nwoko, drew sharp distinction between effective artistic commentary and political acts that might end in the silencing of an important voice.

Others were not sure that political and artistic acts could be separated. Traditionally, said Albert Opoku, the artist and citizen were one, and others felt that this mutual condition still obtained. Kofi Awooner urged that the artist must undertake direct political action when the circumstances were compelling. The Ghanaian journalist, Elizabeth Ohene, argued that such involvement extended to all intellectuals. Not only did they possess special eloquence that stimulated public awareness, as celebrities they also had the power to call attention to political inequities in ways not open to the ordinary citizen. And she cited the hue and cry following detention for both Kofi Awooner and Wole Soyinka, a publicity that brought worldwide attention to the arbitrary action of those in power.

These were subsidiary matters, however. The main issue remained— should the humanist in Africa follow the Western lead or look to ancestral virtues? Was modern Africa to be cast in the mold of the West or would she emerge unmistakably African, an ancient culture reborn in modern idiom?

As stated, the question seemed almost philosophical. At Bellagio, however it took shape during discussion of a most material issue— the application to African economies of high technology. Once again it was Dennis Austin who provoked debate. The question of effective African societies goes well beyond the role of the university, said Austin. The new nations of Africa have not begun to deal with their enormous problems of modernization. Technology must be introduced on a massive scale, Austin continued, but will Africans be able to master its use, can they afford its cost, and are they going to adapt it successfully to African needs? Evidence of failure is everywhere to behold, said Austin. Telephone services in most countries do not work. New superhighways produce monumental traffic jams and appalling statistics of death and destruction. Simple devices like air conditioners or elevators are normally inoperative. A chronic lack of spare parts and other material shortages keep machines idle and unproductive. Aqueducts fail to deliver water to dependent urban populations. Power supplies are so uncertain that individuals and institutions are often obliged to install their own generators.

The list is almost without end, Austin went on, and the resultant economic atrophy and public apathy have been dangerously destructive to the aspirations of new societies. Many of Africa's problems of modernization originate with international affairs not readily controlled, but mismanagement of technology is basically internal and its effect has been enormous. The African humanist must not deceive himself into thinking he can deal with the complexities of modern life by a romantic return to an idealized past of village crafts and communal labor. The answer lies in Western technology, said Austin.

Here was a heavy indictment, the more so for its validity. Those present seemed momentarily stunned into agreement. As architect and designer, the Nigerian Demas Nwoko was perhaps best-qualified to respond to Austin, and he turned at once to the task. Nwoko began in agreement. It was true, he conceded, there could be no thought of going back to traditional technologies. The most modern machines and processes were essential to African development. What had gone wrong, said Nwoko, was not the utilization of high technology but the unreflecting wholesale import of machines designed for other places and other needs, and often at costs beyond limited African budgets. For example, he pointed out the ubiquitous nonfunctioning air-conditioning systems were frequently the victims of insufficient electric circuits, which invited fire as well as breakdown. Better to erect buildings, at least in domestic architecture, that avoided such expensive installation and maintenance, featuring cheap and effective natural cooling systems. Such designs have long existed, Nwoko assured his listeners, designs that had evolved over many generations of dealing with problems of tropical habitation in a preindustrial society.

On first hearing, Nwoko's comments seemed paradoxical, calling for a return to the African past, a rejection of the very Western technology he was urging. There was no inconsistency, however. Indeed the argument was calculated to reconcile the worlds of Africa and Europe, drawing them together in a synthesis that closed the gap between the exigencies of modern living and the yearning to recapture and express a genuinely African culture in the contemporary world. It was a design for living that reached both backward and outward. What we need, Nwoko insisted repeatedly, is the best technology in machine, design, and process, but always created to meet an African condition. The African necessity comes first, he said. The solution must be an African solution.[1]

## Technology and African Culture

Through the words of Demas Nwoko, the Bellagio delegates began to sense a way out of their dilemma, a solution that would modernize yet retain qualities of African life that satisfied and sustained, that would resolve the old ambivalence over Africa and the West. Here was a catalyst that unified the conference in an enthusiasm of achievement and prospect. If technology drawn from any corner of the globe could be made to serve a genuinely African need, why not the same for education, the arts, history, literature?

Nwoko's remarks were not born of an insubstantial eloquence, momentarily intoxicating but visionary. He spoke with a practicality that reflected twenty years of experience as designer, architect, and town planner, his most recent work concentrated in the very problem of adapting high technology to industrial development in an African setting.

After schooling, Nwoko had established himself in his native Nigeria, principally at Ibadan, where he had been associated for a number of years with the theater program of the University of Ibadan. More recently he had returned to his home village of Idumuje Ugboko, in Bendel State, located some sixty miles east of Benin. Sharing his time between Ibadan, where he maintained a studio, and Idumuje Ugboko, Nwoko had become increasingly preoccupied with the exigencies of industrial growth in Nigeria, and by extension, with the problems of national development in a modern African state.

Nwoko had come to feel that much of the faltering pace of development in Africa lay deeper than in the laws of economics or the vagaries of politics, that it was buried in habits and attitudes inherited from colonial times. At Bellagio he chided his fellow countrymen, accusing them of a twenty-year independence celebration while they neglected the important business of capitalizing on a new freedom. Educated Africans have failed to provide the energy and initiative necessary to build new nations, Nwoko has remarked. They have concentrated on a hunt for jobs, which they have alternately exploited and neglected, building fine houses in their home villages while professional responsibilities languished. In part, says Nwoko, this has come from the tendency to look on government as something foreign, a linear descendant of the old colonial regime, something to be used to advantage, perhaps cheated, certainly not an object of support. Where Marxist notions have held sway, the alienation from government has been deepened by the widely-held image of a socialist state responsible for all matters, a universal sow to be thoroughly milked for personal gain.

Much of this attitude, Nwoko continues, has originated in the Westernized cities, with their impersonal ambience that erodes loyalties and breeds exploitation. In the village, Nwoko points out, there emerges a totally different sense of civic responsibility. There, everyone belongs, everyone is responsible, everyone has something to gain through mutual support. The cities are dirty, dangerous, and inefficient, says Nwoko. Nobody is responsible. No one cares. Taxes are avoided, services break down, community morale is nonexistent. In the village the old values endure—the streets are cleaned by all, contributions for municipal support are freely given, crime dissolves before law and order, and a tidy, safe, healthy community results. In Idumuje Ugboko, Nwoko recalls, the village had determined a few years earlier to be rid of all dogs because of the threat of rabies and incidents in which children had been frightened and molested. There being no available veterinary service, dogs in the neighborhood were forthwith exterminated and no more permitted; Nwoko and others coming to live in the village were forced to dispose of their pets. Despite the permissive laws of the state, this community action was effectively enforced, a circumstance that would have been impossible in the city.

For Demas Nwoko there was a lesson to be learned. In a setting of community stability and pride, new industry could be built, not the village crafts of former times but a fully mechanized modern industrial establishment based upon the latest technology. A labor supply was available in the local population that, properly trained, would have as much pride in job achievement as it did in village efficiency. A manufactory would no longer be a foreign establishment, some white man's institution. It would become part of the local scene, meeting a local need, and supported with local pride. The key, says Nwoko, is domestic. "If you import somebody else's solution, you will always be behind," he is fond of saying. As with the rat who sees the powerful elephant and tries to fit the elephant head onto a rat's body, the result is disaster.

This remove to the village is a calculated risk, for across Africa population trends are running strongly in the opposite direction. The cities are building up huge concentrations of unemployed, people low in economic productivity and living amid an urban ugliness that breeds civil disobedience and political chaos. Nwoko is convinced, however, that the village is the place where industrial growth must take place. Thus far, Nwoko points out, industry is an alien and ill-understood phenomenon, superimposed from abroad. Even under African management it is the "white man's job," an exotic accretion with hours of work and a production discipline that mean nothing beyond the wages they bring.

Nevertheless, industry, wage labor, and cash-crop agriculture have become part of everyday life in Africa. As with the railroad workers in *God's Bit of Wood*, these foreign institutions have entered the nervous system of the modern African. He does not understand them well; they are not part of his heritage. But he needs them; they are part of his life. Therefore, says Nwoko, we must bring industry to the village. The labor is supplied from the vicinity and the workers live at home in a stable and familiar domestic atmosphere. "I am trying to get industry into the culture of the people," Nwoko insists, adding that this cannot easily be done in the city, which itself spawns an alien culture.

In prospect it is a formidable task. Nwoko recalls how engineering students at his school in Zaria thought exclusively in terms of academic diplomas and the glamor of an executive position in some government department, never giving thought to the problems of building roads and raising bridges. An advanced diploma meant a well-paying job. Positions were guaranteed by government decree. If the work were not done, it did not matter. The foreign contractor hired expatriates to do the job, adding the expense to the overall cost of the contract. Here was an invitation to corruption, inefficiency, and waste, which must be replaced, Nwoko warns, while Nigeria still can rely on its oil supplies to support a modernizing economy.

Consequently Demas Nwoko has returned to Idumuje Ugboko, a farming community of four thousand where he was born. Nwoko feels that a large country like Nigeria is bound to develop regional economic specialties, and he thinks there is an opportunity for industrial development in Bendel State. Others like himself are coming back to start small industries, prodded by the necessity to bring development and the good things of the city to their hometowns, where they expect one day they will return to live. In the village, they begin on a modest scale, avoiding major missteps and basing their activities firmly in local custom. They learn from practical experience how to run an efficient industry. Working for themselves, not for the government, they grasp the concept of productivity. Situated in the village, they rely on local manpower and seek to instill an understanding and sense of purpose in their workers. Responding to local custom and tradition, they develop an industry that is socially responsible in terms of wages, working conditions, benefits, and pollution.

"Independence should have meant a type of mental, psychological cutoff, a reappraisal, and then a fresh start," says Nwoko. "It didn't happen, but it has to happen sometime." During the civil war in Nigeria, he points out, the Biafrans utilized kerosene and palm oil to run their equipment. They had to and it worked; necessity brought invention. Now we must fit technology and culture to each other, Nwoko insists, altering each to meet the demands of the other. "You are bringing in something," he says, "so you must make the culture take it in, digest it, make it part of the system." In the village setting a factory dare not cheat the worker. At the same time the laborer no longer stays home from work to attend the funeral of a relative, as he did when he held a "white man's job." Now he understands that his job is part of his life, part of a new and changing culture.

At Idumuje Ugboko there is a conscious experiment to modernize the village, and, if successful, to provide a model for other efforts at development. To some extent it is a family affair. Demas Nwoko's oldest brother, Albert, the obi, Nwoko III, recently retired after many years of government service in Benin and has returned to assume his place as head of the village and to lend the authority of his office to the plans for industrialization. Another brother, Martin Nwoko, has given up an important position in the Imo State educational system to direct the affairs of the village comprehensive school that is being designed, among other things, to educate cadres of technicians and supervisors for the industrial establishment that Demas Nwoko has begun to erect on a site at the edge of town.[2]

Nwoko's factory consists of two open sheds that shield concrete platforms one-hundred meters in length and about half as wide. Between these two is a third structure, a skeleton of piping, all erected with local labor, the piping having been cut and assembled with nothing more complex than a homemade metal tripod and a set of pulleys. Nwoko has installed heavy machinery in the form of lathes and presses, his intention to produce furniture and fittings for home and public use, but soon he hopes to manufacture spare parts that would be available to other plants for the upkeep of their own machinery. Nwoko is confident that there will be a good market for his furniture and fittings; for example, he is finishing work on a state theater in Benin and must provide the interior seating and appointments. As for spare parts, the demand is unending to overcome the breakdown of equipment that has been a major problem inhibiting industrial growth in Africa.

Ultimately, however, Nwoko hopes to concentrate on the manufacture of prototypes that other plants can use for their own production. He might design a chair or a table, for example, and then produce the templates, patterns, and dies necessary for the manufacture of that particular piece of furniture, selling these forms to others but making no effort to manufacture a finished product of his own. There need be no limit to the utilization of high technology, Nwoko explains. Machines with multiple heads, their actions computerized, could replace single units performing individual functions. Nwoko himself would be free to work at his village home, transmitting sketches and instructions electronically to his studio in Ibadan by visual reproduction, thus avoiding time-consuming travel. For Nwoko, these are all design problems requiring design solutions, the technical details to be worked out by engineers hired for that purpose.

Indeed, Nwoko approaches the whole business of industrial production as a problem in design. At Ibadan, Nwoko had difficulty holding workers; they often left his studio after a lengthy training period because there was no loyalty to Ibadan as a community and no sense of identity with a job beyond the salary it provided. At Idumuje Ugboko local attractions can create labor stability while on-the-job training instills an understanding of the work, bringing identification and pride in the product. Special housing is already under construction to offer comfort and security, and the comprehensive school will be able to give training in science and technology along with the arts, thus creating skilled labor ranging from electricians and carpenters to computer programmers. Social services are not neglected so that familiar ceremonies like traditional religious rites can be practiced as they always have. Thus, for Nwoko, technology moves to become a part of modern African life, but it is a technology domesticated and responsive to African needs just as African customs evolve to include the machine as an integral and appreciated part of modern living.[3]

*The Evolution of an African Designer*

Looking back over the years, Demas Nwoko might feel that his whole life and training have been an apprenticeship for the work in which he is now engaged. As a child he was fascinated by architecture and spent his spare moments observing the construction of new houses, even improving his efficiency as a petty trader so that he might have more leisure time to devote to his avocation. Later, when matriculating at the College of Arts, Science and Technology in Zaria, Nwoko found the architecture curriculum unimaginative, unconcerned with creative design and the practical problems of building. Classes stressed technical mastery of mechanical drawings, based upon what he regarded as outmoded architectural styles inappropriate to a tropical environment. "If you people are architects," said Nwoko, "then I will have to be something else," and he transferred to the school of art.

Here was direction and determination early exhibited. "My idea of architecture," Nwoko observed, "was to design buildings, not to . . . try to get a perfect angle on the drawing board. . . . You have a perfect drawing but when you are building the house you find you have to change it anyway. . . . So what's the perfect drawing about?" Architectural drawings lacked details, he pointed out, and these had to be provided later by the builder—the contribution of the architect was at best insufficient. Freehand drawing seemed a more relevant prerequisite to the young aspirant designer, a medium that would permit the sketching of ideas that could later be converted into blueprint.

For Nwoko scholasticism in training was a lesser part of the problem. More serious was the continual utilization of architectural designs created for other times and far-off places. He could see no connection between temperate-zone construction and equatorial needs; moreover, when Western architects addressed themselves to building problems in the tropics, they introduced, in Nwoko's judgment, misguided solutions, such as structures sited for a maximum breezeway that was thought to keep interiors cool. If they had troubled to examine the traditional architecture of Africa, says Nwoko, they might have seen their error. The open construction merely allowed the hot exterior air to circulate throughout the building. "You might as well be outside," Nwoko observes, adding that expensive air-conditioning is no alternative answer.

Traditional architecture in Africa, Nwoko continues, is based upon the creation of a cool interior air bubble, insulated against noonday heat. The buildings, therefore, are enclosed and sealed, impervious to external temperatures. When Nwoko left school and settled in Ibadan, he eventually acquired a site where he started construction of a studio and house that was adapted from traditional patterns. The old houses had largely disappeared, Nwoko observes, because people had come under European influence and began to erect hot, stuffy dwellings topped with ugly, rusting corrugated iron roofs that offended the eye as they parboiled their occupants.

"I had no money," Nwoko recalls. "I couldn't afford the cinder blocks imported for all the fine houses. So I looked around. And I saw that the ground was of clay and laterite. It was there. It was free. So I said, 'Fine,' and we made our bricks for nothing." It was the traditional solution to which Nwoko added the improvement of a cement binder that provided greater durability against the weather and time.

The building was also traditional. Nwoko's structure was basically a rectangle surrounding a central court open to the sky, the opening defined by a slab-sided plastic funnel about eight-feet square that tapered downward and hovered over a shallow tiled basin situated slightly below floor level. Here, in season, the rains fell and were drawn off by drains, but the surrounding quarters, with their polished Japanese-style wood floors, remained secure and dry. Flying above, neither birds nor insects were encouraged to plunge into what looked from their perspective like a bottomless pit; hence, there was no problem with unwanted pests.

The purpose of the central vent, however, was the control of temperature, and was linked to louvered openings situated along the outside walls near ground level. The key was convection currents. Throughout the day the interior gradually heated, so that by evening it contained warm air in contrast to the declining temperatures of the external night atmosphere. The imbalance caused cool currents to enter through the louvers, sucked in as the hot internal air ascended through the central vent. During the night hours, therefore, the interior was refreshed, and by morning, as external temperatures rose, the house had become a cool bubble, held in place by the surrounding warmth and only gradually losing its freshness in the face of daytime heat. At evening the whole process began again.

Nwoko came to Ibadan in 1961 and for the following decade was primarily concerned with theatrical productions at the university's School of Drama and with the construction of his own studio, which in time came to include workshops and a half-finished theater to supplement office and living space. It emerged as a ruggedly handsome building combining clay bricks and fieldstone, embellished at intervals with decorative cement panels. The structure has withstood the ravages of tropical weather admirably in contrast to the soiled and worn plaster facades that are so characteristic of recent building in Africa. As his work progressed, Nwoko sharpened the clarity of his ideas, which came to focus on local needs and local solutions. "I never wanted to study abroad," Nwoko has observed, adding that foreign solutions were not likely to be useful outside their own context. "I've always wanted to study here, to solve the problems here."

Gradually Nwoko's reputation spread, and in 1969 the fathers of the Dominican mission in Ibadan, impressed with Nwoko's studio, asked him to design a plaque for the altar of their chapel. They went on to explain that they hoped eventually to build a permanent chapel to replace their temporary facilities. "Has the chapel been designed?" Nwoko wanted to know. It had not. "Well," he continued, "instead of just making you a plaque for the altar, I might as well make you a design that looks like an African [shrine.]" It was to be his first attempt at an architectural drawing.

The initial sketch was freehand, but when he thought he had what he wanted, Nwoko started to translate the design into an architectural drawing. "Of course it was crude, very crude," Nwoko later admitted, but the Dominican fathers liked his ideas and arranged for Nwoko to make a formal presentation to a church committee that had come from the United States to examine his proposal. Nwoko presented a paper that ranged widely over the problems of architecture and religious expression before centering on his plan for a Dominican chapel. The presentation and ensuing discussion went on all night, with sharp questioning from the Dominican order's own architects, but in the end Nwoko was able to convince the doubters. He built the chapel and later added other buildings, including cloisters, a refectory, and residences.

Once again Nwoko was able to put into effect ideas long germinating, particularly those stressing local solutions to local problems. The air-bubble principle was used to create a chapel interior of cool tranquility, contrasting with the tropical heat outdoors. The central vent was located in a tower that soared 150 feet and supported a

3,000-pound bell at its crest. To hoist the bell into place Nwoko had hoped to use the motor crane of a European contractor in Ibadan. The crane proved to be unreliable, and Nwoko turned to his African work crew for help. Could they raise the bell? Nwoko asked. They said they could and proceeded to do so with the classic technology of pulleys and an inclined plane.

Other building projects followed—several homes, including Nwoko's own dwelling in Idumuje Ugboko, and finally the arts theater in Benin. Each was a fresh solution to a new problem since Nwoko had no backlog of architectural plans to rely upon. "I never designed anything until the need arose," he observes. "It was the purpose that put the building together, and the image I wanted to court. That created the form."[4]

Here is classic eclecticism. Nwoko's African solution to an African problem is only a determination that the local need be met, that design fulfill that need, whether it be created afresh or borrowed from the traditions of Africa or those of other cultures. The theater at Benin is a good example of Nwoko's capacity to reach out for workable expedients wherever he finds them. "That theater," says Nwoko, "is the model theater that tries to solve theater design problems." The solutions have been drawn from many sources and its mechanics are based upon the latest in high technology, but, as Nwoko observes, "Benin's solution is really Greek plus Japanese."

Approached from the outside, the Benin theater looks faintly like a small sports stadium, an oval of marked horizontal stripes that alternates dark adobe bricks with lighter bands of concrete. The auditorium forms a semicircular amphitheater seating about 750 and descending to an orchestra that can provide further seating or double as a platform stage. Nwoko chose the Greek amphitheater for his model because of its similarity to the seating of folk theater and also because it enabled him to solve acoustic problems. He had already confronted acoustical questions in his theater building in Ibadan and so was now able to transfer his solutions to Benin, principally in the shape and texture of walls and ceiling.

The forestage at Benin runs the total width of the theater, with proportionate backstage depth and ample wings and flies that rise several stories to contain scenery and drops, all mechanically operated. Thus, the design of the auditorium is drawn from ancient Greece while the stage and backstage, which takes a good half of the total floor space, is patterned after the Japanese Kabuki theater. Nwoko recalls his residence in Paris in 1961 at a time when theater designers began to influence theater architecture, disturbed by the failure of architects to deal effectively with problems of sight lines, acoustics, or backstage facilities. Now, at Benin, Nwoko has made use of the Kabuki concept that stresses the importance of the performer, a point of view that contrasts with the neglect of the performing artist in the Western theater. The Benin installation is provided with innumerable practice rooms and makeup rooms, storage facilities and office space. There are wide corridors for easy access and several stories of working space to take care of the largest of performing companies.[5]

Nwoko's design interests stretch in many directions. It was to be expected that he would create the stool and sceptre used for the investiture of his brother as Obi Nwoko III, and it was equally certain that he would design the seats for the Benin theater, to be turned out by the furniture plant now in place at Idumuje Ugboko. Nwoko's furniture is architectural, reminiscent in this respect of the work of Frank Lloyd Wright. For some, Nwoko's seating may seem heavy, both in weight and design, but, as usual, Nwoko has a reason for his action. Nigerians are hard on public property, he points out. Whatever is produced must be durable as well as comfortable. Hence Nwoko creates rugged chairs and other furniture and urges new designs for public transport, including airplanes, that will allow for the enormous loads that the typical Nigerian carries with him on every journey. School furnishings too must be able to withstand much punishment. Present classroom equipment, he points out, has a life expectancy of two years or less. This means expensive replacement that taxes limited funds. "As the plan for mass education builds up," Nwoko warns, "the importance of retaining gained grounds in the provision of physical facilities is very important."

This throws the emphasis on local production, says Nwoko, for foreign manufactories are interested in high turnover and quick replacement. African artists, Nwoko urges, must create local designs for local industries. "The right design," he says, "can only be produced by a patriotic citizen whose primary consideration is the success of the Nation." It is a high-minded and perhaps quixotic judgment, but there seems little doubt that it is the guideline that directs Nwoko's own work.[6]

## An African Voice

The ideas of Demas Nwoko, so winningly presented at Bellagio, appeared to offer a promising resolution of the old divisions that had long separated those Africans favoring Westernization and those urging the validity of the African past. As the Bellagio meeting drew to a close, this notion of synthesis was taken up by the Kenyan political scientist, Ali Mazrui. There is no longer any possibility that Africa can turn from Europe, said Mazrui. Past reactions have tended to reject Europe, to glorify indigenous institutions because they were criticized or ignored by the West. Clearly European ideas and institutions have become an integral part of the African present, Mazrui went on. At the same time there is a body of traditional values and institutions that can also serve the present in effective union with what is absorbed from the West.

Africans should no longer be so defensive, said Mazrui. Let us fuse the best of African and Western civilization in a new African culture, but let us go one step further. Let us reach out to practice a "counter-penetration" in a shrinking world by making a positive contribution to modern world civilization. It will not be easy in the face of a dominant Western culture, Mazrui concluded, but, if successful, it will establish a genuine African presence, a welcome African voice, in the modern world.[7]

It was not a new idea, expressed a century earlier by Edward Blyden, and later by Senghor in his Civilization of the Universal. What did seem new, however, was the prospect that, come what might, modern African culture would henceforth comprise an indivisible unity of Western and African inspiration.

# Notes

(Interviews tape-recorded by the author are cited by the name of the individual and the date of the interview, as, for example, Efua Sutherland, March 1, 1981.)

## Prologue

1 *Paris-Dakar* (Dakar), June 21, 1960; Kwame Nkrumah, *I Speak of Freedom* (New York: Praeger, 1961), p. 106; Efua Sutherland, March 1, 1981; *The Spectator* (London), November 25, 1960, p. 804.

2 *New Statesman* (London), November 6, 1964, pp. 692–94.

3 *Reporter* (Nairobi), December 14, 1963, pp. 10–11, 13; December 9, 1963, pp. 10, 11; November 25, 1961, pp. 11–12; *West Africa* (London), February 23, 1957, p. 183; March 2, 1957, p. 207; *Paris-Dakar,* April 27, 1960; *Afrique Nouvelle* (Dakar), May 4, 1960; *Harper's* (New York), October 1966, pp. 74–86; *Daily Times* (Lagos), September 2, September 23, October 5, 1960; *The Spectator,* November 25, 1960, pp. 804, 806; Nkrumah, *I Speak of Freedom,* pp. 109–10; Julius Nyerere, *Freedom and Unity* (Dar es Salaam: Oxford University Press, 1966), p. 72; Julius Nyerere, *Ujamaa: Essays on Socialism* (Dar es Salaam: Oxford University Press, 1968), pp. 3–7.

## 1 Colonial Legacies

1 There are a number of studies dealing with ideas and activities of the individuals described in the early sections of this chapter. Many of these works have been consulted, but most of the discussion and conclusions

have been drawn from my *Origins of Modern African Thought* (New York: Praeger, 1967).

2 *Time* (New York), October 10, 1960; *The Economist* (London), October 8, 1960, p. 131; *Daily Times*, September 21, 1960; *Life* (New York), September 26, 1960, p. 74; *West Africa*, January 9, 1960, p. 35.

3 American Universities Field Service Reports (Hanover, N.H.), RF-3-61, pp. 6–7; *Observer* (London), September 8, 1957; *New York Times*, April 19, 1959.

4 *West Africa*, March 29, 1958, p. 291; *Saturday Review* (New York), October 31, 1970, p. 44; *New York Times*, March 25, 1962.

5 Abubakar Tafawa Balewa, *Nigeria Speaks* (Ikeja: Longmans of Nigeria, 1964), pp. 19–20.

6 *West Africa*, March 2, 1957, p. 211; March 9, 1957, p. 219.

7 American Universities Field Service Reports, VDB-2-65, p. 13, n.5; *New York Times*, March 25, 1962.

8 *Times* (London), March 5, 1959; *Financial Times* (London), March 5, 1959.

9 Kwame Nkrumah, *Africa Must Unite* (New York: Praeger, 1963), pp. 174–75, 181–82, 167–72, 193.

10 *New York Times Magazine*, February 16, 1959.

## 2 Présence Africaine *and the Expression of Cultural Freedom*

1 Julius Nyerere, *Ujamaa: Essays on Socialism* (Dar es Salaam: Oxford University Press, 1968), pp. 1–17, esp. 6 and 12. See Cranford Pratt, *The Critical Phase in Tanzania, 1945–1968* (Cambridge: Cambridge University Press, 1976), for a detailed analysis of Nyerere's ideas on development, esp. chaps. 4 and 8.

2 Sékou Touré, *Expérience Guinéenne et Unité Africaine* (Paris: Présence Africaine, 1959), pp. 79–88; American Universities Field Service Reports, West Africa Series, VDB-8-62, pp. 1–63.

3 Sékou Touré, *L'Action Politique du Parti Démocratique de Guinée* (Paris: Présence Africaine, 1959), pp. 161–68.

4 J. Rabemananjara, April 9, 1981; Mme Alioune Diop, February 19, 1981; *Encounter* (London), January 1957, pp. 52, 56.

5 *Présence Africaine* (Paris), June–November 1956, nos. 8–10, pp. 190–205.

6 Ibid., pp. 9–18; *Encounter*, January 1957, pp. 56–57.

7 *Présence Africaine*, June–November 1956, nos. 8–10, pp. 347–60.

8 Thomas Hodgkin, "The African Renaissance," *The Listener* (London), August 15, 1957; *Présence Africaine*, June–November 1956, nos. 8–10, pp. 363–64.

9 Davidson Nicol, May 11, 1981; *Présence Africaine*, June–November 1956, nos. 8–10, pp. 51–65, 67–68; *Encounter*, January 1957, p. 54.

10 Bakary Traoré, February 19, 1981; Bakary Traoré, "Temoinage," mimeo-

graphed; *Présence Africaine,* October–November 1955, no. 4, pp. 12–15, 36–41; J. L. Hymans, *Léopold Sédar Senghor* (Edinburgh: University of Edinburgh Press, 1971), p. 125; Dieng Amadi Ali, February 20, 1981; Présence Africaine, *Les Etudiants Noirs Parlent* (Paris: Présence Africaine, 1952), pp. 287–303.

11 *Présence Africaine,* June–November 1956, nos. 8–10, pp. 179–89, 207–13, 238–44; *Encounter,* January 1957, p. 57.

12 Hodgkin, "The African Renaissance"; Davidson Nicol, May 11, 1981; *Présence Africaine,* June–November 1956, nos. 8–10, pp. 318–25.

13 *Encounter,* January 1957, pp. 52–53, 58; *Présence Africaine,* June–November 1956, nos. 8–10, pp. 190, 207, 213, 215–16, 221–23, 383; Présence Africaine, *Hommage à Léopold Sédar Senghor* (Paris: Présence Africaine, 1976), pp. 104–6, 107–13; Cheikh Anta Diop, February 19, 1981.

14 George Padmore, *Pan-Africanism or Communism?* (London: Dobson, 1956); James R. Hooker, *Black Revolutionary* (New York: Praeger, 1967).

15 *Présence Africaine,* June–November 1956, nos. 8–10, pp. 193–94; Aimé Césaire, *Letter to Maurice Thorez* (Paris: Présence Africaine, 1957).

16 *Présence Africaine,* June–November 1956, nos. 8–10, p. 213; Mme Alioune Diop, February 19, 1981.

17 Abiola Irele, March 12, 1981; Hymans, *Léopold Sédar Senghor,* p. 172.

18 Bakary Traoré, February 19, 1981; Abiola Irele, March 12, 1981.

19 Hymans, *Léopold Sédar Senghor,* p. 171; *Présence Africaine,* August–September 1955, no. 3, pp. 3–4; Traoré, "Temoinage," pp. 9–10; *Présence Africaine,* October–November 1955, no. 4, pp. 5–15.

## 3 The Visual Arts and African Independence

1 Eliot Eliosofon, *The Sculpture of Africa* (New York: Praeger, 1958).

2 Quoted in H. U. Beier, *Contemporary Art in Africa* (London: Pall Mall, 1968), p. 3; *New York Times,* arts and leisure section, March 1, 1970.

3 *New York Times,* January 29, 1977.

4 Author's diary, March 14, 15, 1981.

5 Albert Opoku, June 6, 1980; Oku Ampofo, March 8, 1979, March 2, 1981.

## 4 The Independent African Theater

1 Wole Soyinka, *Myth, Literature and the African World* (Cambridge: Cambridge University Press, 1976), pp. 2–3.

2 H. U. Beier, "Yoruba Theatre," in H. U. Beier, ed., *Introduction to African Literature* (London: Longmans, 1967), pp. 243–44.

3 Bakary Traoré, *Le Théatre Négro-Africain* (Paris: Présence Africaine, 1958), pp. 17–24.

4  *Theatre Arts* (New York), November 1963, p. 65; R. Crawford diary, November 5, 1963, Rockefeller Foundation Archives, Record Group 1.2, University College, Ibadan, Drama, 1961–63.

5  Geoffrey Axworthy, "Developments in the Nigerian Theatre, 1957–67," *Speech and Drama* (London), Spring 1969.

6  Soyinka, *Myth, Literature and the African World*, pp. 37–39.

7  Geoffrey Axworthy, September 29, 1980; Wole Soyinka, June 7, 1981; Dapo Adelugba, March 10, 1981; Ebun Clark, *Hubert Ogunde: The Making of Nigerian Theatre* (Oxford: Oxford University Press, 1979); Abiola Irele, March 21, 1981.

8  Geoffrey Axworthy, September 29, 1980; Geoffrey Axworthy, "The African Theatre," mimeographed; Geoffrey Axworthy to author, December 15, 1980; Dapo Adelugba, March 10, 1981; Abiola Irele, March 21, 1981; Dapo Adelugba and Geoffrey Axworthy, "Nigeria—Theatre Survey," *New Theatre Magazine* (Bristol, England) 12, no. 2 (1972) : 15–18.

9  Geoffrey Axworthy, September 29, 1980; Axworthy, "African Theatre"; Adelugba and Axworthy, "Nigeria—Theatre Survey"; Axworthy, "Developments in the Nigerian Theatre."

10  Clark, *Hubert Ogunde*, pp. 99–100.

11  Geoffrey Axworthy, September 29, 1980; Geoffrey Axworthy to Chadbourne Gilpatric, May 22, 1963, Rockefeller Foundation Archives, Record Group 1.2, 497R, University College, Ibadan, Drama, Ogunmola; Geoffrey Axworthy to Chadbourne Gilpatric, June 18, 1963, Rockefeller Foundation Archives, Record Group 1.2, 497, University College, Ibadan, Drama, 1961–63.

12  J. Parry to author, May 22, 1959, "Indigenous Drama of Nigeria," Rockefeller Foundation Archives, Record Group 1.2, 495R, University College, Ibadan, Drama, 1959–62.

13  Geoffrey Axworthy, September 29, 1980; Dapo Adelugba, March 10, 1981; Wole Soyinka, June 7, 1981.

14  The details of Soyinka's activities are combined with critical studies of his work in Eldred D. Jones, *The Writing of Wole Soyinka* (London: Heinemann, 1973), and Gerald Moore, *Wole Soyinka* (London: Evans, 1971).

15  *Transition* (Kampala) 31 (1967) : 11–13; *Transition* 42 (1973) : 62–63. The political commentary in Soyinka's writings is examined in R. W. July, "The Artist's Credo: The Political Philosophy of Wole Soyinka," *Journal of Modern African Studies* 19, no. 3.

16  *West Africa*, January 1, 1966, p. 22; *Daily Times*, October 18, 1965.

17  *Kongi's Harvest* in his *Collected Plays* (London: Oxford University Press, 1974), vol. 2, esp. p. 99; Geoffrey Axworthy, September 29, 1980.

18  *Herald Tribune* (Paris edition), October 27, 1961; *The New Ghana* (Accra) 1, no. 11, 12; Nkrumah talk at Experimental Theatre, October 1961, Rockefeller Foundation Archives, Record Group 1.2, 496R, Ghana Experimental Theatre, 1958–61.

19  Efua Sutherland, March 1, 1981.

20 Bill Marshall, February 28, 1981.

21 P. S. Banaag to author, December 26, 1961, Rockefeller Foundation Archives, Record Group 1.2, P. S. Banaag, 1961.

22 Efua Sutherland, March 1, 1981.

23 Ibid.; Louise Crane, *Ms. Africa* (New York: Lippincott, 1973), pp. 47–52.

24 Efua Sutherland, March 1, 1981.

## 5 *Africans Dance*

1 Geoffrey Gorer, *Africa Dances* (New York: Norton, 1962), pp. v–vi, 213; Rockefeller Foundation Archives, author's diary, March 2, 1958, and March 12, 1979.

2 James Anquandah, "Men of Our Time: Dr. Ephraim Amu," unpublished typescript; Ephraim Amu, March 4, 1981.

3 Anquandah, "Men of Our Time"; Ephraim Amu, March 4, 1981; Ephraim Amu to author, November 22, 1960, and J. H. Nketia to author, January 13, 1961, Rockefeller Foundation Archives, Record Group 1.2, 496R, University College of Ghana, African Studies.

4 Author's diary, February 4, 1958, and March 22, 1979, and J. H. Nketia, fellowship application and attachments, Rockefeller Foundation Archives. See also Alan Merriam to author, April 24, 1958, Rockefeller Foundation Archives, Record Group 1.2, Nketia, Joseph H., July 31, 1959.

5 J. H. Nketia to author, October 11, 1960, Rockefeller Foundation Archives, Record Group 1.2, University College of Ghana, African Studies, 1958–62; author's diary, March 22, 1979; J. H. Nketia, *Ethnomusicology in Ghana* (Accra: Ghana Universities Press, 1970), p. 10.

6 Nketia, *Ethnomusicology in Ghana*, p. 10; J. H. Nketia, "The Creative Arts and the Community," contribution to a symposium on building an intellectual community in Ghana, November 25, 1959.

7 J. H. Nketia to author, January 13, 1961, and April 27, 1962, Rockefeller Foundation Archives, Record Group 1.2, 496R, University College of Ghana, African Studies; J. H. Nketia to author, "School of Music and Drama, Interim Report," Rockefeller Foundation Archives, Record Group 1.2, 496R, University College of Ghana, African Studies, 1963–64.

8 Albert Opoku, June 7, 1980; Albert Opoku, "The Ghana Dance Ensemble, the African Dance Company of Ghana," mimeographed, esp. p. 7; A. A. Y. Kerematen, *Asante Cultural Center* (Accra: Guinea Press, n.d.); Albert Opoku, fellowship application and enclosures, May 3, 1960, Rockefeller Foundation Archives, RG 10; author's diary, March 22, 1979.

9 Albert Opoku, June 6, 1980.

10 Ibid.; Albert Opoku, June 7, 1980; *New York Times*, November 26, 1968, p. 40; Opoku, "The Ghana Dance Ensemble," p. 20.

11 Opoku, "The Ghana Dance Ensemble," pp. 5–6.

12 *New York Times*, November 27, 1968, p. 38; Opoku, "The Ghana Dance Ensemble," p. 12.

13  *New York Times*, February 17, 1959, p. 28, and February 22, 1959, sec. 2, p. 10.
14  Ladji Camera, March 1, 1982; *New York Times*, February 22, 1959, sec. 2, p. 10.
15  Ladji Camera, March 1, 1982; *Présence Africaine*, June–September 1957, nos. 14–15, pp. 202–3, 209.
16  *New York Times*, February 22, 1959, sec. 2, p. 10.
17  Ladji Camera, March 1, 1982.

## 6  *Literary Perspectives of Cultural Independence*

1  Sembene Ousmane, *God's Bits of Wood* (London: Heinemann, 1970), p. 2.
2  Ibid., p. 57.
3  Ibid., p. 106.
4  Ibid., p. 44.
5  Ibid., p. 51.
6  Ibid., p. 13.
7  Ibid., p. 75.
8  Ibid., p. 76.
9  Ibid., pp. 29–30.
10  Ibid., p. 163.
11  Ibid., pp. 180, 181.
12  Ibid., pp. 8, 20, 221, 237.
13  Yambo Ouologuem, *Bound to Violence* (London: Heinemann, 1971), p. 3.
14  Ibid., pp. 4–5.
15  Ibid., pp. 6, 12.
16  Ibid., pp. 18, 24.
17  Ibid., p. 33.
18  Ibid., pp. 94–95. See below, pp. 222–26.
19  Ibid., pp. 160–61.
20  Ibid., p. 167.
21  Ayi Kwei Armah, *The Healers* (London: Heinemann, 1978), pp. 5, 6.
22  Ibid., p. 39.
23  Ibid., pp. 79–84.
24  Ibid., p. 271.
25  Ibid., p. 30.
26  Ibid., p. 255.
27  Ibid., p. 182.
28  Ibid., p. 280.
29  Ibid., p. 269.
30  Ibid., p. 291.
31  Ibid., pp. 308–9.
32  Ibid., p. 270.

## 7 *The Search for a Usable Past*

1 Kwame Nkrumah, "The African Genius," speech delivered at the opening of the Institute of African Studies, October 25, 1963 (N.p., n.d.), p. 3.

2 These ideas have been artfully developed in J. F. A. Ajayi, "The Place of African History and Culture in the Process of Nation Building in Africa, South of the Sahara," *Journal of Negro Education* 30, no. 3, 206–13.

3 *Sierra Leone Weekly News*, February 18, 1893; A. B. C. Sibthorpe, *The History of Sierra Leone* (London: Frank Cass, 1970), preface to first edition.

4 C. C. Reindorf, *The History of the Gold Coast and Asante* (Accra: Ghana Universities Press, 1966).

5 A more detailed analysis of the histories of Samuel Johnson, C. C. Reindorf, and A. B. C. Sibthorpe is found in R. W. July, *The Origins of Modern African Thought* (New York: Praeger, 1967), chap. 13. For Johnson, see also J. F. A. Ajayi, "Samuel Johnson, Historian of the Yoruba," *The Historia* (journal of the University of Ibadan Historical Society) 1, no. 1 (April 1964): 10–18.

6 George Padmore, *The Gold Coast Revolution* (London: Dobson, 1953), pp. 3, 8, 62, 64; see also J. R. Hooker, *Black Revolutionary* (New York: Praeger, 1967), pp. 115–18.

7 J. C. deGraft-Johnson, *African Glory* (New York: Walker, [1966]), esp. p. 192.

8 Théophile Obenga, "Méthode et conception historiques de Cheikh Anta Diop," *Présence Africaine*, no. 74 (second quarter 1970), pp. 5–6, 9; Mercer Cook, ed. and trans., *The African Origin of Civilization* (Westport, Conn.: Lawrence Hill, 1974), pp. xii–xvii.

9 Cheikh Anta Diop, February 19, 1981.

10 K. O. Dike, May 23, 1980; also see *The Listener*, November 28, 1963.

11 K. O. Dike, May 23, 1980; K. O. Dike, *Report on the Preservation and Administration of Historical Records and the Establishment of a Public Record Office in Nigeria* (Nigerian Government Printer, 1954).

12 K. O. Dike, May 23, 1980; Carnegie Corporation Archives, Ibadan University, Historical Research and Travel; Alan Ryder, *Benin and the Europeans, 1485–1897* (New York: Humanities Press, 1969), pp. ix–x; J. F. A. Ajayi, March 19, 1981.

13 *Report of Visitation to University College, Ibadan, January 1961* (Ibadan: University of Ibadan Press, 1961), pp. 58–60; J. F. A. Ajayi, March 19, 1981.

14 K. O. Dike, May 23, 1980; J. F. A. Ajayi, March 19, 1981; Michael Crowder, September 30, 1980.

15 J. F. A. Ajayi, March 19, 1981; J. F. A. Ajayi, *Christian Missions in Nigeria, 1841–1891* (London: Longmans, 1965), p. x; *University College, Ibadan, Calendar, 1961–62* (Ibadan: University of Ibadan Press, 1961), pp. 67–68; *Calendar, University of Ibadan, 1965–66* (Ibadan: University

of Ibadan Press, 1965), pp. 65–66; Eric Ashby, *Universities: British, Indian, African* (London: Weidenfeld and Nicholson, 1966), p. 239.

16  Jan Vansina, "Recording the Oral History of the Bakuba," *Journal of African History* 1, no. 1, 52.

17  Ibid., pp. 45–53; 1, no. 2, 257–70.

18  Alan Ogot, March 25, 1981; R. Oliver to K. Ingham, September 30, 1959, and R. Oliver to author, May 4, 1960, Rockefeller Foundation Archives, Record Group 10, Ogot, Bethwell A., 1962; B. A. Ogot, *History of the Southern Luo* (Nairobi: East African Publishing House, 1967), pp. 11–28.

19  B. A. Ogot to author, March 29, 1960, July 17, 1960, May 5, 1961, Rockefeller Foundation Archives, Record Group 10, Ogot, Bethwell A.; "Report on . . . Field Work, January–December 1961," ibid.; B. A. Ogot, March 25, 1981.

20  B. A. Ogot, "The Concept of Jok," *African Studies* 20, no. 2 (1961); B. A. Ogot, March 25, 1981.

21  Ibid.; Andrew Roberts, ed., *Tanzania Before 1900* (Nairobi: East African Publishing House, 1968), pp. v–xii.

22  Michael Crowder, September 19, 1980, conference, "African Culture and Intellectual Leaders and the Development of the New African Nations," Bellagio, Italy, September 17–22, 1980.

23  R. W. July and Peter Benson, eds., *African Cultural and Intellectual Leaders and the Development of the New African Nations* (New York: Rockefeller Foundation, 1982), pp. 107–11. J. F. A. Ajayi, "In Search of Relevance in the Humanities in Africa," Second World Black and African Festival of Arts and Culture, *Colloquium on Black Civilization and Education, Proceedings* (Nigeria, 1977), vol. 1, 34–40.

## 8  The Idea of an African University

1  Edward W. Blyden, *Christianity, Islam and the Negro Race* (Edinburgh: University of Edinburgh Press, 1967), pp. 71–93.

2  The development of university education in Africa is set forth in detail in Eric Ashby, *Universities: British, Indian, African* (London: Weidenfeld and Nicholson, 1966), pp. 190–235. Graham Irwin to author, February 27, 1982.

3  Ashby, *Universities*, pp. 236–37, 240–42, 308–9; Graham Irwin, November 30, 1981.

4  Author's diary, February 5, 1958; J. F. A. Ajayi, March 19, 1981; Ashby, *Universities*, pp. 236–50, 258–59; Geoffrey Bing, *Reap the Whirlwind* (London: MacGibbon and Key, 1968), pp. 353–54.

5  Ashby, *Universities*, pp. 242–47, 259–60; Kwame Nkrumah, *I Speak of Freedom* (New York: Praeger, 1961), p. 243.

6  Nkrumah's ideas on African development are liberally sprinkled through his writings. See, for example, *Ghana: The Autobiography of Kwame*

*Nkrumah* (New York: International Publishers, 1971), *I Speak of Freedom,* or *Africa Must Unite* (New York: Praeger, 1963).

7   Ashby, *Universities,* pp. 236–37.

8   Graham Irwin, November 30, 1981; Thomas Hodgkin, September 27, 1980; Bing, *Reap the Whirlwind,* pp. 356–60; Ashby, *Universities,* 309–10; Adam Curle, "Nationalism and Higher Education in Ghana," *Universities Quarterly* 16, no. 3 (1962): 232–33; Dennis Austin, *Ghana Observed* (Manchester: University of Manchester Press, 1976), p. 170.

9   Dorothy Hodgkin, September 27, 1980; Graham Irwin, November 30, 1981.

10  Bing, *Reap the Whirlwind,* pp. 359–60; Curle, "Nationalism and Higher Education in Ghana," pp. 234–35.

11  Thomas Hodgkin, September 27, 1980.

12  Curle, "Nationalism and Higher Education in Ghana," pp. 236–41.

13  Ashby, *Universities,* pp. 311–13; Bing, *Reap the Whirlwind,* pp. 363–64.

14  Curle, "Nationalism and Higher Education in Ghana," pp. 237–39; Thomas Hodgkin, September 27, 1980; author's diaries, September 6, 1961, February 27, 1962, December 8, 1961; Bing, *Reap the Whirlwind,* p. 361; F. W. Beecham to chairman, University College Council, May 27, 1961; resolution passed by the Academic Board of the University College, Ghana, May 31, 1961.

15  *Ghanaian Times* (Accra), June 6, 1961.

16  Bing, *Reap the Whirlwind,* pp. 364–65; Thomas Hodgkin, September 27, 1980; Graham Irwin, November 30, 1981.

17  Thomas Hodgkin, "Ghana Politics, 1961–1965," unpublished typescript, March 24, 1966, esp. pp. 3, 7–8.

18  C. C. O'Brien, *Writers and Politics* (New York: Pantheon, 1965), pp. 240–44; Thomas Hodgkin, September 27, 1980.

19  Thomas Hodgkin, September 27, 1980; O'Brien, *Writers and Politics,* pp. 244–51; Austin, *Ghana Observed,* pp. 172–74; Hodgkin, "Ghana Politics, 1961–1965"; C. C. O'Brien to author, March 30, 1982, July 30, 1982; author's diary, March 22, 1979.

## 9   Organizing Africana

1   *Investment in Education* (Ashby Report) (London: St. Clements Press, 1960), p. 23; Davidson Nicol, "The Realities of Ashby's Vision," *Universities Quarterly* 15, no. 4 (1961): 378.

2   Author's diary, February 4, 1958; Eric Ashby to author, January 9, 1983; Eric Ashby, *Universities: British, Indian, African* (London: Weidenfeld and Nicholson, 1966), p. 241.

3   J. F. A. Ajayi, March 19, 1981; P. C. Lloyd memorandum of October 24, 1961, "The Functions of the African Studies Institute," J. E. Black diary, October 4, 1962, Rockefeller Foundation Archives, Record Group 1.2, 497,

University College, Ibadan, African Studies, 1961–62; J. F. A. Ajayi to author, December 14, 1982.

4 R. W. July and Peter Benson, eds., *African Cultural and Intellectual Leaders and the Development of the New African Nations* (New York: Rockefeller Foundation, 1982), pp. 56, 57–58, 60, 71.

5 Michel Crowder, September 30, 1980.

6 Kwame Nkrumah, *The African Genius* (N.p., [1963]), pp. 2–3.

7 A. M. Opoku, June 6, 1980.

8 Thomas Hodgkin, September 27, 1980.

9 Ibid.; author's diary, January 31, 1961, "Appendix I, African Studies, Institute of African Studies," note by Mr. Thomas Hodgkin, Rockefeller Foundation Archives, Record Group 1.2, 496R, University College, Ghana, African Studies, 1958–62; J. H. Nketia, March 22, 1979; Ghana Institute of African Studies papers, foreword to first issue of institute bulletin.

10 R. K. Davidson diary, November 7, 1963, Thomas Hodgkin to author, August 12, 1963, author to Chadbourne Gilpatric, May 22, 1963, Rockefeller Foundation Archives, Record Group 1.2, 496R, University College, Ghana, African Studies, 1963–64; M. Field to Kwame Nkrumah, n.d., Ghana Institute of African Studies papers; report of Institute of African Studies (Ghana), 1963–64.

11 July and Benson, eds., *African Cultural and Intellectual Leaders*, pp. 66–71; J. H. Nketia, March 22, 1979; Ghana Arts Council papers.

12 July and Benson, eds., *African Cultural and Intellectual Leaders*, pp. 72–76; "University of Ghana, School of Music and Drama," Rockefeller Foundation Archives, Record Group 1.2, 496R, University College, Ghana, African Studies, 1963–64.

13 K. Thompson diary, March 25, 1961, Rockefeller Foundation Archives, Record Group 1.2, 497, University College, Ibadan, African Studies, 1961–62; K. O. Dike, May 23, 1980.

14 University College, Ibadan, *Calendar, 1962–63* (Ibadan: University of Ibadan Press, 1962), pp. 95–98, 110; "Draft Proposal for the Establishment of an Institute of African Studies," Rockefeller Foundation Archives, Record Group 1.2, 497, University College, Ibadan, African Studies, 1961–62.

15 *Calendar, University of Ibadan, 1963–1964* (Ibadan: University of Ibadan Press, 1963), pp. 141–42; *Calendar, University of Ibadan, 1965–1966* (Ibadan: University of Ibadan Press, 1965), pp. 184–87. Chadbourne Gilpatric diary, October 26, 1962, Rockefeller Foundation Archives, Record Group 1.2, 497, University College, Ibadan, African Studies, 1961–62.

16 J. F. A. Ajayi, March 19, 1981; author's diary, April 23, 1964; author to J. E. Black, June 23, 1966, Rockefeller Foundation Archives, Record Group 1.2, 497, University College, Ibadan, African Studies, 1963–66.

## 10   The African Personality and Europe

1   Philip D. Curtin, *The Image of Africa* (Madison: University of Wisconsin Press, 1964), pp. 363–87.

2   J. C. Carothers, *The African Mind in Health and Disease* (Geneva: World Health Organization, 1956), pp. 71–82.

3   Ibid., pp. 84–94, 101–4.

4   Ibid., pp. 107–10, 171.

5   O. Mannoni, *Prospero and Caliban* (London: Methuen, 1956), pp. 11, 38–88.

6   R. W. July, *The Origins of Modern African Thought* (New York: Praeger, 1967), pp. 212–20.

7   L. S. Senghor, *On African Socialism* (New York: Praeger, 1964), pp. 13, 71; L. S. Senghor, "African-Negro Aesthetics," *Diogenes,* no. 16 (Winter 1956), pp. 23–24.

8   Jean-Paul Sartre, *Black Orpheus* (Paris: Présence Africaine, 1962), esp. pp. 31, 44, 59–60, 61, 62.

9   Irene Gendzier, *Frantz Fanon* (London: Wildwood House, 1973), pp. 4–5.

10  Frantz Fanon, *Toward the African Revolution* (New York: Grove Press, 1967), pp. 17–27; Frantz Fanon, *Black Skin, White Masks* (New York: Grove Press, 1967), pp. 110, 112.

11  Fanon, *Black Skin, White Masks,* pp. 122–23, 124, 129–31, 132–33.

12  Ibid., pp. 93, 115–17, 135.

13  Frantz Fanon, *The Wretched of the Earth* (New York: Grove Press, 1966), pp. 206–48, esp. 212, 225, 233, and 243.

14  Gendzier, *Frantz Fanon,* pp. 72–88.

15  D. D. Nicholas, D. A. Ampofo, et al., "Attitudes and Practises of Traditional Birth Attendants in Rural Ghana," *Bulletin of the World Health Organization* 54 (1976) : 343–47; Albert Opoku, June 6, 1980.

16  P. A. Twumasi, *Medical Systems in Ghana* (Accra-Tema: Ghana Publishing, 1975), p. 108; T. A. Lambo, "A Form of Social Psychiatry in Africa," *World Mental Health* 13, no. 4, 6–14.

17  Lambo, "A Form of Social Psychiatry in Africa," pp. 1–5; T. A. Lambo, *First Pan-African Psychiatric Conference, Report Abeokuta, Nigeria, 1961* (Ibadan: Government Printer, n.d.), pp. 60–64.

18  K. Wiredu, *Philosophy and an African Culture* (Cambridge: Cambridge University Press, 1980), pp. 32, 37–38, 48–49; P. J. Hountondji, *African Philosophy: Myth and Reality* (Bloomington: Indiana University Press, 1983), p. 53.

19  Wiredu, *Philosophy and an African Culture,* pp. 28, 29, 40–42, 47.

20  M. Towa, *Essai Sur la Problématique Philosophique dans l'Afrique Actuelle* (Yaoundé, Cameroon: Editions Cle, 1979), pp. 35–59, esp. 41 and 48; Peter Bodunrin, "The Question of African Philosophy," *Philosophy,* no. 56 (1981), p. 167.

21  Hountondji, *African Philosophy,* pp. 34–44, 48, 50, 97–101.

## 11 *An African Voice*

1 The papers presented at the Bellagio conference are combined in R. W. July and Peter Benson, eds., *African Cultural and Intellectual Leaders and the Development of the New African Nations* (New York: Rockefeller Foundation, 1982).

2 Demas Nwoko, March 13, 1981; author's diary, March 14–15, 1981.

3 Author's diary, March 14–15, 1981; Demas Nwoko, March 15, 1981.

4 Demas Nwoko, March 15, 1981; author's diary, February 16, 1979.

5 Author's diary, March 16, 1981.

6 *New Culture* 1, no. 7 (June 1979): 2–3.

7 July and Benson, eds., *African Cultural and Intellectual Leaders*, pp. 24–25.

# Bibliography
## Sources and Works Mentioned or Cited

### Archives

Carnegie Corporation Papers, New York.
Ghana Arts Council Papers, Accra.
Ghana Institute of African Studies Papers, Legon.
Rockefeller Foundation Archives, Pocantico Hills, N.Y.

### Manuscripts and Tapes

Anquandah, James. "Men of Our Times: Dr. Ephraim Amu," typescript (author's copy).
Axworthy, Geoffrey. "The African Theatre," mimeographed (author's copy).
Conference on African Cultural and Intellectual Leaders and the Development of the New African Nations. Bellagio, Italy, September 1980, proceedings tapes (author's possession).
Hodgkin, Thomas. "Ghana Politics, 1961–1965." London: Chatham House, March 24, 1966, typescript (author's copy).
Interview tapes with Dapo Adelugba, J. F. A. Ajayi, Oku Ampofo, Ephraim Amu, Geoffrey Axworthy, Michael Crowder, Amady Ali Dieng, K. O. Dike, Mme Alioune Diop, Cheikh Anta Diop, Dorothy Hodgkin, Thomas Hodgkin, Abiola Irele, Graham Irwin, Camera Ladji, Bill Marshall, Davidson Nicol, J. H. Nketia, Demas Nwoko, B. A. Ogot, Albert Opoku, J. Rabemananjara, Wole Soyinka, Efua Sutherland, Bakary Traoré (author's possession).
Nketia, J. H. "The Creative Arts and the Community," contribution to a symposium on building an intellectual community in Ghana, November 25, 1959, offprint, n.d., n.p. (author's copy).
Opoku, Albert. "The Ghana Dance Ensemble, the African Dance Company of Ghana," mimeographed (author's copy).
Traoré, Bakary. "Temoinage," mimeographed (author's copy).

## Newspapers and Periodicals

*Afrique Nouvelle*, Dakar

*American Universities Field Service Reports*, Hanover, New Hampshire

*Daily Times*, Lagos

*Economist*, London

*Financial Times*, London

*Ghanaian Times*, Accra

*Harper's*, New York

*Herald Tribune*, Paris

*Life*, New York

*Listener*, London

*New Culture*, Ibadan

*The New Ghana*, [Accra]

*New Statesman*, London

*New York Times*, New York

*New Theatre Magazine*, Bristol, England

*Observer*, London

*Paris-Dakar*, Dakar

*Présence Africaine*, Paris

*Reporter*, Nairobi

*Saturday Review*, New York

*Spectator*, London

*Speech and Drama*, London

*Theatre Arts*, New York

*Times*, London

*Transition*, Kampala

*West Africa*, London

## Articles

Ajayi, J. F. A. "The Place of African History and Culture in the Process of Nation Building in Africa, South of the Sahara." *The Journal of Negro Education* 30, no. 3 (Summer 1961).

———. "Samuel Johnson, Historian of the Yoruba." *The Historia* (journal of the University of Ibadan Historical Society) 1, no. 1 (April 1964).

———. "In Search of Relevance in the Humanities in Africa." Second World Black and African Festival of Arts and Culture, *Colloquium on Black Civilization and Education, Proceedings*, vol. 1 (Nigeria, 1977).

Axworthy, Geoffrey. "Developments in the Nigerian Theatre." *Speech and Drama*, Spring 1969.

———. "Nigeria—Theatre Survey." *New Theatre Magazine* 12, no. 2 (1972).

Baldwin, James. "Princes and Powers." *Encounter*, January 1957.

Beier, H. U. "Yoruba Theatre," in H. U. Beier, ed., *Introduction to African Literature* (London: Longman, 1967).

Bodunrin, Peter. "The Question of African Philosophy." *Philosophy*, no. 56 (1981).

Curle, Adam. "Nationalism and Higher Education in Ghana." *Universities Quarterly* 16, no. 3 (1962).

Hodgkin, Thomas. "The African Renaissance." *Listener*, August 15, 1957.

July, R. W. "The Artist's Credo: The Political Philosophy of Wole Soyinka." *Journal of Modern African Studies* 19, no. 3 (September 1981).

Lambo, T. A. "A Form of Social Psychiatry in Africa." *World Mental Health* 13, no. 4 (November 1961).

Nicholas, D. D., D. A. Ampofo, et al. "Attitudes and Practises of Traditional Birth Attendants in Rural Ghana." *Bulletin of the World Health Organization* 54 (1976).

Nicol, Davidson. "The Realities of Ashby's Vision." *Universities Quarterly* 15, no. 4 (1961).
Obenga, Théophile. "Méthode et Conception historiques de Cheikh Anta Diop." *Présence Africaine*, no. 74 (2nd quarter, 1970).
Ogot, B. A. "The Concept of Jok." *African Studies* 20, no. 2 (1961).
Senghor, L. S. "African-Negro Aesthetics." *Diogenes*, no. 16 (Winter 1956).
Vansina, Jan. "Recording the Oral History of the Bakuba." *Journal of African History* 1, no. 1 (1960).
Zeitlin, Arnold. "Ghana's Young Theatre." *Theatre Arts* 47, no. 11 (November 1963).

*Books and Pamphlets*

Abraham, W. E. *The Mind of Africa.* London: Weidenfeld and Nicolson, 1962.
Ajayi, J. F. A. *Christian Missions in Nigeria, 1841–1891.* London: Longman, 1965.
Armah, Ayi Kwei. *The Healers.* London: Heinemann, 1978.
Ashby, Eric. *Universities: British, Indian, African.* London: Weidenfeld and Nicolson, 1966.
Austin, Dennis. *Ghana Observed.* Manchester: Manchester University Press, 1976.
Balewa, Abubakar Tafawa. Nigeria Speaks. Ikeja: Longman of Nigeria, 1964.
Beier, H. U. *Contemporary Art in Africa.* London: Pall Mall, 1968.
———. *Introduction to African Literature.* London: Longman, 1967.
Bing, Geoffrey. *Reap the Whirlwind.* London: MacGibbon and Key, 1968.
Blyden, E. W. *Christianity, Islam and the Negro Race.* Edinburgh: Edinburgh University Press, 1967.
*Calendar, University of Ibadan, 1965–66.* Ibadan: University of Ibadan Press, 1965.
Carothers, J. C. *The African Mind in Health and Disease.* Geneva: World Health Organization, 1956.
Césaire, Aimé. *Letter to Maurice Thorez.* Paris: Présence Africaine, 1957.
Clark, Ebun. *Hubert Ogunde: The Making of Nigerian Theatre.* Oxford: Oxford University Press, 1979.
Cook, Mercer, ed. and trans. *The African Origin of Civilization.* Westport, Conn.: Lawrence Hill, 1974.
Crane, Louise. *Ms. Africa.* New York: Lippincott, 1973.
Curtin, Philip. *The Image of Africa.* Madison: University of Wisconsin Press, 1964.
deGraft-Johnson, J. C. *African Glory.* New York: Walker, [1966].
Dike, K. O. *Report on the Preservation and Administration of Historical Records and the Establishment of a Public Record Office in Nigeria.* [Lagos]: Nigerian Government Printer, 1954.
Diop, Cheikh Anta. *Nations Nègres et Culture.* Paris: Présence Africaine, 1955.
Eliosofon, Eliot. *The Sculpture of Africa.* New York: Praeger, 1958.

Fanon, Frantz. *Black Skin, White Masks.* New York: Grove Press, 1967.
———. *Toward the African Revolution.* New York: Grove Press, 1967.
———. *The Wretched of the Earth.* New York: Grove Press, 1966.
Gendzier, Irene. *Frantz Fanon.* London: Wildwood House, 1973.
Gorer, Geoffrey. *Africa Dances.* New York: Norton, 1962.
Hooker, James. *Black Revolutionary.* New York: Praeger, 1967; London: Pall Mall, 1967.
Hountondji, P. J. *African Philosophy: Myth and Reality.* Bloomington: Indiana University Press, 1983.
Hymans, J. L. *Léopold Sédar Senghor.* Edinburgh: Edinburgh University Press, 1971.
*Investment in Education* (Ashby Report). London: St. Clements Press, 1960.
Johnson, Samuel. *The History of the Yorubas.* Lagos: CMS Bookshops, 1921.
Jones, Eldred D. *The Writing of Wole Soyinka.* London: Heinemann, 1973.
July, R. W. *The Origins of Modern African Thought.* New York: Praeger, 1967; London: Faber, 1968.
———, and Peter Benson, eds. *African Cultural and Intellectual Leaders and the Development of the New African Nations.* New York: Rockefeller Foundation; Ibadan: University of Ibadan Press, 1982.
Kerematen, A. *Asante Cultural Centre.* Accra: Guinea, n.d.
Lambo, T. A., ed. *First Pan-African Psychiatric Conference, Report Abeokuta, Nigeria, 1961.* Ibadan: Government Printer, n.d.
Mannoni, O. *Prospero and Caliban.* London: Methuen, 1956.
Moore, Gerald. *Wole Soyinka.* London: Evans Bros., 1971.
Nketia, J. H. *Ethnomusicology in Ghana.* Accra: Ghana Universities Press, 1970.
Nkrumah, Kwame. *Africa Must Unite.* New York: Praeger, 1963; London: Heinemann, 1963.
———. *The African Genius.* N.p.: [1963].
———. *Ghana: Autobiography of Kwame Nkrumah.* New York: International Publishers, 1971.
———. *I Speak of Freedom.* New York: Praeger, 1961; London: Heinemann, 1961.
Nyerere, Julius. *Freedom and Unity.* Dar es Salaam: Oxford University Press, 1966.
———. *Ujamaa, Essays on Socialism.* Dar es Salaam: Oxford University Press, 1968.
O'Brien, C. C. *Writers and Politics.* New York: Pantheon, 1965.
Ogot, B. A. *History of the Southern Luo.* Nairobi: East African Publishing House, 1967.
Ouologuem, Yambo. *Bound to Violence.* London: Heinemann, 1971.
Ousmane, Sembene. *God's Bits of Wood.* London: Heinemann, 1970.
Padmore, George. *The Gold Coast Revolution.* London: Dobson, 1953.
———. *Pan-Africanism or Communism?* London: Dobson, 1956.

Pratt, Cranford. *The Critical Phase in Tanzania, 1945–1968.* Cambridge: Cambridge University Press, 1976.

Présence Africaine. *Les Etudiants Noirs Parlent.* Paris: Présence Africaine, 1952.

———. *Hommage à Léopold Sédar Senghor.* Paris: Présence Africaine, 1976.

Reindorf, C. C. *The History of the Gold Coast and Asante.* Accra: Ghana Universities Press, 1966.

*Report of Visitation to University College, Ibadan, January 1961.* Ibadan: University of Ibadan Press, 1961.

Roberts, Andrew, ed. *Tanzania Before 1900.* Nairobi: East African Publishing House, 1968.

Ryder, Alan. *Benin and the Europeans, 1485–1897.* New York: Humanities Press, 1969.

Sartre, Jean-Paul. *Black Orpheus.* Paris: Présence Africaine, 1962.

Senghor, L. S. *On African Socialism.* New York: Praeger, 1964.

Sibthorpe, A. B. C. *The History of Sierra Leone.* London: Frank Cass, 1970.

Soyinka, Wole. *Collected Plays.* Vol. 2. London: Oxford University Press, 1974.

———. *Myth, Literature and the African World.* Cambridge: Cambridge University Press, 1976.

Touré, Sékou. *L'Action Politique du Partie Démocratique de Guinée.* Paris: Présence Africaine, 1959.

———. *Expérience Guinéenne et Unité Africaine.* Paris: Présence Africaine, 1959.

Towa, M. *Essai Sur la Problématique Philosophique dans l'Afrique Actuelle.* Yaoundé, Cameroon: Editions Clé, 1979.

Traoré, Bakary. *Le Théatre Négro-Africain.* Paris: Présence Africaine, 1958. (English language edition: *The Black African Theatre and Its Social Functions.* Dapo Adelugba, trans. Ibadan: University of Ibadan Press, 1972.)

Twumasi, P. A. *Medical Systems in Ghana.* Accra-Tema: Ghana Publishing, 1975.

*University College, Ibadan, Calendar, 1961–1962.* Ibadan: University of Ibadan Press, 1961.

Wiredu, K. *Philosophy and an African Culture.* Cambridge: Cambridge University Press, 1980.

# Index

Aborigines' Rights Protection Society, 134–35
Abraham, W. E., 220
Achebe, Chinua, 64, 108, 220
Achimota College, Ghana, 52, 53, 87, 97, 161, 189; educational philosophy, 160; and Kwame Nkrumah, 166
Adelugba, Dapo, 65, 70; on African theater, 62–63
African Dance Company of Ghana, 102, 103
*African Glory*, 134, 136–37
*The African Mind in Health and Disease*, 204–7
"African Personality," 18, 101, 181, 201–2
African socialism: and Julius Nyerere, 21–22; and Kwame Nkrumah, 166, 168, 176, 181
African studies, 177, 178, 181; controversy over, 178–83, 196–97; at University of Ghana, 183–92; at University of Ibadan, 193–97
Africans, westernized, 20–21, 23–24, 86–87, 107, 110, 119–20, 157, 167, 215, 220, 226, 228, 230, 233, 235
Agbebi, Majola, 12, 13
Ahmad, Muhammad Jamal, 188
Ajayi, J. F. A., 143, 146, 147; and

African historical research, 155–56; *Christian Missions in Nigeria, 1841–1891*, 144; criticizes African studies, 179–80
Akintola, S. I., 71
Akropong, Ghana, 85, 87, 92
Akwapim, Ghana, 19, 54
Akwapim Six, 52–58 passim, 189
American Society of African Culture (AMSAC), 39, 43
Ampofo, Oku, 99; artistic principles, 55, 56; artistic style, 56–57; cultural nationalism, 57–58; encourages African arts, 53–56, 189; and Ghana Drama Studio, 73; medical and art training, 52–53; medical practice, 217–18
Amu, Ephraim, 52, 57–58, 92, 96, 97, 99; cultural independence, 85–87; early career, 85–86; influence, 90–91, 189; musical ideas, 87–89, 90
Anene, J. C., 143, 146; *Africa in the Nineteenth and Twentieth Centuries*, 146
Antubam Kofi, 54–55
Armstrong, Louis, 4
Art, African: and Akwapim Six, 52–56; and Benin bronze workers, 48–50; traditional sculpture, 48–49
Arts Theatre, Benin, 241–42

Arts Theatre Group, Ibadan, 64–65, 66
Arusha Declaration, 22
Asante Cultural Centre, Kumasi, 97, 98, 101, 190
Asare, E., 53, 54, 55
Ashby, Sir Eric, 170; and African studies, 178; and African universities, 161
Assimilation: in Francophone Africa, 8–10, 34, 41, 202; in literature, 119–20; and university education, 160
Attoh Ahuma, S. R. B., 12, 184
Atwia, Ghana, 78–80
Austin, Dennis, 229, 231
Awooner, Kofi, 229, 230, 231
Axworthy, Geoffrey, 61–62, 63, 69–70; on African theater, 62; at Ibadan, 64–65, 66; and Ogunmola company, 66–67

Ba, Ahmadu Hampate, 188
Baldwin, James: and *Présence Africaine* congress, Paris, 1956, 25, 26, 27, 28, 30, 35, 36
Balewa, Abubakar Tafewa, 15, 16
*Les Ballets Africains*, 103–6
Balme, David, 201; at University College, Gold Coast, 161–62, 163–64, 166, 167, 169, 171, 172; and western culture, 179
Banda, Hastings, 71
*Bantu Philosophy*, 224
*Before the Blackout*, 71
Bellagio Conference, 228–29, 231, 232, 233
Bergson, Henri, 210, 224
Biesheuvel, Simon, 203
Bing, Geoffrey, 171
*Black Orpheus*, 32, 210–11, 214
*Black Skin, White Masks*, 212
Blyden, Edward W., 52, 131, 243; and African culture, 12, 13; racial ideas, 158, 209; and university education, 158–59
Bodunrin, Peter, 220, 223–24
Boilat, Abbé P. D., 10, 107, 226
Bond, Horace Mann, 35, 36

*Bound to Violence*, 116–20
Busia, Kofi, 75, 92, 167; and African studies in Ghana, 185, 189; and African studies at Ibadan, 195–96

Carothers, J. C.: and the African mind, 204–7
Casely Hayford, J. E., 12, 14, 108, 135, 169, 184, 226
Césaire, Aimé, 41, 43, 44; and American blacks, 37; and communism, 40–41; and European colonialism, 25–27, 28, 29; and Negritude, 29, 32, 33, 39, 108, 213–14
Character, African, 29, 59, 60–61, 62, 75, 82–83, 110, 115, 120–26, 129–30, 131, 156, 158, 201, 204–7, 209–10, 210–11, 212–17, 218–19, 222, 223, 226, 233
*Christian Missions in Nigeria, 1841–1891*, 144
Christianity: and colonialism, 34
Church Missionary Society (CMS), 10–11
Cities, African, 234
Civilization of the Universal: and L. S. Senghor, 209, 243
Clark, Ebun, 62
Clark, J. P., 64, 70
Cobblah, John, 53, 54
College of Technology, Kumasi, 87, 90, 97
Convention Peoples' Party, 57, 100, 134, 135, 165, 172, 173, 175, 183, 185
Cook, Mercer, 35; and Aimé Césaire, 37–38; and Alioune Diop, 41
Cowell, Henry, 92
Crowder, Michael: on African history, 154–55; supports African studies, 182–83
Crowther, Samuel Ajayi, 10–11, 131, 226
Culture, African, 47, 48–51; and African studies, 177, 183–84, 185–87, 189; and Aimé Césaire, 25–27, 34, 40–41, 42, 213–14; and Alioune Diop, 43–44; and Anglophone Africa, 34; and Bellagio confer-

ence, 228, 230, 231; and dance, 82–
84, 97, 98, 100, 102, 191; and early
support, 11–14; and Frantz Fanon,
216–17; and history, 133, 138–39,
147–48, 150–52; and Julius
Nyerere, 21–22; K. O. Dike on,
193–94; and Kwame Nkrumah, 18,
165–66; and literature, 109–12,
121–22, 126, 191; and L. S. Senghor, 29–30, 209–10, 213–14; and
modernization, 231–32, 234–35, 236,
237; and philosophy, 220–26; and
psychiatry, 217, 218–19; and
Richard Wright, 27–28; and scientific racism, 202–7; and Sékou
Touré, 22–24; and theater, 60–61,
62, 63, 66–68, 73, 75–77, 191–92;
traditional, 48, 49, 56–57, 201, 227,
228, 230; and universities, 158–59,
164, 166, 169, 181, 192
Cultural ambivalence, African, 7–8,
13–14, 19, 23, 26, 27–28, 30, 39,
50–51, 52, 55, 62–65, 68, 72–73,
85–87, 108, 113–14, 131, 139, 157–
58, 158–59, 164, 167, 212–14, 220–
21, 223, 225, 227–29, 231, 232, 233,
234, 235, 243

Dadié, Bernard, 63
Dakar Festival of Negro Art, 1966,
72–73
Dance, in Africa, 82–84; and A. M.
Opoku, 96–103, 191; and politics,
101, 102
A Dance of the Forests, 68, 70–71
Danda, 66
Danquah, J. B., 58, 75, 107, 135, 184
D'Arboussier, Gabriel, 31
Darwin, Charles, 203
Davidson, Basil, 188
Davis, John A., 35, 38, 40; on
American blacks, 36–37
deGraft, Joe, 77, 78, 96, 190, 191
deGraft-Johnson, J. C., 136–37; and
African Glory, 136
Dei-Anang, Michael, 75
De Mille, Agnes, 98
Depestre, René, 31–32
Diagne, Blaise, 12

Diagne, Pathé, 230
Dike, K. O., 148, 195; and African
historical studies, 140–45, 220; and
African studies, 178, 179, 181, 193–
94, 195–96; Benin research scheme,
142–43; historical publishing,
143–44; and Nigerian archives,
141–42
Diop, Alioune, 24, 27, 29, 31, 32, 33,
35; and African independence, 31,
43–44; and Présence Africaine
congress, Paris, 31; and Society of
African Culture, 43
Diop, Cheikh Anta, 137–39, 146, 154;
and American delegation, 1956
Paris congress, 38; historical
philosophy, 137, 138–39, 140; and
Pan-Africanism, 123
Dominican Mission, Ibadan, 240–41
Du Bois, W. E. B., 35–36, 38, 40, 138

Egungun, secret society, Nigeria, 49,
59–60
Ekello, Thomas, 34, 36
L'Enfant Noir, 108
Enwonwu, Ben, 52
Esquisses Sénégalaises, 107
Ethiopia Unbound, 108
Ethnophilosophy, 221–22, 225
Les Etudiants Noirs Parlent, 31, 32
European colonialism, 34, 135–36;
and African history, 141; and African reactions, 7–8, 11–14, 21–22,
58; and Aimé Césaire, 25–27; and
Alioune Diop, 43–44; and Christianity, 34; cultural legacies, 18–
19; economic legacies, 16–18, 20;
and Frantz Fanon, 216; and literature, 108, 114–15, 118–20, 120–26;
political legacies, 14–16; and
Richard Wright, 27–28; and scientific racism, 202–3; and universities, 157–59, 160–61, 163–64
European Economic Community, 16,
18
Existentialism, 202, 215

Facelli, Kante, 105
Fagg, William, 48–49

Fanon, Frantz, 39, 220, 227; ideas on race, 212–17; and psychiatry, 217, 218
Fanti Confederation, 134
Field, Margaret, 188
Fifth Pan-African Congress, Manchester, England, 184
First International Congress of Black Writers and Artists, 24–44 passim, 47
Fodeba, Keita, 63; artistic principles, 104–5; *Les Ballets Africains*, 103–6
Fontaine, William T., 35
Fourah Bay College, 157, 170
Franklin, Albert: on *Black Orpheus*, 32–33
Freeman-Grenville, G. S. P., 188
Frobenius, Leo, 118

Gadeau, Coffi, 63
Gambia: and independence, 3
Gandhi, Mohandas, 58
Gelede, secret society, Nigeria, 59–60
Ghana (Gold Coast), 19, 52, 53, 55, 85, 126; cultural nationalism, 58, 74–75, 181; economy, 17, 174–75; and independence, 1, 3, 16, 74–75, 135–36, 166–67; and university education, 161–76 passim
Ghana Arts Council (Gold Coast Arts Society) : founded, 54, 99, 190
Ghana Dance Ensemble, 94, 101–2, 191
Ghana Drama Studio, 73–74, 76, 78, 79, 80, 94, 191
Ghana Experimental Theatre, 74, 75, 77, 191
Ghana Music Society, 94
Ghana Society of Writers, 75
*Ghanaian Times*, 171–72
*God's Bits of Wood*, 109–16, 235
*The Gold Coast Revolution*, 134–36
Gorer, Geoffrey, 82–83, 84
Gowon, General Yakubu, 72, 101
Graham, G. S., 144
Graham, Martha, 98
Grant, William, 158
Guinea, 23–24; and Keita Fodeba, 105–6
Gyampo, F. A., 53, 54

*The Healers*, 120–26, 220
Hegel, G. W. F., 203, 210
Hill, Polly, 188
History, African, 158; and A. B. C. Sibthorpe, 131–32; and African philosophy, 223, 224–25; and C. C. Reindorf, 132–33; and Cheikh Anta Diop, 137–39; and George Padmore, 134–36; at Ibadan University, 140–47; and J. C. deGraft-Johnson, 136–37; objectives, 129; and oral traditions, 138, 147–53; problems and future, 154–56; and Samuel Johnson, 133
*History of Sierra Leone*, 131–32
*History of the Gold Coast and Asante*, 132–33
*History of the Southern Luo*, 153
*History of the Yorubas*, 133
Hodgkin, Thomas, 93, 170, 173; and Institute of African Studies, University of Ghana, 185–87, 188, 189, 195; on Kwame Nkrumah, 173
*The Horn*, University of Ibadan, 64, 69
Horton, James Africanus Beale, 10, 52, 131, 202; and an African university, 156–57, 178
Hountondji, Paulin, 221, 230; on African philosophy, 224–26
Houphouet-Boigny, Félix, 16, 18, 108
Humanitarianism, European, 8–9, 11
Humanities, African, 47–48, 177, 220, 228, 229, 230, 231

Idumuje Ugboko, Nigeria, 50, 233, 234, 235, 236, 237, 241, 242
Independence, African, 1–4, 14; Aimé Césaire on, 41–42; Alioune Diop on, 31, 43–44; and Bellagio conference, 228, 229, 230; cultural, 47–48, 52, 68–70, 74–75, 81, 85–87, 93–96, 97, 99, 126, 181, 227, 228, 230; and Gambia, 5; and Ghana, 3, 74, 136; and Guinea, 22–24; and history, 129–31, 135–36, 138–39; in Kenya, 3; and Kwame Nkrumah, 168, 175–76, 181; in literature, 115, 116, 126; and L. S. Senghor,

42–43; and modernization, 228, 230, 231, 236; and philosophy, 223; and Tanganyika, 3, 4, 21–22; in Zambia, 1–3
Institute of African Studies, University of Ghana, 78, 84, 93, 94, 130, 153, 170, 175, 180, 189, 193; program, 96, 186–88
Institute of African Studies, University of Ibadan, 153, 192–97
Institute of Art and Culture (Ghana Arts Council), 190, 191
Investment in Education (Ashby Report), 177, 178
Irele, Abiola: on African philosophy, 230; on African theater, 63
Ivey, James W., 35

James, Marcus, 34
Johnson, James, 158
Johnson, Samuel, 134; and *History of the Yorubas*, 132
Johnston, Harry: *Colonization of Africa*, 140
*Journal of the Nigerian Historical Society*, 146

Kagamé, Abbé, 225
Kaunda, Kenneth: and African independence, 2–3
Kenya: and African independence, 3
Kerematen, Alex, 97
King, Martin Luther: and African independence, 1
Ki Zerbo, Joseph, 154, 188
Kofi, Vincent, 51
*Kongi's Harvest*, 72–73
*Kusum Agoromba*, 80
Kwame Nkrumah Ideological Institute, Winneba, 176
*Kwamina*, 98, 100
Kwei Armah, Ayi, 120, 121, 123, 124; and *The Beautyful Ones Are Not Yet Born*, 120; and *The Healers*, 120–26, 220

Ladji, Camera, 105
Lambo, T. A., 218–19
Lamming, George, 34–35

Laye, Camera, 108
Legon, Ghana, 162, 166, 167, 168, 169, 170, 174, 176, 181, 183, 187
Lessing, Doris: on Zambian independence, 2–3
*Les Lettres Françaises*, 31
Lévy-Bruhl, Lucien, 203, 205, 210, 224
Literature in Africa, 107–8; and *Bound to Violence*, 116–20; and *God's Bits of Wood*, 109–16; and *The Healers*, 120–26
Lods, Pierre, 83
London University: and African education, 160, 161, 162, 163
Lovanium University, Zaire, 159

Macaulay, Herbert, 12, 14, 226
Mampong, Ghana, 52, 54, 55
Mannoni, O., 207–8
Marx, Karl, 210
Marxism, 38, 40, 134, 233; and Aimé Césaire, 40–41; and Kwame Nkrumah, 165, 169, 184; and Negritude, 30, 31, 32, 33; at *Présence Africaine* Congress, Paris, 1956, 35–36
Mazrui, Ali, 243
Medicine, African: and Frantz Fanon, 217, 218; and Oku Ampofo, 217–18; and T. A. Lambo, 218–19
Mensah, A. A., 191
Mensah Sarbah, John, 14, 169, 184, 226
Meyerowitz, H. V., 52, 53, 189
*The Mind of Africa*, 220
Modernization, 20–21, 139, 222, 224, 227, 228, 230, 231, 232, 235, 236, 237
Morton-Williams, Peter, 188
Music in Africa: and Ephraim Amu, 84–91; and J. H. Nketia, 92, 93–96, 191
Myrdal, Gunnar, 204

Nadel, S. F., 204
National Congress of British West Africa, 135
National Liberation Movement, Ghana, 100

National Theatre Movement, Ghana, 190

National Union of Nigerian Students, 65

Nationalism, African, 57–58, 134, 135; and higher education, 163, 164, 166, 167, 169, 171–72; and history, 129–30, 134–35

*Nations Nègres et Culture*, 137, 138

Negritude, 155, 201, 202, 212, 220, 222, 227, 230; and Aimé Césaire, 29, 32, 33, 39, 108, 213–14; criticism of, 30–33; and Frantz Fanon, 213, 214, 215, 216–17; and Keita Fodeba, 105; and L. S. Senghor, 29–30, 31, 39, 108, 209–10, 224

Neocolonialism, European, 165, 168, 176; cultural, 18–19, 131, 159–61, 163–64, 169, 178–79, 193, 201, 212–17, 223, 224, 225, 226, 227; economic, 16–18; political, 14–16

Nicol, Davidson, 29, 34, 170

Nigeria: Civil War, 72; and independence, 1, 3–4, 15, 16, 108–9; National Archives, 141–42; University of Ibadan, 140–47, 178, 192–97; Western Region political crisis, 71–72

Nigerian Institute of Social and Economic Research, 194

1960 Masks, 70

Nketia, J. H., 97, 99, 101, 102; artistic objectives, 93–96, 102; early training, 91–93; and Institute of African Studies, University of Ghana, 185, 188, 191, 195; and School of Music and Drama, University of Ghana, 189, 191–92; supports African studies, 180–81, 229

Nketsia, Nana Kobina, 170, 172

Nkrumah, Kwame, 23, 57, 58, 106, 108, 116, 134, 135, 175, 190, 193, 224; and African culture, 181, 184–85, 186, 190; and African history, 130; on African independence, 1, 4, 17–18, 21, 165–66; and "African Personality," 18, 101, 181, 201–2; and dance, 100, 101, 102; and Efua Sutherland, 74, 76; European eco-nomic connections, 16–18; and Institute of African Studies, University of Ghana, 183–84, 185; and neocolonialism, 17–18, 165, 168, 169; and Pan-Africanism, 18, 123; political acumen, 172–73, 184–85; and university education, 164, 166, 169–70, 171, 173, 229; and Wole Soyinka, 71, 72–73

Nkrumaism, 176

Nwoko, Demas, 51, 230; and African modernization, 232, 233, 234, 235, 236–37; and Benin bronze workers, 50; and design ideas, 237–39, 240–43; and *Palm-Wine Drinkard*, 67, 68

Nwoko, Martin, 236

Nwoko III, obi, Idumuje Ugboko, Nigeria, 50, 236, 242

Nyerere, Julius, 224; and African independence, 3, 4, 21–22

O'Brien, Conor Cruise: educational philosophy, 174; and University of Ghana, 173–76

*Odasani*, 75–76, 77

Ogot, B. A., 154; and oral history, 148–53; and problems of African history, 155, 156

Ogunde, Hubert, 62–63, 66, 67, 73

Ogunmola, Kola, 66–68, 70, 73

Ohene, Elizabeth, 230–31

Okae, J. D., 54

Okigbo, Christopher, 64

Okoampa, Chief Nana, 78

*Okyeame*, 75, 189

Okyere, J. C., 53, 54

Oliver, Roland, 144, 148, 149, 150

Omer Cooper, J. D., 146

Opoku, A. A., 54

Opoku, Albert M., 94, 98, 100, 102, 189–90, 191, 230; background and training, 96–97; dance ideas, 97, 98, 99, 100–101

Oral traditions: in history, 138, 147–53

Orisun Theatre, 71

Oruka, Henry, 220

Oshogbo, Nigeria, 51, 66

Ouologuem, Yambo, 116, 117, 118, 119, 120; and *Bound to Violence*, 116–20

Ousmane, Sembene, 109, 115, 116; and *God's Bits of Wood*, 109–16

Padmore, George, 137; *The Gold Coast Revolution*, 134–36; *Pan-Africanism or Communism?*, 40

*Palm-Wine Drinkard*, 67, 68, 70

Pan-African Congress, Manchester, England, 1945, 135–36

Pan-Africanism, 123, 156; and Cheikh Anta Diop, 137, 138–39; and communism, 40–41; and Kwame Nkrumah, 130, 135–36, 166, 168, 176

*Pan-Africanism or Communism?*, 40

Philosophy, African, 220–26, 227

Poto Poto, 51, 83

Prempeh II, 89

*Présence Africaine:* cultural review, 24, 27, 29, 43, 44, 137, 190, 224

*Présence Africaine:* First International Congress of Black Writers and Artists, 24–44 passim, 47; and United States delegation, 35–39

*Présence Africaine:* Second International Congress of Black Writers and Artists, 24, 215

*Prospero and Caliban*, 207–8

*Rassemblement Démocratique Africain*, 37

Rattray, Captain R. X., 204

Reindorf, C. C., 133, 134; philosophy of history, 132–33

Rhodesian National Gallery, 51

Ryder, Alan, 146; quoted, 143

el Salahi, Ibrahim, 51

Sankore mosque, Timbuktu, 157

Sartre, Jean-Paul, 32, 33, 215; and *Black Orpheus*, 210–11, 214

School of Drama, University of Ibadan, 61, 66

School of Music and Drama, University of Ghana, 78, 84, 90, 93, 94, 102; program, 96, 189, 191–92

Scientific racism, European, 2–3

Second International Congress of Black Writers and Artists, 24, 215

Second World Black and African Festival of Arts and Culture, Lagos, 1977, 49

Selassie, Bereket Hapte, 188

Selassie, Haile, 58

Senghor, Léopold Sedar, 32, 37, 38, 39, 41, 224, 243; on African independence, 1, 21, 42–43; and American delegation, *Présence Africaine* Congress, Paris, 38, 39; Civilization of the Universal, 29, 209; and Negritude, 29–30, 108, 202, 209–10, 213–14

Sibthorpe, A. B. C., 133, 134; and African history, 131–32

Smith, H. F. C., 146

Society of African Culture, 43, 190

Sowande, Fela, 52

Soyinka, Wole, 64, 67–68, 220, 231; and Civil War, Nigeria, 72; defines African drama, 62; and new African drama, 68–71; and Western Region, Nigeria, crisis, 71–72

Sutherland, Efua, 94, 96, 189, 190, 191, 220, 230; and Atwia, 78–80; and Ghana Drama Studio, 74–77; and Kusum Agoromba, 80; as playwright, 75–76, 77; theatrical ideas, 75, 76, 77, 78, 79, 80, 81

Taban lo Liyong, 230

Tanganyika: and independence, 3, 4, 21–22, 23

*Tarikh*, 146

Teilhard de Chardin, Pierre, 210

Tempels, Placide, 224, 225

Theater in Africa, 191; character, 59–62; and Efua Sutherland, 73–81; and Ogunmola, 66–68; and University of Ibadan, 64–66; and Wole Soyinka, 68–71, 72–73

*A Thousand Years of West African History*, 146, 147; and J. F. A. Ajayi, 147

Touré, Sékou, 17, 21; and African independence, 22–24, 108; and Keita Fodeba, 106
Towa, Marcien, 220–21, 222–23, 224, 225
Traoré, Bakary, 63
Travelling Theatre, University of Ibadan, 61–62, 65–66, 67
Trowell, H. C., 204
Tutuola, Amos, 67

*Ujamaa*, 22
UNESCO: history of Africa, 156
United Gold Coast Convention, 135, 184
Universities, African: and African studies, 177, 178–97, 229; in British colonies, 159–61; early efforts for, 157–59; and modernization, 229
University Arts Theatre, University of Ibadan, 61, 62, 64, 71
University College, Cape Coast, 171, 175, 187
University College, Gold Coast, 161–76 passim, 180, 185
University College, Ibadan, 140, 141, 144, 145, 193
University of Dakar, 159, 160
University of Ghana, 170, 180, 187
University of Ibadan: and African history, 140–41, 143–47, 153, 154; and African studies, 179–80, 192–97
University of Science and Technology, Kumasi, 170, 187

Vansina, Jan, 147, 148, 149, 150
Villages, African, 233, 234, 236

Westernization, 8–9, 19, 139, 202; and Abbé Boilat, 10; and African reaction, 9–11, 14; and African theater, 62, 63–64, 75; and Aimé Césaire, 25–27; and Blaise Diagne, 12; in cities, 233; in education, 157, 159, 160, 161, 163, 164, 167, 177–78, 181; and Edward Blyden, 12, 13; and Ephraim Amu, 85–87; and Herbert Macaulay, 14; and J. A. B. Horton, 10; and James Johnson, 12–13; and Julius Nyerere, 21–22; in literature, 109–10, 113–14, 119–20; and Majola Agbebi, 12, 13; and modernization, 228, 230, 231–32; and philosophy in Africa, 221–23, 224, 225, 226; and Richard Wright, 27–28, 30; and S. A. Crowther, 10–11; and S. R. B. Attoh Ahuma, 12; and University College, Ghana, 91
Wilks, Ivor, 188
Wiredu, Kwesi, 220, 225; and African philosophy, 221–22
*The Wretched of the Earth*, 215–16
Wright, Richard: Cheikh Anta Diop on, 39; at *Présence Africaine* Congress, Paris, 1956, 27–28, 29, 30, 35, 39, 222

Zambia: and independence, 1–3

Library of Congress Cataloging-in-Publication Data
July, Robert William.
An African voice.
Bibliography: p.
Includes index.
1. Africa—Civilization—20th century. 2. Humanities
—Africa. I. Title.
DT14.J85   1987   960'.3   87-5388
ISBN 0-8223-0717-0
ISBN 0-8223-0769-3 (pbk.)